CONNECTING THE DOTS OF IDENTITY

MODERN ABSTRACT RELIGIOUS VERBAL IMPRESSIONISM ROLE PLAY IDENTITY ARRAY

JOHN LOUIS THOMAS

COPYRIGHT AND DISCLAIMER

REDNLOVE

Rednlove2@gmail.com

Copyright © 2024 by John Louis Thomas

Connecting The Dots Of Identity

All scripture references are from the Holy Bible. Authorized King James Version. Copyright 1989. World Bible Publishers, Inc.

Internet references are taken from popular web browsers in the years 2019, 2020, 2021, 2022, and 2023. Some sources may require updates or additional information regarding the validity of their content.

"This work is licensed under the Creative Commons Attribution 3.0 Unported License. To view a copy of this license, visit http://creativecommons.org/licenses/by/3.0/."

Briefly, this license allows intellectual property to be shared among content creators within limits. If you alter the material, you may not distribute it. You may copy and redistribute the material but not for commercial purposes. If your platform is commercially oriented and you post *Connecting The Dots Of Identity* content, you violate the terms of the Creative Commons License. This is the letter of the law. In the spirit of the law, if you profit from the content, you incur an obligation to remit a portion of the profit to the license holder. The license holder provides content, the content creator extends content.

The main goal in granting a Creative Commons license is to facilitate the distribution of the work by screen capture, text, voice, closed captioning, subtitles, or sign language. By extension, this includes translation from the English language.

Content creators may reproduce a chapter not to exceed the length of one chapter per thirty-day period on the same website or URL (Universal Resource Locator). Any chapter may be selected. Permission is granted to copy and distribute unaltered material under the same Creative Commons License conditions of Attribution, Non-Commercial, and Non-Derivative means.

Categorically, the license pays particular attention to voice narration of individual chapters by readers to post on websites or blogs for promotional purposes not to exceed the length of one chapter per 30-day period on the same website or URL (Universal Resource Locator). Any portion of the book representing a chapter may be selected for reproduction.

No narrator or agent of the narrator may offer copyright content for sale per the non-commercial aspect of the license.

The Creative Commons License emphasizes permission to provide text-to-speech access when reading is restricted, inconvenient, or undesirable.

The licensee must include details of attribution to the licensor.

Example as a chapter-by-chapter audiobook:

Title of Publication.

Author.

Publisher Name/Email Address.

Date of Publication.

Selected Chapter Name to Be Read.

Selected Chapter Number to Be Read.

Total Number of Chapters In Publication.

Narrator Name.

Narrator Contact Information.

Narration Date.

At the beginning of narration – Title of Publication, Chapter (number and title), by (Name of Narrator).

At the end of narration – the words "The End."

Name or link to purchase the publication.

Text To Speech (TTS). This is a service that converts written material to an audio program that simulates the human voice. These paid and free services assist those who are visually impaired, have limited reading opportunities, or prefer narration for various reasons. Consider TTS for someone to access *Connecting The Dots Of Identity* on Android, IOS, Windows, and other platforms using a desktop, laptop, tablet, or smartphone.

Connecting The Dots Of Identity is not intended to modify, subvert, or infringe on Christian orthodox theology.

Connecting The Dots Of Identity is strictly an artistic verbal impression of religious principles. It is an art project rendered by an artist.

Connecting The Dots Of Identity expressly discourages any representation as a church.

Connecting The Dots Of Identity does not qualify as a church. The essential elements of a church include order of service, worship, discipleship, prayer, sacraments, discipline, leadership, teaching, missions, and fellowship.

Connecting The Dots Of Identity supports the local church, away church, and spiritual social gatherings.

Editor: Polgarus Studios

Cover Design: Sidney Nicholas

DEDICATION

To you.

I sacrifice my life for you.

I love you.

Contents

GLOSSARY OF COLORS

These are some of the primary, secondary, and tertiary colors used to paint Modern Abstract Religious Verbal Impressionism-Role Play Identity Array. There is no other way to present *Connecting The Dots Of Identity* other than to make use of vivid expressions.

AGNOSTICISM

The conclusion that knowledge of a Supreme Being, God, is doubtful, inaccessible, and unknowable. Therefore, theism, and atheism, cannot be known or proven. Proof of non-conversion to theism, and the ongoing functional lifestyles of an atheist, confirm an agnostic's conviction that theism is man-made.

Agnosticism doesn't acknowledge the doctrine of spiritual blindness, that God intentionally withholds knowledge of Himself. However, they must admit to blindness in the sense they have no spiritual eyesight. They do not perceive God. Therefore, He’s incomprehensible. He's also incomprehensible to everyone else.

Initially, this is true. Spiritually seeing God is an involuntary action by the Holy Spirit as proof of God's Election-Predestination program, existing before the foundation of the world. Scripture asserts no one perceives then chooses to follow Jesus Christ unless God initiates the process. The default position from birth is a belief in the self and disbelief in the God of the Bible. This is the Demonstration of Free Will.

ANGELS

First-Class Angels—accept God's will for their life.

Second-Class Angels—Satan and others decline God's will for their life, but do not abandon Heaven.

Third-Class Angels—Abaddon (Hebrew), or Apollyon (Greek), and others are those that left Heaven for the Earth in the hope of securing a redeemer for angels via procreation with human females. An audacious mission to match God's solution to human disobedience.

ARMINIANISM

The religious doctrine attributed to Jacobus Arminius (1629-1725) that affirms man's Free Will in the salvation plan of God, rather than God's determined will as the only factor.

ATHEISM

The system of thought that a Supreme Being, God, does not exist. Although they are proponents of objectivity and science, atheists possess no knowledge or proof of their negative position or agreed-upon evidence of absence.

Atheists reject the Reformed theology principle that God withholds knowledge of Himself except to the Elect. Though their knowledge of God is from General Revelation (nature) and Special Revelation (scripture), atheists are spiritually blind. Being so blinded, they are functionally agnostics. They can't know God and, therefore, you can't know God either. Otherwise, we would all know God. Why wouldn't we?

This contrasts with theism, which holds that an Intelligent Essence has always existed throughout various belief systems and makes itself known in a variety of means.

AUTHENTIC AND INAUTHENTIC IDENTITY

Authentic identity is the primary identity of a 100 percent human being that is recognized by the Lord before the foundation of the world. This is referred to as the Super-Spiritual Identity, or SSID.

The inauthentic identity is a secondary identity engaged in the Demonstration of Free Will initiated by Adam and Eve subject to the forces of heredity, environment, and experiences.

The inauthentic identity may be transformed by the Holy Spirit (Holy Spirit Identity or HSID). They are born again. Those who are not transformed are:

a) The control group that proves unless the Holy Spirit intercedes, no one ever perceives or chooses to follow God. Their roleplay ends. They join the SSIDs.

b) Compromised by evil spirits (Evil Spirit Identity or ESID). They may not be 100 percent human. An inauthentic identity must be transformed at death, before death, or after death or will have no corresponding SSID in Paradise on Judgment Day.

BLIND EYES CHART

The Blind Eyes Chart is an informal attempt to highlight nonphysical aspects of identity-array roleplay blindness using a questionnaire and a brief essay.

Nonphysical roleplay blindness refers to spiritual blindness, intentional blindness, and unintentional blindness. This follows from an inability or unwillingness to perceive objective morality, thereby deferring to subjective morality. The intent of the chart is to help clarify the disparity in roleplayers' perceptions of good/bad and right/wrong. (Glossary – Objective Morality and Subjective Morality).

A thirty-point yes/no questionnaire on spiritual blindness follows with a brief essay defining spiritual, intentional, and unintentional blindness. (*Connecting Dots Of Identity-1*, Chapter 17, *Connecting Dots Of Identity-2*, Chapter 17).

BOOK OF LIFE / LAMB'S BOOK OF LIFE (Spiritual books)

The blessed heavenly "book" that contains (God-given) names of the individual persons who are assured of salvation before God created the world (refers to bible verses implying names, writings, books, etcetera).

CALVINISM

The belief system of John Calvin (1615-1772) declares grace (salvation by the grace of God) rather than works (salvation by man's efforts). Five primary points feature the acronym T.U.L.I.P. (Total depravity, Unconditional election, Limited atonement, Irresistible grace, Perseverance of the saints).

CREATIONISM

Creationism is a secondary view (following Traducianism and Designationism defined in this section) that centers around WHEN souls or spirits are created, and HOW souls or spirits are created.

When – (1) at conception, (2) before conception, or (3) after conception.

How – (1) by parents, or (2) by God.

Creationism follows that the SOUL or SPIRIT is created by God at conception. This may include fractions of time before conception or after conception. A human being's BODY (physical identity/mental identity) is created in sin by sinful parents. God cannot be the creator of sinful persons. Creationists hold that a man is essentially a soul WITH a body, versus traducianists, who hold a man is both soul AND body.

CHRISTIAN REFORMED IMPRESSIONISM

The imagery of Christian Reformed theology as spiritual impressions, featuring suppositional constructs outside orthodoxy. This includes:

–A pre-life ontological identity based on Election/Predestination.

–An inauthentic present-life roleplay identity based on heredity, environment, and experiences.

–Everyone who is 100 percent human goes to Heaven based on Election/Predestination.

–Only those less than 100 percent human, Satan, and his angels go to Hell.

–Jesus Christ as the 100 percent human (and 100 percent God) perfect Roleplayer assured salvation for Elect Roleplayers.

–Life is a Demonstration of Free Will, initiated by Adam and Eve, and also influenced by the Nephilim (fallen angel/human female offspring).

–Salvation is by grace and not by works. Free Will to choose God was abrogated when Adam and Eve chose their own will for their lives rather than God's will for their lives. Only a flawless person can choose God; a flawed person cannot. All progeny from Adam and Eve are flawed. By grace, the Holy Spirit affirms salvation to inauthentic Roleplayers, confirming unless He arrives, Roleplayers cannot, do not, and will not choose God's will for their life.

–Since the UNSANE (Glossary) aren't able to open their spiritual eyes, and the SANE (Glossary) aren't able to do so for them, the responsibility of the SANE is to serve God by reintroducing God to the UNSANE. This is done by illustrating that God saved them before they were born. Who they are presently is a construct of heredity, environment, and experience derived from a Demonstration of Free Will, in contrast to God's Determined Will for human beings—AND angels—before the foundation of the world.

DESIGNATIONISM

A third view regarding WHEN and HOW a soul is created is Designationism (see Creationism and Traducianism defined in this section).

God has determined specific souls before He created the world, which correspond to specific humans conceived after creation. The soul, or spirit, (Spiritual Identity-SID) is created in sin as SID-Negative. Moving from pre-birth to birth through childhood, the child gravitates SID-Positive or SID-Negative depending on heredity, environment, and experiences.

Therefore, Designationism comes first. God elects souls before He creates the world. Traducianism comes second from parents. Creationism comes third as God identifies the Pre-Life Elect by giving the Holy Spirit — a reborn soul. (From Christian Reformed Impressionism)

EGO-CENTRACISM

The belief that it is the right of a living creature to demand and pursue the best interests of said creature. Restriction of this right therefore undermines the viability and autonomy of a flawless living creature. It's my life and not God's life through me. Otherwise, I may not be actually alive.

EGO-SKEPTICISM

A result of uncertainty regarding the nature of identity (who am I, what should I be doing, why am I here?). This includes unreliability of General Revelation (nature or science), Special Revelation (scripture), sense perception, and limitations of mental ability. Generally, a begrudging acknowledgment that autonomic systems of the body such as heart, lungs, glands, and brain, and other immutable aspects of the body such as race, height, and age contribute to confirming a lack of access and authority regarding identity.

Where God's Determined Will is perceived as non-religious natural forces of macroevolution, similar feelings of Ego-Skepticism apply.

Lucifer – A lack of confidence in God's Determined Will that restricts the freedom of a flawless creature, leading to resentment and discontent with life.

Serpent, Adam, Eve – Doubt and lack of confidence stemming from a lack of access to the control of essential determining factors that define physical, mental, and spiritual details of identity.

Roleplayers – Helplessness at lack of access to physical, mental, and spiritual details that confirm the utter dependence on heredity, environment, and experiences affecting the purpose and reason to live. Additionally, given the limited access to the self, access to the knowledge of others is also limited. Therefore, the ability to communicate and coordinate with others elicits feelings of suspicion, mistrust, and uncertainty.

EXCLUSIVISM

The belief that there is one way and one way only that will satisfy God's provision for salvation, such as Jesus Christ. The view includes religious liberty as everyone's right to freely worship without prohibition. It is the opposite of INCLUSIVISM (Glossary).

FREE WILL DEMONSTRATION

Human life as it began in the Garden of Eden, whereby flawless living creatures (Serpent, Adam, and Eve) illustrate freedom to pursue God's will for their lives or pursue their own will for their lives. Roleplay (pursuit of Free Will based on heredity, environment, and experiences) provides conclusive proof that Free Will leads to death and eternal damnation.

GENERAL REVELATION AND SPECIAL REVELATION

The biblical explanation of how God is revealed to us. General Revelation by the way we perceive the world through our senses, experiences, and natural laws of the universe. Special Revelation by the words God has given through oral tradition and the written word.

GODLY MARRIAGE MATERIAL

The person who accepts who they are as the *inauthentic* identity imposed by heredity, environment, and experience. Therefore, if the *authentic* identity is recognized by God, who granted salvation before the foundation of the world, life is a responsibility to assist the Holy Spirit in healing spiritual blindness. The secondary responsibility is addressing intentional and unintentional blindness, as defined by the Blind Eyes Chart. In the interim, every effort is made to overcome the effects of identity flaws that inhibit the attractiveness to bond with others who follow *Connecting The Dots Of Identity* – especially Single-Persons Champions.

GOD'S DETERMINED WILL

God's provision that established salvation for His Elect individuals before He created the world is His Determined Will. This affirms that autonomous human beings and spirit beings possess everlasting life. God's Determined Will is that flawless identities possess autonomy but will never disobey His will for their life. There are two classes:

1) Super-Spiritual Identities (SSIDs) – The Pre-Life Elect individuals identified in scripture who are guaranteed salvation before the foundation

of the world. Also portrayed as Christian Reformed Impressionism and Election-Predestination.

2) First-Class Angels – Spirit creatures who never exercise Free Will to disobey God.

The contrast is:

Non-Limited Free Will: Free Will to obey or disobey God. The Second-Class Angels, Third-Class Angels, The Serpent, Adam, and Eve were created flawlessly with this status.

Limited Free Will: The Serpent, Adam, and Eve became estranged from God by exercising Non-Limited Free Will to disobey God. Second and Third-Class Angels also became estranged from God when they disobeyed. Disobedience to God becomes Limited Free Will as there is no longer an ability to obey God flawlessly.

IDENTITY ARRAY

The eight-part identity model of personhood: SSID, HSID, SID, ESID, PID, MID, CID, MID. They are Super Spiritual ID, Holy Spirit ID, Spiritual ID, Evil Spirit ID, Physical ID, Mental ID, Childhood ID, and Dream ID.

INCLUSIVISM

The belief system asserts there are many paths to God. No one path or set of paths is more efficacious to salvation than others. It is the opposite of EXCLUSIVISM (Glossary) which maintains there is only one path to salvation – such as Jesus Christ.

INSANITY CHART (See complete chart in Chapter 17 and *Connecting The Dots Of Identity-2*, Chapter 17 and Chapter 27)

A crude shortcut to a classification of thinking and behaving.

Sane

The status of Pre-Life Elect individuals (Holy Spirit Identity-HSID) who possess a Christian worldview while continuing the Demonstration of Free Will through heredity, environment, and experience. They affirm objective morality as the standard of thinking and behaving, based on the transcendent, universal, top-down imperative from God of the Bible. The sane include people who are Holy Spirit immature: spiritually minded people who have yet to receive the Holy Spirit, and people whose mental impairment prevents them from consistent Christian participation.

Unsane

People who ascribe to atheists, agnostics, and non-Christian worldviews. They are spiritually blind but broadly mentally competent. Their profile is a cynical, derisive, contemptible view of objective morality—the standard of thinking and behaving based on the transcendent, universal, top-down imperative from God of the Bible.

They are against godliness unless God overrides their Free Will. They portray the Demonstration of Free Will through heredity, environment, and experience. (See Blind Eyes Chart)

Insane

Group A – The group of people who are 100 percent human, who suffer mental impairment from heredity, environment, and experience. They may be sane, adult Christians, but in general, they are mentally irresponsible. Additionally, the unsane also may suffer insanity from the effects of heredity, environment, and experience.

Group B – The group of people who are less than 100 percent human. Their mental identity also suffers the effects of heredity, environment, and experience. These are most likely ancestors of the Nephilim.

LUCIFER'S POSTULATE

Before "Lucifer" became Satan, a leading angel (X) inquired of God to receive unlimited freedom of behavior (omnipotence). The essence of living for a flawlessly created being is to behave as one desires without negative consequences. Considering God is omnipresent, omnipotent, and omniscient, He is capable of correcting any misbehavior on the fly. This renders true autonomy and freedom to the flawlessly created being, while eliminating any negative aspects of actions.

God declined the request, based on granting omnipotence to a created being without granting omniscience. However, God will provide a live Demonstration of Free Will. Non-angelic flawless human beings will have limited omnipotence (behavior) and limited omniscience (knowledge). The Demonstration will help prove God's will for His creatures is better than the creature's will for itself.

MARVI-RPIA

Modern Abstract Religious Verbal Impressionism-Role Play Identity Array. The name intends to convey a pseudo-orthodox view of religion featuring an artistic impression of Reformed theology.

MINISTER OF ART

Your humble servant, the author of CD1/CD2. Also, anyone who appreciates the artistry of Christian Reformed Impressionism by promoting or improving the imagery.

MONISM

The thoughts regarding the source of reality. Broadly, monism holds that everything is derived from one primary source INDEPENDENT of everything else. It differs from PHYSICALISM (materialism) in that physicalism holds that everything is derived from one primary source, though that source is NOT independent of everything else.

Monism affirms a distinction in physical, mental, and spiritual states. Physicalism affirms a "meat all the way down" aspect of human identity, which includes consciousness and mental states as products of the physical brain and other anatomical systems.

MORAL RELATIVISM

The view is that any standard of thinking and behaving is dependent upon the individual and circumstances. Context rules the adjudication of an agent to express themselves in any manner that enhances the quality of life, irrespective of other factors. Objective moral standards, such as rape, murder, and theft, are without standing and subject to reformation.

NEPHILIM AND NEPHILIM ONE-DROP RULE

The Nephilim are the living product of the sons of God (see Third-Class Angels in this section) and the daughters of men (human females). The offspring are destroyed in the Flood with every other person except the eight people of Noah's family. One (or more) of the eight persons saved is thought to genetically pass on a fraction of Nephilim genetic material from a relative who perished in the Flood.

Since Noah and Missus Noah are ostensibly blessed by God, and the three sons were blessed by God in scripture that leaves one or more of the three wives of Noah's sons as suspects.

Given that Shem was the progenitor of Abraham, and from Abraham came Jacob, and from Jacob came Judah, and then forward to Jesus, Missus Shem was most likely pure. Given that Canaan is cursed by Noah, and Canaan is a son of Noah's blessed son Ham, perhaps Canaan has the so-called "drop of Nephilim blood" from Missus Ham. This may also set the example for the children of Missus Japheth.

It should also be noted that even though Jesus avoided the cursed line that included Jeconiah, Jeconiah's curse was later modified. Even more so, all the ancestors of Jesus's mother and stepfather were sinners (cursed) until blessed by Jesus's birth. Every 100 percent human being was cursed until redeemed by Jesus.

(This One-Drop Rule refers to the dominant status of Negro blood in any ambiguous Negro person, thereby classifying them as Negro. This one-drop-of-blood practice was legally and socially in effect in times past, especially in the United States, but also elsewhere, and currently in effect among some Native American and Alaska Native tribes as proof of eligibility for membership).

OBJECTIVE MORALITY

Standards of thinking and behaving are based on transcendent, universal, top-down imperatives from the God of the Bible that apply to everyone. This contrasts with Subjective Morality, which bases standards of thinking and behaving on individual human preference rather than God.

ONTOLOGICAL STATUS

Human individual identity BEFORE the world was created. The essence of individual personhood being of necessity by the assertion from multiple examples in scripture. A determined, uncreated, identified immaterial essence.

PARADISE

The secondary name used for Heaven and/or the location with the Lord outside of time.

PELAGIANISM

Pelagianism is a heterodox Christian theological position. Pelagius (354-418 AD): Theologian. Philosopher. The British Isles. Noted antagonist to Saint Augustine. Believed no sin nature came from Adam; we are born spiritually neutral. We can choose God by individual Free Will. No such thing as predestination. Denied atonement by Jesus Christ. We should emulate Jesus. We are able to lead a sinless life or God would not command what man cannot achieve. Denounced as a heretic at the Council of Carthage (418), Council of Ephesus (431), and Council of Orange

(529). Semi-Pelagianism: Denial of full efficacy of grace for salvation until human initiative begins.

PHYSICALISM

Holds everything is derived from one primary source, but that source is NOT independent of everything else. Physicalism affirms a "meat all the way down" aspect of human identity which includes consciousness and mental states as products of the physical brain and other anatomical systems. As opposed to MONISM, everything is derived from one primary source that is INDEPENDENT of everything else.

PLURALISM (RELIGION)

The belief is that all religions have the blessing of God to achieve salvation. God honors sincere efforts to pursue love, honor, and peace with others, especially other religious belief systems. A community where diverse religious rights are protected from non-religious entities. This view relates to religious liberty.

PRE-LIFE ELECT

Individual persons (as opposed to a collective group of persons) guaranteed salvation before birth and before the world was created, and function as roleplayers of Free Will.

REDEEMER/ANTIDOTE/REMEDY/SOLUTION/MEDIATOR

The embodiment of God Himself via procreation of the Holy Spirit and Virgin Mary. By becoming 100 percent human and retaining 100 percent divinity, He provides correction to the error posed by Adam and Eve that created (physical) death and eternal damnation (spiritual non-life).

ROLEPLAY

Autonomous human beings were created by God to demonstrate Free Will, beginning with Adam and Eve. Also, Jesus Christ, being 100 percent God and 100 percent human, became a Free-Will Roleplayer as a 100 percent human to live a perfect life in place of Adam and Eve. After living perfectly, He died so as to conquer death by resurrection for all 100 percent human beings.

Our identity emanates from three basic influences—heredity, environment, and experience. HEVEX is the acronym.

Heredity-Roleplay

The identity we possess is a composite of ALL the identities in the TOTAL ancestral line. Heredity isn't as basic as mother, father, grandparents, and great-grandparents. Heredity isn't necessarily a research project that discovers the ancestral line of the past 100 to 500 years.

Heredity from the biblical record is comprised of EVERYBODY back to Mister and Missus Noah. The Nephilim, being less than 100 percent human, are also a possible ancestral component. Receding further, our identity begins with Adam and Eve—flawless humans who became flawed. Coming forward, the environment and experience contribute to determining what essentially an inauthentic identity is.

Environment-Roleplay

Parenting. Family members. Friends. Peers. Neighbors. Education. Associates. Culture. National Government. Local Government. Neighborhood quality. Air quality. Water quality. Soil quality. Nutritional quality. Ambient Sound quality. Weather quality. Personal products. Medicines. Toxins. A collective of material and immaterial components that contribute to identity.

Experience-Roleplay

Life events that are remembered, forgotten, repressed (accessible but avoided), subconscious (inaccessible), embellished, or inaccurate. This includes non-physical "experiences" such as imaginations, dreams, and impressions.

Other than birth and death, the most significant event upon inauthentic identity is the Holy Spirit's arrival. Preceding this, who we are could be summarized by heredity, environment, and experience until we join our authentic identity in Paradise. In the interim, our identity doesn't respect OBJECTIVE MORALITY, the standard of thinking and behaving defined by God. We respect SUBJECTIVE MORALITY, standards of our own defined as we see fit. This state of mind is spiritual blindness. It's the default position that NEVER changes until the Holy Spirit intercedes.

In this regard, what we see in Free Will roleplay is sanity and unsanity (see Insanity Chart):

1–Sane persons who project a high level of individual integrity.

2–Sane persons who project low to high levels of individual integrity.

3–Unsane persons who project low to medium levels of integrity.

ROLEPLAYER—TEAM PLAYER—TEAM COMPANION

ROLEPLAYER is a term to imply a contrived, temporary, inauthentic identity. It is the manifestation of heredity, the environment, and experiences before birth, at birth, and beyond birth. God developed procreation through Adam and Eve for two reasons: to prove the error of their Free Will through successive generations and correct their error via the antidote Jesus Christ. Like actors on a stage, we assume the character imposed on us, though it is not our true identity (Super-Spiritual Identity or SSID).

TEAM PLAYER is the union of two or more roleplayers. A Roleplayer loses their Roleplayer status by a 100 percent commitment to combine identities, typically through marriage. Roleplayers retain their contrived, temporary, inauthentic identity. As Team Players, they continue the Demonstration of Free Will, susceptible to procreation, thereby creating new Roleplayers who join the team. Ideally, both parties follow the impression conveyed by *Connecting The Dots Of Identity*, which suggests Godly Marriage Material, Team Companion, and a Single-Persons Champion before reaching Team Player status.

TEAM COMPANION is a relationship to a person or persons who communicate heart-to-heart regarding Connecting The Dots Of Identity impressions.

Godly Marriage Material (dating). Bronze.

Team Companion (friend, not marriage material). Silver.

Single-Persons Champion (unattached, not dating). Gold.

Team Player (engaged or married). Gold.

If you come to accept some of the tenets of MARVI-RPIA, you could be in the process of becoming Godly Marriage Material, assuming you are unattached. The next step is being a suitable Team Companion to a Single-Persons Champion. The process you go through begins with being the best single person you can be.

As you evaluate the effects of heredity, environment, and experience that formed what could be considered your inauthentic identity, you realize you're not limited by your appearance, your intellect, or your experiences.

SINGLE-PERSONS CHAMPION

Someone who never married, is divorced, or widowed. A person who has yet to meet another person worthy of changing their single-person status. In the interim, they think and behave in a manner that gives honor and service to the Lord by exemplifying and promoting Jesus Christ with 100 percent commitment.

Although finding a spouse has never been easier than it is today, the Single-Persons Champion doesn't pursue marriage. They're as neutral as possible, even while casually dating and making friends. The Single-Persons Champion motto is: “It’s up to YOU to make it impossible for ME to remain single.”

SPECIAL REVELATION AND GENERAL REVELATION

The biblical explanation of how God is revealed to us. General Revelation by the way we perceive the world through our senses, experiences, and natural laws of the universe. Special Revelation by the words God has given through oral tradition and the written word.

SUBJECTIVE MORALITY

The reliance on human definitions for good/bad, right/wrong, and risk/reward rather than a theistic definition. It is characterized by a cynical, derisive, contemptible view of objective morality.

SUPRALAPSARIAN (ANTE LAPSARIAN) (refers to a lapse in time)

Refers to the timing when God decrees individuals to salvation. This view maintains that (1) God chose individuals before He created the world, and (2) He creates the world. Contrast is then shown between the saved and unsaved of the world.

SUBLAPSARIAN and INFRALAPSARIAN (refers to a lapse in time)

This view holds that (1) God created all individuals, and (2) They all sin. Then God provides salvation to an elect number.

TRADUCIANISM

Traducianism is a secondary view (following Creationism and Designationism, defined in this section) that centers around WHEN souls or spirits are created and HOW souls or spirits are created.

When: (1) at conception (2) before conception (3) after conception.

How: (1) by parents (2) by God

Traducianism proposes the soul or spirit is created at conception by one or both parents. Although the soul is essentially immaterial, it is nonetheless transferred through procreation. The child is created in sin inherited by the parents.

Traducianism continues that God initiated physical and spiritual essence all at once with Adam and Eve. They were not conceived in sin. Only afterward when Adam and Eve fell was sin inherited from parents, not from God. The question of Jesus inheriting sin from the Virgin Mary is mitigated by the Holy Spirit, who implemented procreation.

UNIVERSALISM

In the sense of a religious principle, Universalism teaches that God's presence is in all individuals and is sufficient to assure all will achieve salvation, and that none be condemned. God is love. His love covers any and all circumstances, from conception to death. Hell is not a physical place of eternal torment for human beings. No humans go there. All humans go to Heaven. Jesus Christ paid for all sin, for all time.

PREFACE

Taking notes on life led to a notebook, which led to a journal, which led to a manuscript. As the journal grew, it seemed best to divide it into subjects. The most important subjects became religion, philosophy, psychology, and sociology. Then, it became 90 percent religion.

I developed a personal "perfect" prayer that I pray each night. I developed a Spiritual Day once a month, devoted to only spiritual things. I honored the Sabbath Day. I became a member of a church for twenty-five years.

Then, the pandemic hit.

So, no physical church attendance for a while. But that was not a time to relax. It was a time for fellowship and communication in other ways. Here was an opportunity and a challenge to continue spiritual growth while still supporting the churches.

Over the years, the background of my religious study research centered on question-and-answer programs. Thousands of questions and thousands of answers. This helped formulate an image of spiritual reality and how that coincided with physical and mental experiences. In the task of collating and preserving thirty years of notes into the computer, an idea began to form. Following up on the idea led to the possibility of an unorthodox religious project. Rather than promote the project as theology, it seemed better to simply share the project as an artistic impression of theology. This was especially fitting as I have no aspirations of ministry, teaching, or writing.

The impetus for presenting this material is to offer an alternative to the current imagery of theism, agnosticism, and atheism. By *Connecting The Dots Of Identity* via Modern Abstract Religious Verbal Impressionism, who I am, who you are, and what is happening is no longer such a mystery. God could have a similar plan. Certainly, His plan will be better than any we devise. But this so-called Plan B, compared to God's Plan A, may be appealing to you. Plan B certainly isn't conventional, but that may not matter. What matters is how well it stands up to everything else.

INTRODUCTION

Goliath stands tall and strong in modern days. He screams at the people of God every day—all day. God is NOBODY! God is not love. God is not moral. God is not here. Goliath speaks for the media, big tech, and big business. Goliath speaks for academia, politics, and celebrities. Goliath says follow us and live. He says following God of the Bible leads nowhere.

Connecting The Dots Of Identity says NOT SO! There's a way of looking at spiritual reality that will reintroduce you to who God may be.

We know the God of the Bible does not open everyone's spiritual eyes. A large segment of the world's population lives and dies in spiritual blindness. Those who have their spiritual eyes open do so in varying degrees of awareness and acuity. As the sighted attempt to help the blind, their efforts are well-meaning but often misguided.

A large number of people don't know God. They only know people who know *of* God, until God meets them Himself. We who follow the God of the Bible have a responsibility to sacrifice our lives for the sake of the environment of people. The environment improves to the extent that people in the environment improve. The improvement is defined as honor and respect for life. And life is that dynamic essence imparted to Adam and Eve by God, passed down to us via procreation. Adam and Eve exercised their Free Will to disobey God. They died, day by day, for about a thousand years.

As their children, we inherited the Error of Free Will rather than obeying God's Will for our lives. The Demonstration of Free Will must play out to prove the error made by flawless creatures. A flawless creature must be free to show independence from God. That applies to angels as well as human beings. We are free agents and not robots, puppets, or automatons.

However, this freedom was severely compromised when angels and humans acted on their Free Will to oppose God's will. Now, so-called freedom is restricted to thinking and behavior outside of God's beneficence—His active goodwill. In the case of angels, good angels remain within His good grace, the evil angels without.

Human beings become the cosmic display of what may result from the deviation of God's will to the will of the creature. Fortunately, God provided a Remedy for humans—Himself! God would take the form of a human being to correct the error of Adam and Eve.

God's intercession via the Holy Spirit to open our spiritual eyes dramatizes the fact no one chooses God's will. We choose our own will, constantly. We're free to follow the path of error until God overrides it.

Connecting The Dots Of Identity can't silence Goliath. Goliath will continue to taunt the people of God and defy the God of the Bible. *Connecting The Dots Of Identity* and *Connecting The Dots Of Identity-2* are here to function as David to defend the privilege and honor of following God. Goliath doesn't know God. That must not be OUR fault. We must do all in our power to introduce God to Goliath.

But why doesn't God just open everyone's eyes? Why all the mystery, misery, and mayhem? God, if You are there, SHOW US!

Yes. That is what the CD1/CD2 is all about. Showing God's presence to you. God could certainly make Himself known to everyone in an instant. But if He did so, why continue life after Jesus Christ died? Jesus lived a perfect life. Jesus conquered death. Jesus guaranteed salvation for everyone chosen before the foundation of the world. Let Judgment Day commence. The End. But that didn't happen.

Life is about proving the error a flawless living creature makes to choose its own will rather than God's will. The Serpent, Eve, and Adam chose death rather than God's will to not pursue knowledge of good and evil. Lucifer and a group of other angels chose their own will rather than God's will. They were flawless. Their Free Will was not corrupted. Ours is – thanks to Adam and Eve.

Apparently, their dissension must be visible across a specific number of lives before the end of the Demonstration of Free Will.

But the great news is that ROLEPLAY of our inauthentic identity—that identity forced upon us by heredity, environment, and experience—is not our authentic identity. Our authentic identity is the Pre-Life Identity, saved before the foundation of the world.

CD1/CD2 will attempt to paint an image of why life continues after Jesus Christ conquered death. Hint: it won’t be eschatology (study of the end times) or prophecy (divine revelation).

CHAPTER 1

PRE-LIFE AUTHENTIC IDENTITY

"Talent hits a target no one else can hit. Genius hits a target no one else can see."

Arthur Schopenhauer, philosopher

Five years ago, that was a great quote. It still is, but I recently reconsidered it. *How does it help YOU if I hit a target you can't see?* Maybe it's not a target to you. A significant part of genius may be defining a target and why it can't be seen. Can a genius be a person of very ordinary mental ability? What if you are simply the best person, at the best time, in the best position, to suggest the best target with significant life-changing value? People should then see the same target and agree it's a target of value.

The answers you have been searching for have produced good answers, great answers, and, of course, wrong answers. But you don't stop searching. That's why you're here.

What's fortunate about you being here is you won't have to resort to multiple sources over multiple years. *Connecting The Dots Of Identity* books 1 and 2 (CD1 and CD2) share readily available imagery. It's an impression that reveals a great Plan B to compare with God's magnificent Plan A.

The Table of Contents and the Glossary of Colors is a forewarning of what to expect. What you'll see over two volumes of *Connecting The Dots Of Identity* is:

1) a defined Pre-Life Elect person. A person saved before the foundation of the world is NOT the same as a born-again Christian.

2) why Lucifer and a group of angels rebelled, and other angels did not.

3) why the Serpent, Eve, and Adam fell.

4) who the sons of God in the Book of Genesis who married human females are?

5) why it only SEEMS that God didn't start over when Adam and Eve fell, but has done so.

6) what the meaning of life is.

7) why life is unfair until life has a new image.

8) why people are bad, with a new definition of "badness."

9) how individual identity has an eight-image array.

10) why some people are Elect by God and others not.

11) why the Bible is trustworthy.

12) why Jesus is the ONLY way to salvation.

13) why there are many religions and no religions (atheists).

14) how is it that all go to Heaven and none go to Hell in a righteous religious system.

15) fifty Questions and Answers session (CD2 only).

A few chapters from now, you'll see 100 Bible verses related to Election/Predestination. A hundred verses! A whole chapter! The point of that is to confirm the validity of the principle in scripture. And from this? From this, we have confidence that God has indeed saved persons before the foundation of the world. That is, He KNOWS them and SAVES them before they are born.

> According as he hath chosen us in him before the foundation of the world, that we should be holy and without blame before him in love (Ephesians 1:4).

But how can He know someone BEFORE they are someone? And, if they are already saved, why are they conceived by their parents? Some die in the womb. Some are aborted. Some die in the first days of life.

Yes, it would be great to have good answers. Answers are forthcoming in subsequent chapters. You decide how good they are.

When we factor in why such a book as *Connecting The Dots Of Identity* was written, the obvious question is why such a book hasn't appeared before. If Election/Predestination is so prominent in scripture, and it is prominent, *what does CD1/CD2 imply that 2,000 years of Biblical scholarship has missed?*

It has missed a METHOD of being unorthodox while maintaining orthodoxy. Typically, being unorthodox is denial, opposition, and subversion of widely held essential Christian beliefs.

CD1/CD2 is an unorthodox expression, while upholding the core beliefs of Christianity. It does so by using ART as the method of expression. *The expression is an IMPRESSION of orthodoxy,* not orthodoxy itself. Using artistic expression provides freedom to apply religious words in new ways.

As it stands, Election/Predestination has a terrible reputation. The understanding is that God chose certain people for salvation and did NOT choose others. One group goes to Heaven, the other group to Hell.

Additionally, Jesus is the ONLY way to salvation, and no one can come to God except through Jesus. And no one can come to Jesus unless God initiates the action. No one does so on their own. People are spiritually blind until God opens their eyes. This is the *works* versus *grace* principle. Works is man doing the work for his own salvation. Grace is God granting grace to save specific people.

So, man does NOT have Free Will. Destiny is settled before the world is created. *Then why be born? Why did Jesus arrive? Why get up tomorrow morning?*

CD1/CD2 portrays the person saved before the foundation of the world could be your AUTHENTIC identity residing in Paradise, a person that is not alive. A person that is a so-called Super-Spiritual Identity. God saved THAT person.

The life that does live is your INAUTHENTIC identity, the identity forced upon you via heredity, environment, and experience. You are a relative by heredity of EVERYONE who ever lived, beginning with Adam and Eve. This is an identity imposed on you without your interest, knowledge, or consent.

But why does the inauthentic identity feel so authentic? Because it's the identity you've been taught. No acceptable imagery of identity has been defined that supersedes the standard of heredity, environment, and experience. Now there is. It's imagery that comes from an artistic impression of Reformed theology, the person saved before the world was created.

And how does that matter?

It matters if it enhances the boundary of reality. The reason you're alive could be to demonstrate the error of a flawless creature exercising Free Will to disobey God.

Test A was the drama of the Serpent, Adam, and Eve. They were flawless creatures inserted *into* time and space. A flawless living creature, to be flawless, must be autonomous, independent from God. God knows what's best, but a flawless creature must experience that for itself. *The Serpent, Adam, and Eve began the Demonstration of Free Will.*

Test B was among spiritual beings *outside* time and space. The angels may have inquired about a form of omnipotence, behavior as desired without peril, transgression, or error. Perhaps God would wink and make the necessary adjustments on the fly. But God is not a 24/7 repairman. He is God, His Majesty, The Blessed Forever, amen. He counseled that such desire was detrimental to communal life and the environment. However, *God will construct a Demonstration of Free Will with non-angelic creatures – namely, human beings.*

God's gift of sharing His life with a creature is an attribute of true love. However, to have value, *life must be autonomous, offering a sense of independent ownership*. By providing a demonstration to the heavenly hosts, they will have an opportunity to witness a flawless creature's will versus God's will for the creature.

This Demonstration is so important that God will allow disobedience. The object of disobedience for the non-angelic creatures is introduced as the Tree of the Knowledge of Good and Evil. The beauty of the Garden environment only has this one representation of risk, uncertainty, and doubt. What will flawless creatures do?

The error of choosing the creature's will, not God's will, does occur. The Serpent, Adam, and Eve all exercise Free Will to oppose God. The angels observe.

–One group of angels condemns exercising Free Will to oppose God (First-Class Angels).

–Another group applauds opposition and even accuses God of animal, human, and angel design flaws (Second-Class Angels).

–A third group leaves Heaven to marry human females (Third-Class Angels).

God promised a Redeemer to reinstate the loss of life to human beings. Angels should likewise produce a redeemer via procreation should they ever disobey God. That mission failed. God brought the Flood. Mankind starts anew with the family of Noah.

The Demonstration of Free Will continues, in Heaven and on Earth.

The first group of angels love and obey God. They remain in Heaven. The second group, who accuse God of design flaws, continue their accusation of God, and act to prove human inferiority to angels. The third group of angels who left Heaven to marry females are captured and imprisoned in chains of darkness at the time of the Flood.

On Earth, which is now completely transformed by the Flood, human beings no longer live 1,000 years. Their lifespan is reduced to about 100 years. The other insidious matter is traces of the angel and human female experiment advances from Noah's family. More on that later in the Nephilim chapters.

Now, from Adam and Eve to Noah and his family, the mission continues to produce a Redeemer via procreation. The secondary mission is proving the error of flawless creatures disobeying God. This is the Demonstration of Free Will. We're all ROLEPLAYERS, exercising Free Will through the forces of heredity, environment, and experience. Free Will inherited from Adam and Eve is corrupt. No one is able to choose God's will. We choose our own will.

If God does not intercede to change our hearts, we will never choose Him. However, our salvation was secured before we were born. *This is our authentic identity.*

The inauthentic identity is our ROLEPLAY assignment from heredity, environment, and experience. When this life ends, we transition to authenticity – the identity saved before the foundation of the world.

Those who do not receive the Holy Spirit after conception, throughout life, and finally at death are NOT lost. They were also saved before they were born.

Our inauthentic identity on Earth:

a) proves the error of flawless creatures choosing THEIR will, not God's.

b) proves NO ONE can choose God (works). God must choose them (grace).

It takes a while to lay out the details of an artistic worldview. I'm not a writer. I'm not a theologian. I'm not an intellectual. I'm nobody, really. But I have a compulsion to share. It's good leverage versus the theist. It's good leverage versus the atheist. You don't ever have to say a word, but you have words. Words that heal. Words that comfort. Words that are meaningful. Words that live forever.

However, as the author, I do not believe in CD1/CD2. It's not theology. It's art. You don't believe in art. You appreciate it; or you don't.

CHAPTER 2

DESIGNATED ROLEPLAY

One day, you are violently removed from your long-established place of residence. You're delivered into a strange new environment. As you loudly protest, one of the voices nearby sounds very familiar. That voice belongs to your mother. It turns out this is the day of your birth. You are a couple of minutes old.

We were all born in a certain year, in a certain country, to certain parents. This was without our knowledge and without our permission. We were assigned gender, ethnicity, height, weight, appearance, intellect, health, and assorted undefined attributes. Some of us never made it out of the womb. Some of us die in the first few years of life. As we go about our lives, we are influenced by forces beyond our control.

Atheism or science purports you never have control. An unknown number of effects manipulate and direct your actions below the level of awareness. Even your choice of clothing, dinner, and spouse are all influenced by a complex model of human evolution. Similar to the imagery of a domino falling in response to being struck by another domino, events in your life are caused by prior events.

Can you prove this is an incorrect assumption by doing something random? No. Randomness is part of the matrix. General evolution, or materialism, suggests the universe behaves in an unintelligent, purposeless, unguided act of generating itself until energy is depleted, if energy can be depleted. Reality is nothingness that becomes something that returns to nothingness. This nothingness is indescribable until science acquires a sufficient model of what “no thing” actually is. In the interim, atheism and theism have no agreement on a reliable definition of nothing.

For theism, no thing can’t make something. No thing will always be nothing. No thing can’t do any thing. It is no thing.
But life derived from non-life, matter from non-matter, energy from no-energy, is acceptable to billions of people. This describes reality. This describes human identity. It’s a wonderful mystery until science figures it out.

Theism maintains that life has a Creator, life has a purpose, and there is an afterlife. Therefore, human identity is transcendent. As we grow and mature, our identity continues to be determined by heredity, environment, and experiences, but God knows and understands you as an individual. God works with you to assist you in life's difficulties. *Furthermore, God didn't make you this way. The human blueprint was pristine. Adam and Eve made you this way. Adam and Eve corrupted the blueprint.*

So begins connecting assorted dots of identity. An impression of religion began that was abstract rather than conventional. It became "modern abstract religious verbal impressionism"—MARVI. The "RPIA" came about through attention to scriptures regarding people who are identified BEFORE the world was created versus people who are identified AFTER the world was created.

What is the significance of these two classes of identities?
Identity is not what atheists declare. Identity is not what theists declare. *Identity is what scripture declares. Scripture declares identity does not begin at birth. Identity began before the world was created. Scripture declares in numerous verses that identity is Pre-Life.* The identity that begins in life, at birth, is a "role play" identity of Free Will. This was initiated by Adam and Eve.

Free Will roleplay is the drama of God proving autonomous, human, flawless living creatures will die if they disobey God's will for their lives. Adam and Eve disobeyed. They died. We inherited death. We inherited the role of proving Free Will leads to death. God saved His elected individuals before He created the world. That is us. We are in Paradise. The earthly persons born after Adam and Eve are our roleplay identities, inauthentic identities that do not define who we really are.

This is the best way to place God back on His throne—the God we all know who must be love, must be omniscient, must be omnipotent, must be omnipresent. *The God who does not send people to Hell because they are born at the wrong time, wrong place, to wrong parents, or in the wrong circumstances of life.* We know God is fair.

Yet, all around us, we see unfairness. The atheists say that's life. Make the best of it. The theists say God knows best. Trust in God. But how can you trust theists who excuse God for all the chaos, confusion, misery, and death we see day after day? How can you trust atheists who contend life is an accident, has no purpose, and goes back to nothing at death?

We say we trust religion. We say we trust science. Do we really trust them with our whole lives?

Rather, let's trust 100 Bible verses (Chapter 6) that declare we were established before the world was established. From this perspective, our earthly birth is a roleplay demonstration of Free Will, initiated by Adam and Eve. *We are not compelled to accept the secondary identity beginning at conception/birth as primary and authentic.* Our authentic identity is a Pre-Life Elect person in Paradise. God says so in scripture.

This book is an art project. It renders an image using religious words. The words paint a picture of an impression derived from seventy years of spiritual exposure. This impression is based on a biblical ontological identity, existing before birth. This is the Pre-Life Elect person acknowledged by God before He created the world. *We might say Group A persons are outside time. They are separate and distinct from Group B persons who are created inside time, starting with Adam and Eve.*

Of course, you're skeptical. It's new, but it sounds like another religious doctrine. However, here's the difference. It's art. It's an impression of the Bible. I don't believe it. I don't expect you to believe it. It's simply undeclared and unspoken leverage for all the assertions coming from theists, atheists, and agnostics. CD1/CD2 is there if you ever need it. It's an extremely positive outlook on pre-life, life, and the afterlife.

CHAPTER 3

THE SECOND-BEST NEWS OF ALL TIME

Do you watch the local, national, or international news every day? Do you avoid the news shows because of too much bad news? Is the so-called "Good News" of Jesus Christ really good news to you?

Here's a bulletin! There is another news item that is the SECOND-BEST NEWS in the history of mankind. It's called *Connecting The Dots Of Identity*, subtitled Modern Abstract Religious Verbal Impressionism-Role Play Identity Array (MARVI-RPIA).

Good news? What good news? The Good News of Jesus Christ is only good news if you believe in Jesus. Arguably, a large portion of the planet does not believe in Jesus. Many who say they do surely have doubts from time to time if they're honest.

Connecting The Dots Of Identity, MARVI-RPIA, readily admits it is not to be believed. It's an impression. It's an art project. You don't believe in art. You appreciate it or you don't. But it is good, and it is new. It's "gooder" than anything you've heard that is based on theology, and newer than anything you've heard based on theology.

We can agree that the concept of Jesus is good. His whole life was based on goodness. But why news? What is newsworthy about Jesus Christ? His story is 2,000 years old.

1) *The Messiah has been born.* The Promise made by God to Adam and Eve that their colossal error would be corrected through procreation has

been fulfilled. This is NEW, as it comes to each individual when God opens their spiritual eyes.

2) *Jesus rose from the dead.* This has never happened before and has not happened since. This is NEW as it comes to each individual when God opens their spiritual eyes.

3) *There is an afterlife*. Jesus, who led a 100 percent sinless, perfect life, assured our salvation to be with Him in the future after our life ends in the present. It's such a certainty, it's as if it's already happened. This is NEW, as it comes to each individual when God opens their spiritual eyes.

This all sounds great. It sounds a little *too* great, in fact. And nobody, that means NOBODY, will believe it unless God opens their spiritual eyes. Free Will to believe the Good News is NOT POSSIBLE! God does ALL the actions in the salvation process. God HAS DONE all the salvation action BEFORE He created the world. This is predestination. This is God's election program of individuals.

The proposal of identity before the world is created, an identity before birth, is relatively new in the context of Free Will, predestination, and our present identity. Mainstream religion does not teach this. Certainly, outside religion, it makes no sense. There can't be two simultaneous identities.

This has opened a gap for a specific project—an art project. I'm an artist. As a Christian, over the years I've developed an *impression* of Christian Reformed theology. However, because I am not a theologian, philosopher, intellectual, or writer, the project will have its doubters. The impression is not meant to counsel, instruct, teach, or suggest a belief system.

Since I don't claim to be a man of God—pastor, prophet, or apostle—what is my intention, you might ask? To illustrate and present the second-best

Good News ever heard: EVERYONE GOES TO HEAVEN; NO ONE GOES TO HELL.

This is not "Universalism." Universalism is rejected by orthodox Christian teaching for its views on Hell, salvation, and Free Will. MARVI-RPIA also rejects Universalism. (See the Glossary of Colors and Chapter 17, “Role Play. Identity Array”).

By sharing this second-best greatest news, I hope to achieve the following:

- Fulfill God's command to seek truth and share truth in love for God, neighbor, and self.
- Assist in revealing reality via General Revelation (nature) and Special Revelation (Bible).
- Increase optimism and decrease pessimism by promoting Christian Reformed imagery.
- Mitigate suffering in the world by providing evidence of an alternate authentic identity.
- Respond to atheists and agnostics concerning concepts of religious principles.
- Offer *Christian Reformed Impressionism* as support for a spiritual worldview.

And this is supposed to be art? It is. As you know, art has many mediums and dynamics of expression. MARVI-RPIA is another form, different from others to be sure, but a form of art.

No, not text-based art. This isn't using words or phrases as an illustration of a work of art. No, not ekphrasis, which means using language to describe or comment on a work of art. No, not a descriptive technique commonly used in art or religion.

When thinking of art, typically we think of seven or so categories: architecture, cinema, literature, music, painting, performance, and sculpture. MARVI-RPIA doesn't quite fit. Literature? No, I don't write that well. Perhaps graffiti, unauthorized trespassing on religious turf? Maybe. It is unorthodox. It is expression.

It's not strictly theology, though it borrows heavily from religious verbal expression. The intent is to utilize the expression of art and the expression of spirituality. It won't attempt to cram religion down your throat. No threats of Hell (by not doing this) and offers of Heaven (by only doing this). This is something you haven't received from artists of the gallery or pastors of the church.

R.C. Sproul mentions in his YouTube lectures ("Defending Your Faith" - Message 4) that there are four "laws" we utilize to believe or disbelieve something when in doubt:

1. The law of non-contradiction (reason)

2. The law of causality (cause and effect)

3. The law of the basic reliability of sense perception (our five senses)

4. The law of the analogous use of language (words that compare/describe)

Doubt is healthy. It suggests your mind is open to options. R.C. Sproul reminds us to be responsible and to follow rules that help us think.

On the other hand, while you're thinking, an analogy of art may help bridge the gap between the possibility of religion and your intuition about religion. There is beauty in religion. The beauty is all too often mired in trying to connect the dots to produce a cohesive image. There are so many unsatisfactory answers to pressing religious questions that most people just give up.

Don’t give up. The second-best Good News is here. And it’s very, very, very good.

CHAPTER 4

THE BIBLE AS DOCUMENT OF MERIT

As popular as the Bible is, it's extremely hard to read, even for Christians. It's hard to set aside time and make yourself open it. It's hard to know where you should start reading. Old Testament? New Testament? Which book? Which chapter? Which verse?

If you are not a Christian, will reading the Bible change your identity? Will you be the same person? What will your family think? Your friends? Your associates at work? A time may come when you are finally ready to go to the Bible, never mind what others think.

The Bible purports to document the history of the world. Books other than the Bible also claim to document the history of the world. Since people have varying opinions about what constitutes historical accuracy, the truth may seem hard to find. It actually is hard to find.

Modern archeology affirms confidence in the historical accuracy of biblical texts. Other branches of the sciences also complement the Bible, insofar as scripture reflects life in antiquity. Bibles sell well, year after year. Many copies are being read worldwide even where the Bible is prohibited. People want to know firsthand what religion is about.

Also consider Jesus Christ. Like the Bible, Jesus is certainly more widely studied than any other person in history. The very best minds in the world have both praised and denied Him. Is it possible such a person could be born of a virgin, lead a sinless life, die, and come back to life? Is it possible He could be 100 percent human and 100 percent God? Are these possibilities worth pursuing?

No, says one group. They hold there is no credibility in any religious worldview. They're atheists. Atheists claim to follow science rather than faith, objectivity rather than subjectivity. Alongside atheists are agnostics. They aren't confident that affirming objective truth is even feasible. They don't know about God because they don't think God is knowable. Otherwise, they would know Him as well as any theists would know Him. What little they do know about God is insufficient to represent a worldview. So, they live as atheists.

For an average person, the Bible as a standard for objective reality raises problems. The Bible is hard to understand. The Bible has utterly ridiculous stories. The Bible has contradictions. The Person considered to be the most significant Person who ever lived, Jesus Christ, may not be real. However, He is the main One who confirmed the reliability of the Bible!

Jesus's historicity is absolutely credible, even for atheists. This historical figure attributed to Himself the identity of God. Though found not guilty of breaking Roman law, religious leaders demanded Jesus be crucified for religious reasons and released an infamous convicted criminal in His place. Jesus was put to death. Direct and circumstantial evidence document His resurrection. This seems a fairly good case for why the Bible is highly esteemed.

Going further, a follow-up question is: Who actually wrote the Bible? Various individuals? Groups of churches? God?

Any human being could write any book and say God inspired them to write it. Anyone could say they had a spiritual dream or vision or visitation from an angel. And from this comes a religious protocol for a religious document. How many people see God? How many people hear God? Many confess to doing so every single day. If such godly visitations are truly from God, they should be added to the treasure of religious documents. *The next step is an evaluation toward inclusion into holy scripture.* How many books of the Bible would we then have? How many Bible translations would we have?

Even more problematic and sinister: *How could we know godly revelations were truly from God?* Satan is known as the Great Deceiver. He employs ministers of light.

> And the great dragon was cast out, that old serpent, called the Devil, and Satan, which deceiveth the whole world: he was cast out into the earth, and his angels were cast out with him (Revelation 12:9).

> And no marvel; for Satan himself is transformed into an angel of light. Therefore it is no great thing if his ministers also be transformed as the ministers of righteousness; whose end shall be according to their works (2 Corinthians 11:14-15).

Does God have any protection in place that GUARANTEES we know His words? If God is God, He surely does.

> And it came to pass in the 4th year of Jehoiakim the son of Josiah king of Judah, that this word came unto Jeremiah from The Lord, saying, Take thee a roll of a book, and write therein all the words that I have spoken unto thee against Israel, and against Judah, and against all the nations, from the day I spake unto thee, from the days of Josiah, even unto this day... Then Jeremiah called Baruch the son of Neriah: and Baruch wrote from the mouth of Jeremiah all the words of the Lord, which he had spoken unto him, upon a roll of a book (Jeremiah 36:1-2, 4). The Spirit of The Lord spake by me, and His word was in my tongue (2 Samuel 23:2).

As He spake by the mouth of His holy prophets, which have been since the world began (Luke 1:70).

Knowing this first, that no prophecy of the scripture is of any private interpretation. For the prophecy came not in old time by the will of man: but holy men of God spake as they were moved by the Holy Ghost (2 Peter 1:20-21).

All scripture is given by inspiration of God, and is profitable for doctrine, for reproof, for correction, for instruction in righteousness (2 Timothy 3:16).

For I testify unto every man that heareth the words of the prophecy of this book, If any man shall add unto these things, God shall add unto him the plagues that are written in this book. And if any man shall take away from the words of the book of this prophecy, God shall take away his part out of the book of life, and out of the holy city, and from the things which are written in this book (Revelation 22:18-19).

When the Book of Revelation verse 22 warns not to add or take away from this book, it would mean the whole Bible. Deuteronomy also warns not to add or subtract from the word of God. Considering there is no Old and New Testament Bible, no compilation of inspired documents without chapters or verses in existence BEFORE the Book of Revelation, it stands to reason God envisioned and guided the translated versions of original documents. Jesus Christ gave His approval of Old Testament documents, and He was the standard and overseer for New Testament scripture.

Ye shall not add unto the word which I command you, neither shall ye diminish ought from it, that ye may keep the commandments of the Lord your God which I command you (Deuteronomy 4:2)

People may ask: How can the Bible simply guarantee itself to be true, since the Bible itself is the source of the statement?

The greatest person who ever lived isn't guarantee enough? Jesus Christ Himself confirmed the reliability of scripture. Being God, Jesus as a person of the Trinity actually wrote the Bible.

The essential issue regarding trust in the Bible is more than how the Bible came to be written or which documents have the most accurate translations. The Council of Chalcedon helps us understand why the Bible has such transcendent stature.

The Council of Chalcedon, the fourth ecumenical council of the Christian church, was held in Chalcedon (modern Kadiköy, Turkey) in 451AD. Convoked by the emperor Marcian, it was attended by about 520 bishops or their representatives and was the largest and best documented of the early councils. It approved the creed of Nicaea (325), the creed of Constantinople (381) subsequently known as the Nicene Creed, two letters of St. Cyril of Alexandria against Nestorius, which insisted on the unity of divine and human persons in Christ, and the Tome of Pope Leo I, which confirmed two distinct natures in Christ. It rejected the Monophysite doctrine that Christ Council of Chalcedon had only one nature. The council then explained these doctrines in its own confession of faith (https://www.britannica.com/event/Council-of-Chalcedon).

The Council further expanded on four specific characteristics of Jesus's dual nature—how Jesus as God and Jesus as Man were to be defined, *without change, without confusion, without division, and without separation.* In other words, without mixing of the two beings, one being is compromised by the other.

R. C. Sproul has a series of lectures called *"Hath God Said"* (Ligonier Ministries, 2021). Sproul highlights three ways objections are made regarding how the Bible was written.

One: God simply dictated and men wrote (dictation method).

Two: God intervened and wrote for the men using the men's own hands (mechanical method).

Three: God spoke through the men to render the men puppets, robots, and avatars (replacement method).

If there are errors, they are not from the original manuscripts. God's intentions were correctly rendered. Errors may occur following the original texts—omissions, additions, damaged manuscripts, etcetera.

What Sproul explained later in the same lecture series is an objection from critics on the authenticity of Jesus's testimony. They said Jesus confirmed the truthfulness and trustworthiness of the Bible, *but Jesus was also human. Humans are not 100 percent reliable.* Jesus could not be faulted if He was not 100 percent accurate about every single thing He said. Sproul affirms Jesus was 100 percent human. What Sproul added was extremely important in understanding why the Bible is infallible, meaning it can't be untrue.

This is because Jesus had to be 100 percent human to be our Redeemer. He had to be human to pay for our human sins. Jesus, as a human being, lived a 100 percent sinless, perfect life. *That gave Him the authority to be the One who saves us and proves His identity as Lord of all.*

Let's review the Bible story. God created the heavens and the earth from nothing. God created oceans, trees, plants, animals, then human beings—Adam and Eve.

God placed Adam and Eve in Eden inside a garden. The humans were told many things, and among them was not to eat of the Tree of the Knowledge of Good and Evil or they would die. Adam and Eve did eat because one of the animals in the Garden, the Serpent, suggested doing so would be beneficial, not detrimental. Adam and Eve did eat—and they died, just not immediately. When confronted by God, the humans shifted the blame. God said because this had occurred, the Serpent was cursed, the humans were cursed, and the environment was cursed. However, God promised the humans they would receive an Antidote for this catastrophe via progeny. Adam, Eve, and the Serpent were then cast out of the Garden.

Within the next thousands of years, the progeny from Adam and Eve became so corrupt that God destroyed every human being except eight of them in the Flood. Later, as humans began to repopulate the earth, God showed favor to a particular group called Israel. This group of people produced the Antidote to the sin in Eden that gave the world death and cursed the earth. The Antidote was a Child born to the Virgin by the Holy Spirit. This Person was Jesus. Jesus the Christ taught that He was the One sent from Heaven by God to save mankind. He proved His identity by His lifestyle, by His miracles, by His death, and by His resurrection from death.

The Bible takes quite some time to lay out this scenario. After the first four books of the New Testament, which tell of Jesus Christ's ministry, the next twenty-three books attest to the previous books of the Old Testament and the previous four Gospel books of the New Testament.

The atheists say this is all nonsense. Science is the only true belief system, as it is demonstrably provable. Agnostics add that knowledge of reality is inaccessible by human attributes. Other belief systems offer a multitude of philosophies about the nature of reality.

Incidentally, while atheists are known for their disbelief in the God of the Bible, or any religious interpretation of a supremely intelligent being, *they should admit it's possible that God exists, even if the Bible isn't inerrant or infallible.* This came as a reminder from an atheist on a YouTube podcast this year (*Harmonic Atheist*).

And yet, the familiar refrain—the Bible is not God's word. The Bible is the word of men. Yes, they admit, we do read in the Bible that God is the author. However, it is men who are writing the Bible. The argument offered is that the Bible may have begun with the inspiration of God, but what probably transpired was a corruption of the transcripts soon after the first century.

We know there have been iterations of bibles, or words of God, leading up to the King James Version in 1611, widely hailed as the official, widely accepted first Bible. Since then, we now have numerous versions of so-called newly deciphered ancient transcripts that improve the authenticity of previous versions.

Considering the Bible must be the document God wants us to have or we certainly wouldn't have it, and that Jesus Christ supports the Bible and quotes it, it's still amazingly dreadful how many lives it cost to make the scriptures available to us.

The path the Bible has taken to arrive in the twenty-first century is filled with a lot of drama and a lot of blood. And it continues, even today!

Your sense of goodwill and empathy might make you wonder why God didn't render the Bible easy to acquire and easy to read. *Why all the drama and blood?*

There was a LONG time when there were NO scriptures available to read. People heard directly from God, from messengers of God, from the priests, and from the prophets of God. And then, there was a time when there was a Bible, but not many people knew how to read.

There was a time when the public was not allowed to read Bibles; only the clergy could read it.

There was a time when it was illegal for certain people to be able to read anything.

There was a time when possessing a particular Bible translation was a life-or-death decision. Only the approved religion was tolerated.

How many hundreds, thousands, or millions of people were killed because they believed in, shared, or quoted scripture? Include the number one person of all time, Jesus Christ.

How many of you, or people you know, could not care less about a Bible? You only know about it from what you've heard others say. Are you afraid of it? Afraid of what others might think of you if you do read it?

Obviously, many world governments are afraid of the Bible. Various internet searches reveal that in as many as fifty countries, the Bible is prohibited, unauthorized, prosecutable, banned, restricted, or held in contempt. Why? Objective morality. *God as the standard of right and wrong, good and bad, moral and immoral overrules the ruling class.* This undermines authority. That must not happen.

And it doesn't happen. *HUMAN BEINGS are becoming the standard of right and wrong, good and bad, moral and immoral.*

The challenge for Christians is to communicate God's moral superiority revealed in the Bible. Otherwise, being spiritually blind, God doesn't seem any more moral than we are. God elects only certain people to Heaven; the rest go to Hell. God kills thousands who don't follow his rules—men, women, and children. *We know 150,000 people worldwide die every day,* whether they pray to Him or not. If the world is ruled by God, He can't be loving, aware, or moral. The world is deranged! Where is He? Nowhere! We have to be God ourselves.

And the Bible is inerrant? Bible scholars are pro and con on this issue. You be the judge.

And the Bible is infallible? The Bible absolutely MUST be infallible. It's exactly what God wants us to read. Which Bible? Any bible that is faithful to the original manuscript(s) translation.

If the Bible is written by God, using men as a spokesperson, there is nothing that can corrupt this word down through a trillion years, much less a few thousand. *If written by men, so what? That does not matter.* Why?

One, because EVERYTHING is written by men. We read, trust, and quote from books written by men (and women).

Two, because we are not saved by scripture—according to scripture itself! Scripture says we are not saved by what we know. We were saved *before the foundation of the world.* We are saved by grace (Him), not works (us).

> According as he hath chosen us in him before the foundation of the world, that we should be holy and without blame before him in love (Ephesians 1:4).

Therefore, we can have a better understanding of the drama and blood that transpires surrounding the Bible. If the words of God are the Bible, they must be followed, no matter what else in life occurs. If the words are the words of men, and not of God, no amount of coercion can force compliance to those words.

Unless God opens our spiritual eyes, the Bible may only be a document of fiction, fear, and suppression of freedom. It may also be highly regarded but is, in actuality, disregarded.

For now, the point is to reiterate that the Bible has a significant presence in CD1/CD2. Scripture is featured throughout to underscore the importance of a reliable foundation for the artistic impression. God reveals Himself as General Revelation and Special Revelation. General Revelation is how God makes Himself known in nature, such as how the world appears, how the world functions, and its beauty, mystery, and awe.

Special Revelation is the written word—scripture (see Chapter 9, "General Revelation and Special Revelation"). Although CD1/CD2 is art, the art isn't possible without scripture. Perhaps as you go through subsequent chapters, you will appreciate scripture a little more.

Additional support for the Bible as God's word to man:

Refnet. https://listen.refnet.fm

J. Warner Wallace. *Person Of Interest.* Zondervan. 2021. *Cold Case Christianity.* David C. Cook. 2023

R.C. Sproul. *Defending Your Faith Series.* Ligonier Ministries. 2001. YouTube.

Familyradio.org

CHAPTER 5

CHRISTIAN REFORMED THEOLOGY—PART 1

Now, back to trust in the inerrancy of the Bible. If it doesn't matter if we even know a Bible exists, that salvation comes by the grace of God, and that this salvation was granted before the world was created, why are we going through this charade of life? What's the point in the Adam and Eve story, the Flood that killed everyone except eight people, God's people Israel, and the birth, life, death, and resurrection of Jesus? If I am an elect person and my neighbor is not an elect person, then according to predestination, we have no choice in the course of our life to change our destination. *Our destiny is sealed before we were born.*

Yes, that seems to be the pressing view we all have when presented with the Christian Reformed doctrine. How can it be fair for me as the Elect person and fair for my neighbor as the non-Elect person? If what we see and experience in life is how God rules the world from His throne on high, where is the Good News?

These are good questions. Recently, I heard an interview featuring Stephen C. Meyer. Meyer has produced material that documents the theistic implications of science (*The Return of the God Hypothesis*, Harper Collins, 2021). Assuming science supports the existence of God, how is that helpful if people don't know God? What if people don't like what they've heard of God? What if God isn't showing anything religion claims He personifies, like love, hope, healing, or joy?

God does personify love, hope, healing, and much more. Dr. Meyer shows that science helps explain how God makes Himself known. *Connecting The Dots Of Identity* may help make God known through the medium of art.

Let's review whether there is a prominent view of theology that promotes Election and Predestination and if it has any real standing in religious circles.

One of the most conservative and solid Christian doctrines is Christian Reformed theology. Why reformed? The Reformation was a refinement of the Protestant movement initiated by the German monk Martin Luther (1483-1546) in the sixteenth century. Martin Luther borrowed from the teachings of the great Saint Augustine (354-430). Luther held that the dominance of the Catholic church was negligent in its teachings on salvation, thereby compromising the integrity of the Bible. Catholicism taught that a person's works (behavior) and tradition (rituals) were instrumental to salvation. Luther opposed this position to affirm that Jesus Christ, the scripture, faith (from God), and grace (by God) were the true pillars of salvation.

Other great men of note followed in Luther's stance, notably John Calvin (1509-1564). Calvin championed the second wave of Protestant theology. The second wave began to reform and finely tune the break from the Catholic church, as well as other denominations. From here, we see a separation between Luther and the newer reformers. Luther and the newer reformers disagreed on the nature of the Lord's Supper (Eucharist/Holy Communion). Luther believed in an ostensible presence of the Lord's body, while others did not.

As the Reformation gained adherence, another view also gained prominence. This was the Arminian view credited to Jacobus Arminius (1560-1609). Arminianism was a remonstration against the reformed view of salvation. On the one hand, reformists believed in God's sovereignty (absence of man's Free Will) to elect persons to salvation based on grace alone. Arminianism disagreed, saying man has Free Will and, by God's grace AND man's works, he becomes saved. Being omniscient, God has perfect knowledge of who His elect will be, and thus chooses these persons based on foreknowledge.

That simplified background summary starts the ball rolling on Christian Reformed theology. MARVI-RPIA is designed to help understand the significance of Reformed theology. Reformed doctrine is neither easy to explain, nor accept. It is, however, of prominent and significant standing throughout scripture. You can't miss it. You can't deny it. Well, you can deny it, but not without the collision that comes with doing so. On what basis do you deny so many obvious statements in the Bible?

The basis is the statements regarding core concepts of reformed doctrine: predestination, election, grace, and God's sovereignty. They are simply unattractive. They're ugly. They're reprehensible. They take away man's Free Will. They misrepresent God. How can God be so unfair to people? This can't be possible.

Christian Reformed doctrine teaches the predestination of God's chosen people to be saved before He created the world (see Romans and Ephesians). They are called the Elect. Of course, that means those whom God does not choose are not saved. One group is bound for Heaven (elect). The other group is bound for Hell (not elect). Does this seem righteous? Does this represent an accurate representation of God's holy scripture? God is love? God is fair? God is not a respecter of persons?

> Then Peter opened his mouth, and said, of a truth I perceive that God is no respecter of persons (Acts 10:34).

> For whom he did foreknow, he also did predestinate to be conformed to the image of his Son, that he might be the firstborn among many brethren (Romans 8:29).

> According as he hath chosen us in him before the foundation of the world, that we should be holy and without blame before him in love (Ephesians 1:4).

So, how do we understand this? It doesn't seem to make sense. One of the ways we may look at this is to realize our "sense" is compromised by sin. We can know this by acknowledging we are not perfect beings. We make mistakes. We have limited knowledge. Our sense of fairness, justice, and our opinion of God is not entirely reliable. We must admit that for there to be God, He must always be right. He is the epitome of rightness. That means we are the ones at fault, not God. We must be misunderstanding scripture.

What could we be missing?

What is predestination? Elect ones were chosen and saved before the world was created.

Can anyone be saved? No. Only the Elect.

And this is a foregone conclusion? Yes, it already happened before the world was created.

Do we have Free Will? No. Only limited Free Will. Adam and Eve had Free Will. Angels have/had Free Will. Once sin compromises a flawless being, their Free Will becomes limited.

Why Hell if there is nothing humans can do to be saved, but all are dependent on God?

Hell is because every human being (and angelic being) has an eternal spiritual identity. Angels who exercise Free Will to oppose God will become eternal non-living waste matter, relegated to Hell. Non-elect humans are those less-than-100 percent humans compromised by those angels. They also could become non-living waste matter unfit for life, relegated to Hell.

But why would God allow a human to be compromised by evil spirits and risk going to Hell?

To demonstrate how Free Will plays out in human life. God allowed Job, King Saul, Mary Magdalene, and others to be demon-compromised. This wasn't necessarily a condemnation to Hell. Jezebel, Judas Iscariot, and Pontius Pilate were also compromised by the spirit of evil. This is the diversity of human freedom. This is the Demonstration of Free Will.

Additionally, to be compromised by an evil spirit(s) suggests you may not be 100 percent human. You don't have a soul, a spirit. Jesus became 100 percent human to only redeem 100 percent humans, not angels, and not angel-human hybrids (the Nephilim). This also doesn't include aliens from other planets, other galaxies, or aliens derived from artificial intelligence. No soul, no spirit, no redemption exists. Jesus doesn't redeem animals. No soul, no spirit exists.

But why are there good angels who disagree with God—Lucifer, Abaddon, and others?

Why are there good humans who disagree with God, especially Adam and Eve?

Why did the good serpent take it upon himself to act against the life of Eve and Adam?

Free Will is the answer, at least the Free Will possessed by those who were flawless creatures. The Free Will that we, as fallen creatures, have no access to and no knowledge of.

But why would any "good" person exercise Free Will to go against God's perfect will for them?

We're not "good." We can only guess. Our knowledge of flawless creatures' thinking is not accessible. But let's guess anyway.

Autonomy. Freedom. Control. Suspicion of being not truly alive. Objection to being a "robot" or a "puppet."

Let's continue to examine Election and Predestination …

What exactly does it mean to be predestined or elected to salvation? It may be helpful to document many of the scriptures that testify to this.

Have you read the Bible? All the way through? No, not speed-reading but reading with comprehension and patience. Perhaps reading with tools nearby like pen and paper. When you read the Bible this way, you should develop spiritual maturity. As you grow from immaturity to maturity, you'll encounter Bible passages that do not seem believable, seem contradictory, and some you may want to deny.

Let's face it, the Bible is ridiculous in its verse after verse after verse of outlandish pronouncements. That's easy to admit. However, one thing stands out no matter how difficult it is to accept it: Election/Predestination. It's a MAJOR feature in the Bible.

A "topical bible" may be a good reference book to have around. You may then search by topic to find Bible verses that apply to the topic. Thirty years ago, I found *Nave's Topical Bible* in a used bookstore. Words such as *election*, *predestination*, and *chosen* provided many scriptural references. You may be surprised to discover just how many Bible verses contain words referring to an absence of human Free Will. You will find words or phrases such as *set apart, His people, before the foundation of the world, determined, fore-ordained, promised, purposed,* and *Lamb's Book of Life.*

In *Nave's Topical Bible* under the word category "God," there are numerous subcategories. Two such categories are God: Knowledge of and God Call (personal). Here we find many verses that pertain to God's knowledge of us, His chosen individuals, and God's personal calling to us to be His chosen ones.

Not all verses are pertinent to predestination or the absence of Free Will. Some will suggest aspects of how predestination or absence of Free Will is related to our imposed roleplay identity, handed down from ancestor to ancestor back to Adam and Eve.

Rather than have you break stride and turn to the back of this book, the next chapter is a reference to Bible verses that may help convince you how important a part predestination and election plays in scripture.

CHAPTER 6

CHRISTIAN REFORMED THEOLOGY— PART 2

ELECTION – CHOSEN – PREDESTINATION

All verses from the Authorized King James Version of the Bible. How many verses? 106.

(1) And in very deed for this cause have I raised thee up, for to shew in thee my power; and that my name may be declared throughout all the earth (Exodus 9:16).

(2) Only the Lord had a delight in thy fathers to love them, and he chose their seed after them, even you above all people, as it is this day (Deuteronomy 10:15).

(3) For it was of the Lord to harden their hearts, that they should come against Israel in battle, that he might destroy them utterly, and that they might have no favour, but that he might destroy them, as the Lord commanded Moses (Joshua 11:20).

(4) Wherefore the king hearkened not unto the people; for the cause was from the Lord, that he might perform his saying, which the Lord spake by Ahijah the Shilonite unto Jeroboam the son of Nebat (1 Kings 12:15).

(5) But I have chosen Jerusalem, that my name might be there; and have chosen David to be over my people Israel (2 Chronicles 6:6).

(6) Blessed is the nation whose God is the Lord; and the people whom he hath chosen for his own inheritance (Psalm 33:12).

(7) Blessed is the man whom thou choosest, and causest to approach unto thee, that he may dwell in thy courts: we shall be satisfied with the goodness of thy house, even of thy holy temple (Psalm 65:4).

(8) Moreover he refused the tabernacle of Joseph, and chose not the tribe of Ephraim: But chose the tribe of Judah, the mount Zion which he loved. And he built his sanctuary like high palaces, like the earth which he hath established for ever. He chose David also his servant, and took him from the sheepfolds (Psalm 78:67-70).

(9) For the Lord hath chosen Jacob unto himself, and Israel for his peculiar treasure (Psalm 135:4).

(10) The Lord hath made all things for himself: yea, even the wicked for the day of evil (Proverbs 16:4).

(11) Yet now hear, O Jacob my servant; and Israel, whom I have chosen: Thus saith the Lord that made thee, and formed thee from the womb, which will help thee; Fear not, O Jacob, my servant; and thou, Jesurun, whom I have chosen (Isaiah 44:1-2).

(12) And who, as I, shall call, and shall declare it, and set it in order for me, since I appointed the ancient people? and the things that are coming, and shall come, let them shew unto them (Isaiah 44:7).

(13) Remember the former things of old: for I am God, and there is none else; I am God, and there is none like me, Declaring the end from the beginning, and from ancient times the things that are not yet done, saying, My counsel shall stand, and I will do all my pleasure (Isaiah 46:9-10).

(14) Then the word of the Lord came unto me, saying, Before I formed thee in the belly I knew thee; and before thou camest forth out of the womb I sanctified thee, and I ordained thee a prophet unto the nations (Jeremiah 1:4-5).

(15) I have loved you, saith the Lord. Yet ye say, wherein hast thou loved us? Was not Esau Jacob's brother? saith the Lord: yet I loved Jacob, And I hated Esau, and laid his mountains and his heritage waste for the dragons of the wilderness (Malachi 1:2-3).

(16) At that time Jesus answered and said, I thank thee, O Father, Lord of heaven and earth, because thou hast hid these things from the wise and prudent, and hast revealed them unto babes. Even so, Father: for so it seemed good in thy sight (Matthew 11:25-26).

(17) So the last shall be first, and the first last: for many be called, but few chosen (Matthew 20:16).

(18) And except those days should be shortened, there should no flesh be saved: but for the elect's sake those days shall be shortened (Matthew 24:22).

(19) And except that the Lord had shortened those days, no flesh should be saved: but for the elect's sake, whom he hath chosen, he hath shortened the days ... For false Christs and false prophets shall rise, and shall shew signs and wonders, to seduce, if it were possible, even the elect (Mark 13:20, 22).

(20) And he said, Unto you it is given to know the mysteries of the kingdom of God: but to others in parables; that seeing they might not see, and hearing they might not understand (Luke 8:10).

(21) Notwithstanding in this rejoice not, that the spirits are subject unto you; but rather rejoice, because your names are written in heaven (Luke 10:20).

(22) And shall not God avenge his own elect, which cry day and night unto him, though he bear long with them? (Luke 18:7)

(23) All that the Father giveth me shall come to me; and him that cometh to me I will in no wise cast out ... And this is the Father's will which hath sent me, that of all which he hath given me I should lose nothing, but should raise it up again at the last day ... No man can come to me, except the Father which hath sent me draw him: and I will raise him up at the last day ... It is written in the prophets, And they shall be all taught of God. Every man therefore that hath heard, and hath learned of the Father, cometh unto me (John 6:37,39,44,45).

(24) Ye have not chosen me, but I have chosen you, and ordained you, that ye should go and bring forth fruit, and that your fruit should remain: that whatsoever ye shall ask of the Father in my name, he may give it you ... If ye were of the world, the world would love his own: but because ye are not of the world, but I have chosen you out of the world, therefore the world hateth you (John 15:16,19).

(25) As thou hast given him power over all flesh, that he should give eternal life to as many as thou hast given him ... I have manifested thy name unto the men which thou gavest me out of the world: thine they were, and thou gavest them me; and they have kept thy word ... I pray for them: I pray not for the world, but for them which thou hast given me; for they are thine (John 17:2, 6, 9).

(26) Him, being delivered by the determinate counsel and foreknowledge of God, ye have taken, and by wicked hands have crucified and slain ... For David speaketh concerning him, I foresaw the Lord always before my face, for he is on my right hand, that I should not be moved: Therefore, did my heart rejoice, and my tongue was glad; moreover, also my flesh shall rest in hope: Because thou wilt not leave my soul in hell, neither wilt thou suffer thine Holy One to see corruption ... For the promise is unto you, and to your children, and to all that are afar off, even as many as the Lord our God shall call (Acts 2:23, 25, 26, 27, 39).

(27) For to do whatsoever thy hand and thy counsel determined before to be done (Acts 4:28).

(28) And when the Gentiles heard this, they were glad, and glorified the word of the Lord: and as many as were ordained to eternal life believed (Acts 13:48).

(29) And hath made of one blood all nations of men for to dwell on all the face of the earth, and hath determined the times before appointed, and the bounds of their habitation (Acts 17:26).

(30) And he said, The God of our fathers hath chosen thee, that thou shouldest know his will, and see that Just One, and shouldest hear the voice of his mouth (Acts 22:14).

(31) Among whom are ye also the called of Jesus Christ (Romans 1:6).

(32) And we know that all things work together for good to them that love God, to them who are the called according to his purpose. For whom he did foreknow, he also did predestinate to be conformed to the image of his Son, that he might be the firstborn among many brethren. Moreover, whom he did predestinate, them he also called: and whom he called, them

he also justified: and whom he justified, them he also glorified ... Who shall lay anything to the charge of God's elect? It is God that justifieth (Romans 8:28-30, 33).

(33) (For the children being not yet born, neither having done any good or evil, that the purpose of God according to election might stand, not of works, but of him that calleth;) It was said unto her, the elder shall serve the younger. As it is written, Jacob have I loved, but Esau have I hated. What shall we say then? Is there unrighteousness with God? God forbid. For he saith to Moses, I will have mercy on whom I will have mercy, and I will have compassion on whom I will have compassion. So, then it is not of him that willeth, nor of him that runneth, but of God that sheweth mercy. For the scripture saith unto Pharaoh, even for this same purpose have I raised thee up, that I might shew my power in thee, and that my name might be declared throughout all the earth. Therefore, hath he mercy on whom he will have mercy, and whom he will he hardeneth ...
And that he might make known the riches of his glory on the vessels of mercy, which he had afore prepared unto glory, even us, whom he hath called, not of the Jews only, but also of the Gentiles? ... Esaias also crieth concerning Israel, Though the number of the children of Israel be as the sand of the sea, a remnant shall be saved: For he will finish the work, and cut it short in righteousness: because a short work will the Lord make upon the earth. And as Esaias said before, Except the Lord of Sabaoth had left us a seed, we had been as Sodoma, and been made like unto Gomorrha (Romans 9:11-18, 23-24, 27-29).

(34) Even so then at this present time also there is a remnant according to the election of grace. And if by grace, then is it no more of works: otherwise, grace is no more grace. But if it be of works, then it is no more grace: otherwise, work is no more work. What then? Israel hath not obtained that which he seeketh for; but the election hath obtained it, and the rest were blinded. (According as it is written, God hath given them the

spirit of slumber, eyes that they should not see, and ears that they should not hear;) unto this day (Romans 11:5-8).

(35) For ye see your calling, brethren, how that not many wise men after the flesh, not many mighty, not many noble, are called: But God hath chosen the foolish things of the world to confound the wise; and God hath chosen the weak things of the world to confound the things which are mighty; And base things of the world, and things which are despised, hath God chosen, yea, and things which are not, to bring to nought things that are: That no flesh should glory in his presence (1 Corinthians 1:26-29).

(36) But we speak the wisdom of God in a mystery, even the hidden wisdom, which God ordained before the world unto our glory (1 Corinthians 2:7).

(37) But when it pleased God, who separated me from my mother's womb, and called me by his grace (Galatians 1:15).

(38) According as he hath chosen us in him before the foundation of the world, that we should be holy and without blame before him in love: Having predestinated us unto the adoption of children by Jesus Christ to himself, according to the good pleasure of his will, To the praise of the glory of his grace, wherein he hath made us accepted in the beloved. In whom we have redemption through his blood, the forgiveness of sins, according to the riches of his grace; Wherein he hath abounded toward us in all wisdom and prudence; Having made known unto us the mystery of his will, according to his good pleasure which he hath purposed in himself: That in the dispensation of the fulness of times he might gather together in one all things in Christ, both which are in heaven, and which are on earth; even in him:1 In whom also we have obtained an inheritance, being predestinated according to the purpose of him who worketh all things after the counsel of his own will (Ephesians 1:4-11).

(39) Among whom also we all had our conversation in times past in the lusts of our flesh, fulfilling the desires of the flesh and of the mind; and were by nature the children of wrath, even as others. But God, who is rich in mercy, for his great love wherewith he loved us, even when we were dead in sins, hath quickened us together with Christ, (by grace ye are saved;) And hath raised us up together, and made us sit together in heavenly places in Christ Jesus: That in the ages to come he might shew the exceeding riches of his grace in his kindness toward us through Christ Jesus. For by grace are ye saved through faith; and that not of yourselves: it is the gift of God: Not of works, lest any man should boast. For we are his workmanship, created in Christ Jesus unto good works, which God hath before ordained that we should walk in them. Wherefore remember, that ye being in time past Gentiles in the flesh, who are called Uncircumcision by that which is called the Circumcision in the flesh made by hands; That at that time ye were without Christ, being aliens from the commonwealth of Israel, and strangers from the covenants of promise, having no hope, and without God in the world (Ephesians 2:3-12).

(40) According to the eternal purpose which he purposed in Christ Jesus our Lord (Ephesians 3:11).

(41) Put on therefore, as the elect of God, holy and beloved, bowels of mercies, kindness, humbleness of mind, meekness, longsuffering (Colossians 3:12).

(42) Knowing, brethren beloved, your election of God (1 Thessalonians 1:4).

(43) That ye would walk worthy of God, who hath called you unto his kingdom and glory (1 Thessalonians 2:12).

(44) But we are bound to give thanks alway to God for you, brethren beloved of the Lord, because God hath from the beginning chosen you to salvation through sanctification of the Spirit and belief of the truth (2 Thessalonians 2:13).

(45) Who hath saved us, and called us with an holy calling, not according to our works, but according to his own purpose and grace, which was given us in Christ Jesus before the world began (2 Timothy 1:9).

(46) Paul, a servant of God, and an apostle of Jesus Christ, according to the faith of God's elect, and the acknowledging of the truth which is after godliness;
In hope of eternal life, which God, that cannot lie, promised before the world began (Titus 1:1-2).

(47) But we see Jesus, who was made a little lower than the angels for the suffering of death, crowned with glory and honour; that he by the grace of God should taste death for every man (Hebrews 2:9).

(48) Of his own will begat he us with the word of truth, that we should be a kind of firstfruits of his creatures (James 1:18).

(49) Elect according to the foreknowledge of God the Father, through sanctification of the Spirit, unto obedience and sprinkling of the blood of Jesus Christ: Grace unto you, and peace, be multiplied ... Who verily was foreordained before the foundation of the world, but was manifest in these last times for you (1 Peter 1:2, 20).

(50) But ye are a chosen generation, a royal priesthood, a holy nation, a peculiar people; that ye should shew forth the praises of him who hath called you out of darkness into his marvellous light (1 Peter 2:9).

(51) Wherefore the rather, brethren, give diligence to make your calling and election sure: for if ye do these things, ye shall never fall (2 Peter 1:10).

(52) For there are certain men crept in unawares, who were before of old ordained to this condemnation, ungodly men, turning the grace of our God into lasciviousness, and denying the only Lord God, and our Lord Jesus Christ (Jude 1:4).

(53) And all that dwell upon the earth shall worship him, whose names are not written in the book of life of the Lamb slain from the foundation of the world (Revelation 13:8).

(54) These shall make war with the Lamb, and the Lamb shall overcome them: for he is Lord of lords, and King of kings: and they that are with him are called, and chosen, and faithful (Revelation 17:14).

(55) And I saw the dead, small and great, stand before God; and the books were opened: and another book was opened, which is the book of life: and the dead were judged out of those things which were written in the books, according to their works (Revelation 20:12).

Fifty-five references. Fifty-one additional verses. One hundred and six total.
All verses taken from The Holy Bible, authorized King James Version.

CHAPTER 7

CHRISTIAN REFORMED THEOLOGY—PART 3

So, you now have proof of how election/predestination is cited in the Bible. There can be no doubt God wants us to know this is His decree. Certainly, there are voices of opposition to the Reformed view of these passages. They strongly object. They say God does not override man's Free Will. Every person has the freedom to choose God or not choose God. Those unable to choose, such as infants, the mentally/physically impaired, or those otherwise unqualified for sound judgment, are not judged. Others who are judged are judged on their own merit.

Among contested theological perspectives are the infralapsarian and supralapsarian views. These two views, including a third, sublapsarianism, detail the timing of the acts of God relative to how salvation takes place. Lapsarian is from the term "lapse," meaning delay, interval, or gap, relating to timing when God decreed specific events.

SUPRALAPSARIAN (OR ANTELAPSARIAN)

1–God Elects Certain Individuals

2–God Creates All Individuals

3–God Allows the Fall (from Adam and Eve) to All Individuals

4–God Provides Redemption to the Elect Individuals via Jesus Christ

INFRALAPSARIAN AND SUBLAPSARIAN

1–God Creates All Individuals

2–God Allows the Fall (from Adam and Eve) to All Individuals

3–God Elects Certain Individuals

4–God Provides Redemption to the Elect Individuals via Jesus Christ

The issue for the ordering of God's Decrees is to understand the implications of the sequence. How can God elect someone before they are born? Is God righteous and fair to create persons who are not Pre-Life Elect individuals – those destined to damnation?

Even though numerous scriptures attest to the veracity of the supralapsarian sequence—God elects persons He knows, then creates them—it seems most Christian Reformed leaders are in the infralapsarian camp. This is because the first decree entails creating all individuals. None, as yet, are elected or condemned. This seems in keeping with God's loving and fair character.

Proponents of supralapsarianism reiterate God's first decree, creation, is outside time, before the foundation of the world. His plan is elected individuals. That is ordained.

Not only is the personhood of God acting outside time considered, but the concept of "sequence" also involves a definition of time. We may not have such a definition we all understand. J. Ellis McTaggart's publication of the unreality of time is a stirring theory on the nature of the intricacies of "when." McTaggart outlines a technique of challenging chronology by contrasting concepts of time with the labels "A" series, "B" series, and "C" series.

Picture in your mind a disposition of “before” or “after,” in no specific sequence, as in, no change occurs relative to this or that. This may be like reading from a magazine, book, or newspaper. You can start and end anywhere you wish. This represents the B series of time.

The disposition of an event that is "tensed"—A-series of time—as in past tense, present tense, future tense, meaning yesterday, today, and tomorrow occur but don't materially change from being "now." Now is always now. There is before now and after now, but you can't experience any other than right now. Before now is irretrievable, and after now is inaccessible.

The point is time has a dimensionality that defies exact "when-ness." McTaggart does a great job of exploring this. See J. Ellis McTaggart's *The Unreality of Time*. (Mind A Quarterly Review of Psychology and Philosophy. October 1908).

So what? Time is the most precious commodity to the living. When there is no more time, that means your "presence," i.e., being in the present time, is no more. You are either pre-life or in the afterlife. In discussing WHEN God chose individuals, the evidence isn't obvious to everyone. So now, the crux of the matter shifts to "works" and "grace." *If no one can be saved by what they know or what they do (works), yet some are guaranteed salvation (grace), how is it that those who are not guaranteed salvation don't have other options?* Arminianism is such a position.

Jacobus Arminius (Jakob Hermanszoon) was a Dutch Reformed Protestant Christian who lived from 1560-1609. The teaching of Arminius was stated in the Remonstrance of 1610. Arminianism differs from Calvinism in the following ways:

- The divine decree of predestination is not absolute but conditioned upon God's foreknowledge of faith regarding an individual.

- God intended to provide an atonement that was available and sufficient for all men, not just for the elect. Everyone is eligible.

- Man cannot exercise a saving faith on his own but must have God's grace to enable him to do the will of the Lord. God's grace extends to all.

- Though the grace of God is a necessary condition of human effort (works), it does not act irresistibly in man. Man can freely exercise his will to resist.

- Believers are able to resist sin but never so confident that sin is unsuccessful in damnation.

Reformed theology maintains that no one is capable of accepting God. Adam and Eve relinquished pure Pre-Fall Free Will to an impure Post-Fall Free Will. This latter Free Will is not capable of choosing God as their God. They have already made their choice. They chose to be gods themselves. This led to the loss of their dynamic identity in the dynamic Garden of Eden. Fortunately, God promised an Antidote that would be produced through them by procreation. Meanwhile, the progeny inherited the death pronouncement of the parents and the accompanying impairment of function. We became "children of error."

From this, the Reformed view underscores how a man can never choose God. Man is corrupted. His will is no longer free; his will is limited. Limited Free Will means he has the ability to choose such things as spouse, car, house, clothing, food, etcetera. His limitation is that he cannot choose godliness. Sin has corrupted his identity. He does not want God in his life. He wants to run his own life. If and when God is brought in, He will be brought in according to man's conditions.

So here we are. On the one hand, man can do nothing at all regarding salvation. God does everything. On the other hand, the Bible commands us to do certain things, or we have evidence we may not be saved—heading for Hell. Can we ever have the assurance of our destiny? This is where church attendance, Bible teachers, friends, and family may help. As you realize an interest in spiritual matters, your assurance will be affected by what you learn. Additionally, the Holy Spirit witnesses with your spirit.

This book is an attempt to illustrate beauty within and around an otherwise not-so-attractive subject.

> As it is written, "There is none righteous, no, not one: there is none that understandeth, there is none that seeketh after God" (Romans 3:10-11).
>
> No man can come to me, except the Father which hath sent me draw him: and I will raise him up at the last day (John 6:44).
>
> And he said, "Therefore said I unto you, that no man can come unto me, except it were given unto him of my Father" (John 6:65)
>
> The Spirit itself beareth witness with our spirit, that we are the children of God (Romans 8:16).

CHAPTER 8

ELECTION-PREDESTINATION

Christian Reformed theology continues to puzzle and frustrate, no matter the brilliance of the scholars who teach it. Hundreds of years' worth of church councils and renowned erudition haven't produced a view any more attractive than those of former years.

How does a Calvinist tell someone God may not love them? How does a Calvinist tell someone God may love them, but they may still go to Hell if they are not one of the elect? Calvinism, named after John Calvin, has come to mean someone who may not be as strident in their beliefs or teachings as Calvin but is now lumped into the broad group of people who support "grace" alone and never "works" as a means of salvation.

How does a Christian Reformed person tell someone God sending people to Hell is God's perfect justice? Mankind's sins are such that Hell is a just punishment for the offense to the holy, perfect, immutable God. Just be happy that God saves even one person. No one deserves salvation. No, not one.

When hearing the scriptures come at you so cold and hard, and being assured this is what the Bible says, how is this the Good News? For those who have an average understanding of scripture, it turns you away in sorrow and disappointment. There must be something missing.

Missing, indeed, many Christians interject. Surely John 3:16, one of the most famous of all Bible verses, overrules sorrow and disappointment. "For God so loved the world, that he gave his only begotten Son, that whosoever believeth in him should not perish, but have everlasting life."

WHOSOEVER believes! Dry your tears! You can be saved—today!

But these Christians don't realize the “so” in “God so loved the world” does NOT refer to God's *magnitude* of loving the world. Rather, it refers to this *manner* that He gave his only begotten Son. Secondly, the "whosoever believeth in Him" can't be just anyone. We know from the preponderance of other scriptures that NO one will believe in Him unless God takes the initiative. We don't. We won't. We can't.

In this case, you might say, people shouldn't be held responsible for sin if they cannot help it. It exists at birth. They WON'T pursue God because they CAN'T. The Reformist's reply is to say the better explanation is people CAN'T (pursue God) because they WON'T (pursue God). They will not bow down to something/someone they do not know, trust, or see.

Unfortunately, no matter how many scriptures underscore the validity of election, the truth of the Reformed doctrine, and the preaching of Jesus, it still feels unacceptable. They ask, “What am I supposed to do*? If I am not able to choose Jesus Christ but must wait for Him to choose me, what if He doesn't choose me?”*

Once, in 2021, the app Instagram featured a beautiful young girl. Briefly, in a few short sentences, she summed up the feelings of millions of people. She said, “If God is omniscient, He knows me. He knows my heart. If He wants to save me, He would do so. Why would He not do so? Why would He avoid, ignore, or allow me to go to Hell when He can lovingly prevent it? God is love. Right? Well, it seems that there is a very real possibility that God does not exist. Just look around you. Where is He?” (Accessed April 14, 2021)

But God may be where you least expect Him. Remember, a thief on the cross with Jesus was apparently a very wicked person. He apparently knew nothing about God. In his last moments of life, he requested Jesus remember him. He was assured by Jesus he would be remembered. That thief had a moment of hope and positivity in the epitome of a bad situation.

Thief number two on his cross may have also wondered why his life was ending so badly. Why didn't things go right? Now what? Seemingly, there was no hope, and Jesus was right there with him.

Thirdly, what about John the Baptist in his mother Elizabeth's womb? These days, an embryo may have a 30/70, 50/50, or 70/30 chance of avoiding abortion. Not good odds. From the story of pre-birth John, we know God is there even in situations that aren't obvious.

> And he said unto Jesus, Lord, remember me when thou comest into thy kingdom. And Jesus said unto him, Verily I say unto thee, today shalt thou be with me in paradise (Luke 23:42-43).

> And it came to pass, that, when Elisabeth heard the salutation of Mary, the babe leaped in her womb; and Elisabeth was filled with the Holy Ghost ... For, lo, as soon as the voice of thy salutation sounded in mine ears, the babe leaped in my womb for joy (Luke 1:41, 44).

Still not convinced? Has this been too simple an explanation of what can be done to secure your salvation? Do you even believe in salvation, Heaven, or Hell? You may be in the stage of life where you have no confidence in creation or evolution. Maybe there is no way of being truly confident. People just say they're confident. Or you may be in the camp of those who will always be cynical. This camp is distrustful of religious worldviews and also distrustful of nonreligious worldviews. Therefore, make the best of your own life with whatever attributes you may possess.

Any points of agreement so far on what has been said? Before you answer that, there's more. Another group of people fears the Bible may be fundamentally true. These people have underlying resentment, anger, frustration, and outrage. Why? Because of the way the Bible is written! Harold Camping, the deceased founder of Family Radio, initially a California-based group of radio stations, often said God could have written the Bible in such a way any six-year-old child could understand it. God being God, that must be true. We all know the Bible is NOT easy to understand. It is hard to understand. *On top of that, the scripture specifically declares that the Bible is difficult ON PURPOSE:*

> And he said unto them, unto you it is given to know the mystery of the kingdom of God: but unto them that are without, all these things are done in parables: That seeing they may see, and not perceive; and hearing they may hear, and not understand; lest at any time they should be converted, and their sins should be forgiven them (Mark 4:11-12).

> He hath blinded their eyes, and hardened their heart; that they should not see with their eyes, nor understand with their heart, and be converted, and I should heal them (John 12:40).

You can see why people would be outraged. Would Jesus purposely prevent people from being saved or being healed? How does this make any sense?

And the Bible indicates Jesus spoke to the people in riddles, or parables.

> But without a parable spake he not unto them: and when they were alone, he expounded all things to his disciples (Mark 4:34).

Why didn't Jesus talk to them straight? Even the disciples were often given the interpretation in private, later in the day. Maybe because it's easier for people to remember a story rather than sentences or a principle? Maybe not.

Then again, why even have the Bible? God, show Yourself! Appear to us in plain sight, or a vision, or through angels. Let us know Your presence through our five senses. Write the Bible in the sky for all the world to see. Make Your word speak through the oceans, the mountains, through the fish, plants, and animals. You are God! This could be so easy for You.

On Pinterest, April 2021 (taken from Space Dyke on Twitter), there was a one-panel joke called "It's A Beautiful Day to Yell At God.". Three groups of people were yelling at the sun(?):

a) Face us, you coward.

b) Come out. We just want to talk.

c) WTF!

Or what about this? God simply starts all over. Adam and Eve made a terrible mistake. We are all suffering. Two thousand years after Jesus was here, there are still people who have no idea who Jesus was. So, they go to Hell? Forever? Really?

Just start over! There has to be a scenario where Eve doesn't succumb to the Serpent. There has to be a scenario where Adam doesn't agree with Eve. There has to be a scenario where the Serpent doesn't tempt Eve. There has to be a scenario where the Serpent isn't a factor in the Garden of Eden. If Satan is involved, there has to be a scenario where Satan is not a factor.

This is God we are talking about. Omnipotent. Omniscient. So just eliminate Hell. Eliminate bad angels. Eliminate bad Adam, bad Eve, and the bad Serpent. Create a perfect Adam and perfect Eve. Create a perfect

Serpent. Create perfect angels. Is that so hard to do? Fix the problem! You are God!

Well, maybe God did start over! Maybe He started over ten times, one hundred times, one million times, one trillion times. Maybe by fixing the angels, fixing Eve, fixing Adam, fixing the Serpent, fixing the Tree of Knowledge of Good and Evil. All kinds of iterations and permutations of fixing occurred. Of course, God doesn't have to do that. Being omniscient, He knows which scenario is best for His purposes. Once should be sufficient.

That doesn't mean we go back to square one of not having an appealing scenario. There is a view that incorporates orthodox Christian principles yet gives hope and optimism using the Christian Reformed foundation. Heretofore, this has not been readily accessible.

It's an uphill battle to present imagery that, on the one hand, is not intended to represent orthodoxy and, on the other hand, portrays imagery based on orthodox principles. People who are repulsed by God's Election Plan of salvation for those saved before the foundation of the world—VERSUS people who preach God's Election Plan—can never reach an agreement.

The repulsed can never accept that God would send people to Hell on the basis they aren't chosen before they were born. That's not a God that is worthy of following. That God cannot be God.

The non-repulsed accept God of the Bible based on what the scriptures declare. Nothing more, nothing less. God is omniscient and knows best. We must trust Him to be righteous.

Connecting The Dots of Identity makes use of MARVI-RPIA to indicate a possibility of resolving conflict between believers and nonbelievers. Parenthetically, the author is neither called nor qualified to declare "Thus saith the Lord." The reminder is these are impressions, shared from the heart, not theology.

The speaker at the orthodox Reformed church will preach from holy scripture this week that salvation is indeed by GRACE, and there is NOTHING that mankind can do by their own WORKS to be saved. Period. Jesus Christ did ALL the work. We can't get ourselves saved, and we can't lose that salvation once we are saved.

But then, we all hear statements, right along with the messages preached in the worship service, that contradict the GRACE affirmation.

You must repent of your sins.

You must believe in Christ.

You must hear the name of Jesus at some point in your life.

You must be exposed to Special Revelation (scripture). General Revelation (God revealed in nature) is insufficient for salvation.

You must worship God.

You must pray.

You must attend a church.

You must be baptized.

Additionally, there are all manner of "special circumstances" that qualify for salvation:

- Aborted
- Stillborn

- Miscarried
- Mental Deficiency
- Chronological Age

Unfortunately, what is heard in the church may be close to what we read in the book of John.

> Nicodemus answered and said unto him, "How can these things be?" Jesus answered and said unto him, "Art thou a master of Israel, and knowest not these things? Verily, verily, I say unto thee, we speak that we do know, and testify that we have seen; and ye receive not our witness. If I have told you earthly things, and ye believe not, how shall ye believe, if I tell you of heavenly things?" (John 3:9-12).

Nicodemus, the teacher of the nation of Israel, failed to understand that words have at least three dimensions: literal, figurative, and spiritual.

Seeing with spiritual eyes, hearing with spiritual ears, and speaking with spiritual words bring advanced meaning to the way we read scripture. If indeed we were saved before the world was created, we don't have to do anything for our salvation. It's already accomplished.

Modern Abstract Religious Verbal Impressionism-Role Play Identity Array illustrates that there are no "special cases" for salvation. Everyone to be saved is already saved. Everyone who is 100 percent human.

Then why are we here? What's the point of Jesus arriving on the scene to guarantee our salvation?

As *Connecting The Dots Of Identity* outlines, life is a Demonstration of the Error of Free Will. God's Determined Will for flawless beings—human and angel—is infinitely better than individual Free Will. Therefore, what roleplay of human inauthentic identities proves is that, unless the Holy Spirit intercedes, no one will ever choose God's will over their own. This has been shown across a great number of examples, in every possible permutation.

At the conclusion of the Demonstration, 100 percent human Roleplayers join the Super-Spiritual Identities (SSIDs) in Paradise. Non-100 percent human Roleplayers will cease to exist. Jesus Christ was born human to redeem 100% percent humans. Only the Devil and his angels will be sentenced to Hell.

CHAPTER 9

GENERAL REVELATION AND SPECIAL REVELATION

As God is revealed, His imagery may not be seen because of the identity of the subjects. God is revealed in nature (General Revelation). God is revealed in the Bible (Special Revelation).

We know if God is the One who is omniscient, omnipresent, omnipotent, and all-loving, and He can make His presence known to all and can save all from damnation. The question is, why can't His imagery be revealed to all? If You are God, why all the mystery and misery? If You are the definition of whom God is supposed to be, what is going on?

We think we know the answer. There is no God! If there is some God out there who has some of the attributes we assume belong to Deity, WE HATE YOU! We hate you because, apparently, you hate us.

Therefore, the most obvious answer to the question of what's happening is: THERE IS NO GOD! There can't be God.

The Bible indicates God does reveal Himself. Revelation comes from Nature. Revelation comes from Scripture. *MARVI-RPIA illustrates revelation also comes from IDENTITY.* What you come to know is always a function of who you are. Who you are is a function of when you were born, where you were born, who your parents are, how you were raised, your physical attributes, your mental attributes, your environment, and your experiences. Your identity is relevant to how you perceive reality, and what can be revealed to you.

There are three components of revelation: General Revelation, Special Revelation, and Identity Revelation.

Ideally, the most intelligent people in the world should always agree on which views of reality have the best explanation of what reality actually is. The least intelligent will always have the worst explanations of reality. But we don't see this. Stupid people often agree with extremely intelligent people. Extremely intelligent people often think and behave in the stupidest manner imaginable. We all know and love wonderful people we just can't understand. We don't understand how smart people can think what they think. They're not dumb. They've proven their mental prowess. They just don't make sense. They're insane, but not insane.

So, life is not about mental ability. It's other factors. It's influence. Suggestion. Emotion. Denial. Experience. Prejudice. Selective inattention. Intelligence is not enough of an answer.

According to Christian Reformed theology, God chose His elected ones before the foundation of the world (Ephesians 1:4). MARVI-RPIA's impression is that every individual conceived since Adam and Eve is a Demonstration of Free Will. Free Will of autonomous living creatures must play out in a myriad of examples regarding human diversity. *No one can spiritually interpret General Revelation or Special Revelation unless God opens their understanding.* That is the point. Nothing a person thinks or does can get them into the kingdom of Heaven. Only God's grace, not man's works, can accomplish this. Otherwise, God would be a respecter of persons. Some people would be better than others. This makes God unfair ... again

MARVI-RPIA renders an impression of the ontological status of individuals God identified before He created the world. This means no one goes to Hell. No one who is 100 percent human, that is. Scripture says plainly that Hell is created for the Devil and his angels (Matthew 25).

There are demon-compromised persons and individuals impersonating humans that will not be in Paradise.

All human identities are already in Paradise. Life on earth is simply a demonstration of Adam and Eve's interest for their own life rather than God's interest for their life. The penalty is the cessation of life. That is what we are seeing today and every day.

If God has reserved our authentic identity in Paradise before the world was created, and our inauthentic identity here on earth is a demonstration of Free Will, what is the point of a plethora of religions? They all imply God wants us to follow Him. Even religious terrorists say God wants unbelievers to follow Him or the penalty is death. Which God? Which religion? What does it mean to follow Him?

As you think about it, if life is indeed a demonstration of Free Will, then people will think and behave as they are designed to do from forces imposed on them pre-birth, at birth, and after birth. It's Free Will. But they do NOT have Free Will to choose the God of the Bible because their Free Will has been compromised by error. This error was described in the Bible as Adam and Eve exercising pure Free Will to reject God's will for their life. This was symbolized by the Tree of Knowledge of Good and Evil.

Adam and Eve risked the penalty of death to disobey God by partaking of the Tree of the Knowledge of Good and Evil. The offspring of Adam and Eve continue the demonstration. In God's mercy, He modified the death penalty and prolonged it. Then He provided a Remedy for Adam and Eve's error. The Remedy was through procreation. God promised a Redeemer to be born through them that would correct their error. They would be restored to a renewed life forever (Genesis 3:15).

The point in declaring the "Good News" of the Bible is an important part of God's love for people. *God maintains the nature of Free Will by not directly intruding into the mental and physical world.* God could appear in the sky, appear in your dreams, appear in your home, but then EVERYONE's Free Will would be overridden. There would be no further reasons to disbelieve God's salvation plan. Everyone, except the Devil, his angels, and those humans who are compromised by devils, would receive enlightenment.

There's no need to continue a demonstration of Free Will. The End. The credits start to scroll across the sky: director ... producers ... cast ... set design ... music...

But BEFORE the credits roll, it's important to convey the magnitude of the drama. Life is a drama of autonomy from God. Living creatures, human and angelic, are given life by God. It is possibly the most precious gift God grants. The questions angels and humans raise are these: How free are creatures to live the life that God grants? Do God's restrictions erode the quality of life to the point of risking death?

God said angels have the freedom to obey or disobey. God said Adam and Eve have the freedom to obey or disobey. They disobeyed. Why? We would have to ask them. Even if they could tell us, we may not be able to understand. They were flawless creatures in two flawless environments: Eden and Heaven. We are flawed creatures in a flawed environment.

As flawed human creatures with autonomy from God, the life He gave us from Adam and Eve still allows us to disobey Him. The only time we can't disobey is when He intercedes to convert us. This overrides our will. The ones God converts are in contrast to the ones He does not convert. Free Will continues. The Demonstration of Free Will plays out in converted lives and the lives of the unconverted. *This cosmic Demonstration is absolutely necessary.*

Theists witness how there are good angels and there are evil angels. Theists and atheists witness that there are good people and there are evil people. We're all in a mix of life on earth as people demonstrate Free Will. Of course, this Free Will is a function of the attributes imposed upon each person based on heredity, environment, and experiences.

As the persons converted by God seek to enlighten those unconverted, the struggle is uphill. This is because salvation is 100 percent God's action. God utilizes the converted person in His providence, but God's grace is the determining factor in who becomes converted and when. Explaining General Revelation is part of the uphill struggle to enlighten the unconverted.

The unconverted and the converted both see XYZ. The converted's mission of love is to interpret XYZ so the unconverted sees it as God's creation in nature. But the unconverted only see the natural phenomena of nature with no supernatural intelligence directing it. Only when God opens their spiritual eyes do they begin to accept General and Special Revelation.

The few unconverted people I like include David Hume, Sam Harris, Christopher Hitchens, and Lawrence Krauss. Hume and Hitchens are deceased. Harris and Krauss have produced publications and are well-featured on social media. What I like about them is how they think. It's not enough to be passionate and articulate. They have something more. It's the "something more" than appeals to someone like me. I'm speaking of General Revelation—how reality is interpreted by what they perceive. The people who spend their life following clues about life are admirable. The challenge is evaluating their clues.

When we admit any scientific observations are interpreted through an atheistic or theistic lens, we must question the value of the observations. Do you make the case to simply reinterpret the observations to support your worldview?

When Special Revelation is rejected as an aspect of reality, General Revelation takes precedence.

Early in life, everything is accepted. Then we gradually learn about religion and science and become more discerning. By the time we leave the influence of our parents and the education system, our identity has drifted to spiritually positive (SID-POS) or spiritually negative (SID-NEG).

People who think like the four guys I mentioned above reinforce the MARVI-RPIA image of a Demonstration of Free Will. They epitomize the influence of heredity, environment, and experiences on their worldview. Their identity is a function of making the very best of their imposed physical and mental attributes. If God does not intercede in their lives, they will continue seeing the world as nontheists. It's the default position.

As God reveals Himself in General Revelation, atheists interpret His imagery as impersonal science. There is no personal intelligence involved. As God reveals Himself in Special Revelation, atheists read only fairy tales. Angels, devils, Heaven, Hell, miracles, and odd characters are all myths and misconceptions.

The difference between Hume, Harris, Hitchens, Krauss, and many other contributors is that these four sought to improve their world by publicly articulating their worldviews in unique ways. Generally, people follow other people. They don't seem to be motivated to question the neighborhood, the community, or the world. They're accepting. The people who are highly motivated and become public figures that question the status quo should be applauded, those Special and General Revelation proponents or opponents.

Applauded, that is, for helping people understand the nuances of their worldview. It's not what is said that has value to a theist. Atheists all say the same thing: there is no God. It's HOW the so-called "new atheists" say it. *When a new atheist articulates the position of people who don't believe in the God of the Bible, they usually REFINE the views of millions of other atheists.* Theists are now challenged to address the specific points raised by atheists. "New theists" should likewise refine the views of millions of other theists in their response to atheists.

As God has revealed Himself in nature (General Revelation) and the Bible (Special Revelation), we have the context of what life is about. From ancient manuscripts, we have the patriarchs, judges, kings, prophets, disciples, and apostles who relate God's words to us. For nontheists, this is unacceptable. It's all subjective folklore.

We do recognize both theists and nontheists support science. The scientific method has afforded us a framework that we all benefit from. What is the scientific method? Here's a quick summation:

An observation in nature occurs. A hypothesis is formed about the observation. Then, testing is done to see if a repeatable pattern or rule can be established. Refinement is made based on feedback from similar testing. From this, a platform is in place to increase knowledge about observations and questions we have regarding nature—what we experience.

Dr. Krauss implies the discovery of knowledge is better than the arrival at truth because discovery is a process of forwarding progress. When you reach a point where you're satisfied that you've found truth, as most religious people affirm, you stop searching. You should always be searching! You should attempt to go beyond what you've discovered, because life is still a mystery, and so is the nature of reality.

As knowledge is cumulative, what we know, or assume we know, is further defined. How the definition of knowledge is formulated depends on the interpretation of those publicizing the data. While analyzing the data, a theist sees this, an atheist sees that.

Those who hold to a General Revelation explanation of everything, but no spiritual intelligence as God, affirm there is no intelligent aspect to matter, energy, time, space, motion, etcetera. There is no design, only the appearance of design. There is no teleology or purpose, just change.

Those of General Revelation despise having their freedom restricted by a worldview that cannot be proven, is not testable, and has all the characteristics of fiction.

Special Revelation people argue that something cannot come from nothing. The "Big Bang" must start with something. They say the definition of nothing by General Revelation people is not consistent with the definition of "no thing". The General Revelation response seems to suggest that the nothing from which everything began is essentially an *apparent* nothingness, without definition, due to thus far undiscovered models available to us. This is the beauty of discovery. This is the beauty of cumulative knowledge. This is human progress. It's not that we don't know what it actually is that defines the specific point of origin. We know whatever it was, it has to be an "it" and not a "who." Theists call it God, a "who." Nontheists call it an "it," as it should be referred to.

Giving a final word, for now, about no thing, theists might say nontheists refuse the classic definition of nothing because they know nothing would be here now if there ever was absolutely nothing to start with. And the double final word for atheists might be, give us another million years or so, perhaps a billion years, and we will have the definitive answers to almost everything.

Meanwhile, MARVI-RPIA's position is the incessant pursuit of knowledge to define reality is good for Special Revelation (Bible) because it glorifies God in every instance. Atheists reject religious interpretations of their discoveries and maintain they are wholly objective and impersonal. There is no splendor of a divine being residing in the science. They say, in a sense, it is human beings that are the splendor residing in the science—the General Revelation of nature.

Thus, the debate continues.

MARVI-RPIA sympathizes to underscore that nontheists have absolutely no way of understanding and accepting God's salvation plan unless He opens their spiritual eyes. No one is capable of achieving salvation until God intercedes. In the interim, they exemplify the Free Will imposed on them by heredity, environment, and experiences of life. They are a part of the Demonstration initiated by Adam and Eve, just as we all are. On the other hand, theists advocate a worldview that affirms intelligent design with purpose. We are to think and behave in ways that articulate and personify theism that contributes to the quality of everyone's life.

> According as he hath chosen us in him before the foundation of the world, that we should be holy and without blame before him in love (Ephesians 1:4).

> Who hath saved us, and called us with an holy calling, not according to our works, but according to his own purpose and grace, which was given us in Christ Jesus before the world began (2 Timothy 1:9).

> Then shall he say also unto them on the left hand, Depart from me, ye cursed, into everlasting fire, prepared for the devil and his angels (Matthew 25:41).

> The heavens declare the glory of God; and the firmament sheweth his handywork. Day unto day uttereth speech, and night unto night sheweth knowledge. There is no

speech nor language, where their voice is not heard. Their line is gone out through all the earth, and their words to the end of the world. In them hath he set a tabernacle for the sun (Psalms 19:1-4).

Because that which may be known of God is manifest in them; for God hath shewed it unto them. For the invisible things of him from the creation of the world are clearly seen, being understood by the things that are made, even his eternal power and Godhead; so that they are without excuse: Because that, when they knew God, they glorified him not as God, neither were thankful; but became vain in their imaginations, and their foolish heart was darkened (Romans 1:19-21).

And I will put enmity between thee and the woman, and between thy seed and her seed; it shall bruise thy head, and thou shalt bruise his heel (Genesis 3:15).

CHAPTER 10

TRILLIONAIRE

One day, you receive very official-looking correspondence in the mail. When you open it, you read that you are the recipient of a trillion dollars! Right. Another scam! You read on. As it turns out, you are correctly identified as the person to receive a trillion dollars. Why you? Why a trillion dollars? Where is the money coming from? When is the money coming? In what form will the money arrive?

Oh, you think to yourself, *next comes the pitch*. This magnanimous sum will be yours after a transaction fee payable to XYZ company. Please hurry. This offer is void after thirty days. But, no, you read no such disclaimer. No such pitch is found. Is this a legitimate notice?

Let's continue this example of good-news extraordinaire. Let's assume the person sending the letter is a private citizen. His profession is researching ancestral lines, especially for the rich and famous. His newest world-class search technique led him to a contract with a super-rich monarch in a small country. The monarch died and left a fortune to a particular heir. That heir is you. Hal, the Heredity Authentication Logistics inventor, has no ulterior motive. This is simply the most glorious commission he's ever attained.

There are many documents to review. The money is tied to the monarch's possessions, the laws of his country, the identity of the heirs, and the rules and directives for claiming the reward. All that and a specific time frame to act.

Okay. What does this have to do with Christian Reformed theology?

This is making the analogy that accepting election/predestination as a viable worldview is like being the heir to at least a trillion dollars! That is, accepting a version of election/predestination as presented in this artistic impression. Just as in this example of disbelief until the reward can be verified, the task is to provide the details so that you may see the path to the reward.

Assume for a few moments that key components of the Christian religion are 100 percent true.

What US dollar value compares with going to Heaven?

What US dollar value compares with NOT going to Hell?

The trillion-dollar example was used as a starting point. How much is a trillion? Let's compare a trillion to seconds ...

One million seconds is about eleven days. A billion seconds is about thirty-one years. One trillion seconds is about 32,000 years. A trillion is the number one followed by twelve zeros.

A “yes” to Heaven and a “no” to Hell are worth much more. We could say one followed by twenty-seven zeros (octillion) or one followed by thirty zeros (nonillion). A trillion is a more practical dollar amount.

Of course, when you try to place any monetary value on Heaven and Hell, you really can't. Even if you could, most of you don't care. You WON'T care. Not until God opens your eyes. In the meantime, you've come to believe you have only one life. You can't take a chance and throw that life away on a restricted, boring, Christian lifestyle that may not be true.

Yes, it's understandable to be skeptical. However, remember that MARVI-RPIA is only an image. It's an impression of Reformed theology.

Generally speaking, a large segment of any population has misgivings about Reformed theology. Election and Predestination are confusing.

My destiny is sealed, but I still must do stuff.

I'm elected to Heaven, but Hell is still lurking in the background.

It's possible to become a Christian, whether I want it or not.

I don't think I want to be a Christian.

I don't want to go to church every Sunday.

I don't want to be baptized.

I don't want a spirit inside of me.

I can't stand their music.

The sermons are boring.

Abortion is okay.

I think gay people are okay.

Same-sex marriage is okay.

Most consenting sex is okay.

The imagery of *Connecting the Dots of Identity* means there is no expectation of you to be a Christian. The expectation is to simply be yourself—after seeing yourself based on MARVI-RPIA imagery.

In the next chapter, I will introduce myself. Afterward, I will give a brief overview of what the trillion-dollar idea is based on. Then comes the in-depth components of what makes a spiritual concept worth a trillion dollars. I am confident this artistic worldview is valuable to you. Not only does it provide infinite treasure, but it also has enormous healing power. This healing is in the form of mental health, with physical health soon to follow.

So far, a lot of what is said may seem to be boasting. The heartfelt intent is to dismiss any reservation of doubt. MARVI-RPIA is a worldview that compares with other worldviews, feature for feature, yet excels in two major points, specifically Pre-Life and the Afterlife.

How do I know this? Pre-Life? *What is Pre-life?*

Life has to be defined as personhood or identity, and this begins at the point of conception. There is no term for personhood or identity BEFORE conception—conception in the female body, that is. The term Pre-Life is the term for a designation of those persons God knows before they are conceived in their mother's womb.

We know that before there was anything, God was. He is self-existent. He (or They as the Trinity—Father, Son, Holy Spirit) created spirit life as the heavenly hosts or angels. Holy scripture and *Connecting the Dots of Identity* indicate God also guaranteed salvation for persons before He created the world. These persons are the Pre-Life Elected.

The Trinity lives. The angels live. Do the Pre-Life Elect live? Are they alive? Are they conscious? Has God given them a form? Are they spirits? Do they exist only in God's mind, like a thought? We know God speaks, and matter appears. Does God withhold words so the Pre-Life Elect don't appear?

And the afterlife? The afterlife is after life. No one living has such knowledge. And based on the most prominent worldviews, which all have deficiencies—not only about the afterlife but about life—after life is utterly obscure.

I aim to produce the value promised—a trillion dollars. This helps highlight value, but the true value is in the way that amount of money could change your life. We know money isn't everything. However, once you are free from working to make a living, your life should open up. Life begins anew. Money is no longer a hindrance to whatever you desire. You are free from thinking about life as you once thought. Life isn't the same. You're a different person—potentially, a better person. The same applies to election/predestination, now with new imagery.

CHAPTER 11

WHO AM I?

Do you care? Probably not, and it doesn't really matter, but here's a little background.

I'm the son of a pastor. My mother and father considered themselves to be members of the Holiness/Apostolic/Pentecostal/Baptist faith. So, I was forced to be in church throughout my childhood. In those days, people in my circle of influence used the term "saved" as often as "Christian." Are you saved? Are they saved? Did anyone get saved at the church service?

I remember a visit with my relatives. I went to see my grandfather, whom I'd never met. One of his first questions was "Johnny, are you saved?" I said yes, I was. My brother, four years younger, was with me. What did he think of my answer? Did my grandfather ask my brother the same question? I don't remember.

I remember how I used to feel about people who said they were saved. There was an implication of comparison. They were better than me. They accepted Jesus Christ; I had not. They are going to Heaven; I'm going to Hell. They figured life out, I'm stupid. At an early age, I accepted that assessment. When I got older, I resented it. How dare you so-called saved persons be so presumptuous to assume you are a born-again, new creature, child of God with one foot in Heaven? You don't impress me one bit. You seem exactly like everyone else I know, except you don't smoke, drink, or curse. Otherwise, maybe I would consider emulating your life. I do not.

This feeling also applied to my mother and father. Yes, I loved them, but I did not want my life to be like theirs. In their defense, I was a typical young person. I didn't have the maturity to be objective about adult thinking and behavior. On top of that, I had no spiritual maturity. My spiritual eyes and ears were not open. My heart was the heart of the average non-Christian person.

When I finally thought about getting serious with my life, I was about twenty-five years old. I went to college, started reading the Bible, and visited churches. While visiting one large Baptist church in Los Angeles, California, one of the deacons (or elders) asked me if I was saved. I said yes. "Do you speak in tongues?" he asked. I said no. He said, "Well then, brother, you don't have anything." That really irked me. So, apparently, that meant I wasn't saved.

At that point, even though I decided to be baptized there, I wasn't really sure if I was a true Christian. Years earlier, I was baptized as a teenager. My father had not been successful in getting me to speak in tongues. I did try a few times. I may have refused after several attempts. Both my parents spoke in tongues. I never felt comfortable with the charismatic presentation of worship, especially glossolalia (the phenomena of impromptu spiritual utterance). That feeling still holds today, but now I have good reasons to demystify that phenomenon (see *Connecting the Dots of Identity*-2, Chapter 33, Q/A 41).

Fast-forward through my college years, and now I read the Bible during dinner. Also, as part of my continuing education, I studied people like Alan Watts, Baba Ram Dass (Richard Alpert), Sigmund Freud, Emile Durkheim, Max Weber, Lao Tzu, and Roy Masters. I became friends with two of my psychology teachers, Fred Cassidy and Larry Luby. I watched television and listened to all the popular, and not-so-popular, Christian personalities of that time on the radio. People like Garner Ted Armstrong, J. Vernon McGee, Dr. Walter Martin, Jim Bakker, Dr. Gene Scott, George Vandeman, Hal Lindsey, and Dr. Wayne Dyer. I finally settled on Harold Camping. He provided a great ten-year education.

Camping was president of Family Radio, a West Coast-based AM radio station that reached across the United States. His popular programs included reading thirty minutes, nonstop, from the Bible a few times a day. Another feature was playing the classic hymns and songs. Perhaps the most well-known and interesting program was a question-and-answer presentation known as "The Open Forum." People would call the station and ask questions based on the Bible. Camping gave exceptionally good answers. And, yes, this is the same person who infamously predicted the end of the world—twice—in 1994 and 2011!

This is the point when I became exposed to election, predestination, and the Christian Reformed teaching of scripture. Enlightenment didn't happen overnight. After years of hearing questions and answers, it hit me. This now makes sense! I'm not responsible for preventing my family, friends, and associates from going to Hell. Nothing I do can save them. God does all the saving. More to the point, all the saving has been done before anybody was even born!

One day, actually one night, I was lying in bed, thinking about people, salvation, and the events of the day. Suddenly, I bolted upright in bed, just like in the movies! It was as if a tremendous weight was lifted from me. I was free! I couldn't save anybody because *God* saves them. I am to be an example of a Christian, speak to people as a Christian, and sacrifice my life for the good of all and for God. But salvation is not up to me. In fact, I never really wanted to be a Christian. At least, not the kind of Christian I always had in mind. *God came to ME! I did not go to HIM!*

My early Christian life was typical. Christianity has good points, I think, but also bad points. I kept trying to figure out life while keeping Christianity at arm's length. For me, salvation was a gradual process of going to church, reading the bible, meeting with Christians, and moving away from non-Christian thoughts and acts. Some people have a one-day realization and from there begin their new life journey. They can tell you the day they were born again. I can't. Maybe I could say the year I was born again, maybe not.

For me, slowly gaining the knowledge of God's salvation plan meant measurable spiritual growth. I was making progress. However, things were still not moving along as I wanted. I expected that once people knew about God's election program, they would accept it. That was not the case. I thought I knew why, but I was naive. People knew about it. They just didn't like it. The opposition to predestination is well-developed and prevalent throughout the world.

Have you read about Pelagianism? Arminianism? Free Will? Determinism? Materialism? I was motivated to explore these terms. Soon, it became obvious I had no interest and no skill in presenting a case for Predestination. I'm not a philosopher, theologian, teacher, writer, or intellectual. I have a view. I have an opinion. But how was I going to get my point across to people while I lacked any proficiency?

I certainly feel an obligation to share what I know. What I know is extremely valuable. That's why I used the trillion-dollar analogy. I have big, big, BIG news. Yes, the Bible is the Good News, the pie in the sky as some might say. What I'm offering is GREAT NEWS, and not just pie in the sky. I'm offering an image of pie in the sky, a la mode, with caviar, with champagne, and a signed blank check payable to you!

Now, the challenge is to deliver on the promise of a trillion-dollar prize. Since I have no training or skills in the traditional method of teaching worldviews, how will this be done? With zig-zagging steps, fits and starts, and determination.

And what makes me the one to produce such a grand presentation? Here are five indicators that pushed me forward:

1–The clergy doesn't want to be unorthodox, heretical, extra-biblical, or unreliable.

2–Scholars don't want to engage in conjecture, speculation, imagination, or guesswork.

3–Artists don't care. I'm an artist. I'm not a pastor. I'm not an intellectual. My goal is to highlight God's absolutely beautiful salvation plan and share an artistic impression of identity.

4–It's apparent that election/predestination is not well understood. What is understood can't be reconciled with the God of love and fairness. I determined to just do my best. I'm no writer. There's nothing to lose. It's art. It's oaky if no one approve it.

5–No worldview incorporates all the elements necessary to be satisfying. *Connecting The Dots of Identity* – Christian Reformed Impressionism won't satisfy everyone either. Yes. So what? Do it. Go forward.

CHAPTER 12

MINISTER OF ART

What school of art did I attend?

The Art School of Identity. I listened to teachers of the Bible, read the Bible, then compared that to what I observed in life— Special Revelation, General Revelation, and Identity Revelation.

I formed an impression. A collection of these impressions gave me an image. I have written about the images to preserve the details. Soon, I had a journal of these detailed images. From this came an overall impression of what Special and General Revelation taught me about identity.

Only through great personal sacrifice have I made progress in describing spiritual impressions and linking them to roleplay and identity. This approach to combining artistic expression and religion gives me the title of Minister of Art. Do you like the title? It gives a sense of levity to the very serious subject of identity.

By the way, although I consider myself a Minister of Art, in the spirit of Bezaleel and Aholiab, I am by no means called of God or given unique gifts by God. I am more like an illegitimate second cousin of Bezaleel or Aholiab. I live outside the camp. I make toys for the kids. The parents in the congregation don't accept me, or the toys, so they may end up with the servants, strangers, and aliens of the land.

> And the Lord spake unto Moses, saying, See, I have called by name Bezaleel the son of Uri, the son of Hur, of the tribe of Judah: And I have filled him with the spirit of God, in wisdom, and in understanding, and in knowledge,

> and in all manner of workmanship, To devise cunning works, to work in gold, and in silver, and in brass, And in cutting of stones, to set them, and in carving of timber, to work in all manner of workmanship. And I, behold, I have given with him Aholiab, the son of Ahisamach, of the tribe of Dan: and in the hearts of all that are wise hearted I have put wisdom, that they may make all that I have commanded thee (Exodus 31:1-6).

We've all heard the phrase "beauty is in the eye of the beholder." Attributed to Margaret Hungerford, she used it to underscore the concept that beauty is subjective. We love art. What does art do for us? It communicates beauty, and much more. Art stimulates us, communicates messages to us, and inspires us. Why is art in virtually every home? How is it that a seemingly mundane and obscure image goes for millions of dollars at auction? The answers are because art represents an intangible essence that is difficult or impossible to convey other than how it is conveyed.

As Minister of Art, I offer a few quotes that may underscore why *Modern Abstract Religious Verbal Impressionism* was produced.

1) "Love of beauty is taste. The creation of beauty is art." – Ralph Waldo Emerson

2) "Art freedom and creativity will change society faster than politics." – Victor Pinchuk

3) "Art is not what you see, but what you make others see." – Edgar Degas

4) "To reveal art and conceal the artist is art's aim." – Oscar Wilde

5) "Art is a revolt against fate. All art is a revolt against man's fate." – Andre Malraux

6) “Art is the tree of life. Science is the tree of death.” – William Blake

7) “The highest art is always the most religious, and the greatest artist is always a devout person.” – Abraham Lincoln

8) “Art is the lie that enables us to realize the truth.” – Pablo Picasso

9) “The most beautiful experience we can have is the mysterious. It is the fundamental emotion which stands at the cradle of true art and true science.” – Albert Einstein

10) “No great artist ever sees things as they really are. If he did he would cease to be an artist.” – Oscar Wilde

All quotes are taken from thegoldenquotes.net – https://www.thegoldenquotes.net/art-quotes/.

I think "impressionism" as an art form is appropriate for me. Impressionism began around 1860. Some of the famous painters making use of the style were Pierre-August Renoir, Claude Monet, Alfred Sisley, and Frédéric Bazille. I should include post-impressionist Vincent Van Gogh. The characteristics of the works made use of movement in colors, liveliness, perception of the subject(s) rather than realism, and the use of light cues and deliberate brush strokes.

Modern art includes works beginning in the 1860s to the 1970s. It departs from past artists' representations of conservatism and tradition to highlight modern advancements and tests new techniques in individual presentations.

Abstract art is a term to describe meaningful imagery that may or may not have a real-world reference point. Its meaning is not discrete or obvious. Intuition is important.

My project is Modern Abstract Religious Verbal Impressionism – MARVI. I am determined to create a way of conveying my impression of religion verbally. I don't have a calling from God to be a pastor (theology), the intellect of a scholar or teacher (philosopher), or the skill to write well (author). I follow art. I love art. Artists create. From this comes Christian Reformed Impressionism (See Glossary of Colors).

With this brief art summary, I'm introducing a proposal to bring Reformed theology through an impression. That is, describing an impression of Predestination, rendering an image of inauthentic and authentic identity, and offering better news than the traditional Good News being taught by religion. Not that MARVI-RPIA is actually better than the Good News of Jesus Christ. MARVI-RPIA is the *GREAT* news *ABOUT* the Good News of Jesus Christ.

This image is beautiful. It will lift your heart. I guarantee it.

Guarantee it? Who am I? How could I possibly have anything to offer that is that bold? I'm nobody. Yet, I dare offer what has NEVER been offered before in Reformed theology. Am I able to discern what has been missed over two thousand years by the most brilliant minds in history? For two thousand years, has the church overlooked a concept that I have managed to uncover? Am I that arrogant? That haughty? A trillion-dollar concept? Absurd.

You may recall Psalm 119:99. The author is recounting how God has blessed him. He has more understanding than his enemies (atheists), more than his teachers (churches), and more than the many esteemed ancient mentors of the past (internet). This is how I feel as I paint this project. My understanding came with the help of others. It's not that I'm so great. It's timing in history. It's circumstances. It's the opportunity and unique resources only made available in the twenty-first century.

> Thou through thy commandments hast made me wiser than mine enemies: for they are ever with me. I have more understanding than all my teachers: for thy testimonies are my meditation. I understand more than the ancients, because I keep thy precepts (Psalm 119:98-100).

But your cynicism may be warranted if Jesus's Second Coming is in the next one to five hundred years. But what if the world continues for another one thousand years? Two thousand years? Five thousand years or more? That's not likely? Is it possible?

How many thousands of years passed after God promised Adam and Eve the "seed of the woman" would prevail over the seed of the serpent? Adam and Eve may have thought the Redeemer born to them would be within their lifetime. Did they know how many children would be born to them? How many children would be born to their children's children? Did they know an average lifespan in those days would be a thousand years? Child after child after child comes into the world. None are the Promised One.

How many centuries passed after the prophets spoke of the Messiah's appearance?

Thousands of years later, time continues to pass. We try to figure out if there is anything we can do to recognize God's plan for the world and be a part of the plan. We have plenty of clues from scripture. Scripture shows us imagery of history, prophecy, parables, and allegory. If MARVI-RPIA were to make any worthwhile contribution to spiritual thought, *why can't it be the Ontological Assurance of the Pre-Life Elect Identity?*

This reminds me of the Pharisees' discussions regarding Jesus. Surely, if any group would recognize the Messiah, it would be the Pharisees. Their lives were dedicated to religious understanding. How could this well-known neighborhood person, Jesus, possibly be the Messiah? All the evidence was to the contrary. It was impossible based on what they relied on as religious data.

Could they have looked beyond the literal words of scripture to a figurative or spiritual IMPRESSION? Was there any way possible the Jews and the Pharisees could have imagined:

- an angel came to Mary and told her of giving birth to Jesus;
- Joseph was not Jesus's father. The Holy Spirit was Jesus's father;
- Mary was Jesus's mother, a virgin, impregnated by the Holy Spirit; and
- Jesus's brothers and sisters were His half-siblings.

> And in the sixth month the angel Gabriel was sent from God unto a city of Galilee, named Nazareth, [to] a virgin espoused to a man whose name was Joseph, of the house of David; and the virgin's name was Mary (Luke 1:26-27).

Does this help explain how a Pre-Life Elect person could have been overlooked, denied, or discouraged from having an identity before birth?

There are no apparent dots to connect! There's nothing there!

A person has only one composite identity according to theistic teaching. This is physical, mental, and spiritual identity. Personhood is not two individual identities. If this were possible, it would have been part of orthodox teaching by now.

As the years go by, our understanding of scripture increases, not decreases. We have better translations. We have more capable scholars. We have a greater number of people who are exposed to scripture, and therefore a greater number of people who contribute to articulating scripture.

One of the major drawbacks in teaching scripture and comprehending scripture is that not everyone has not read the Bible from Genesis to Revelation. Those who have probably don't remember a lot of what they read. What do they remember? How much of that did they comprehend? Are they able to evaluate at least ten of the television ministries to compare and contrast errors in doctrine? Do they have solid answers to at least twenty of the most frequently asked Bible questions? I faced these issues. I've read the Bible. I continue to read the Bible—every single day. If I don't read, I listen to the Bible being read to me.

Not only that, I write the Bible. I REWRITE the scriptures. I write five verses at a time, every day, longhand, on eight-and-one-half-by-eleven, inkjet paper. I've been doing so for about twenty years. After writing the five verses, I read the chapter. If it is a long chapter containing many verses, that means I may read that same chapter over and over and over. If there are forty-five verses in a chapter, forty-five divided by five is nine. So I write the first five verses and read the chapter. I write the next five verses and read the chapter. Nine days later, I've read that chapter nine times. On to the next chapter.

When I finish all the chapters and all books of the Bible, I will have my own handwritten Bible. Then I will begin a second Bible, from Genesis 1:1. Okay, good for me. So what? What does all that mean? It means I feel *partly* qualified to render verbal imagery about religion. I have a lifelong commitment to reviewing every single word of the Bible. And I write. Longhand. Every. Single. Word.

I live in a unique time in history. All the intellectual giants are readily accessible to me on the internet. In the past, I would spend hours in the city, county, or university library. In the past, I had to take college courses. In the past, I drew on years of radio, television, and print that taught me the many various views on religion. Today, I can do this from the comfort of my home during rain, shine, sleet, or hail. I can save, word for word, whatever I find. I can print whatever I find. I can share whatever I find. My education is an extraordinary path that benefits from THOUSANDS of years of material recently made available. No previous generation has anywhere near the resources available to us today.

Now, finally, I'm ready to submit, for your review, an audacious trillion-dollar value that has made an extraordinary impression on me.

And, by the way, other people are doing the same thing I have been doing. They may be coming to some of the same conclusions I have. Many of us have been exposed to a high level of dynamic resources. Technology must have reached over 90 percent of the world by now. It's progress!

MINISTER OF ART—POSTSCRIPT

A real fear that drags my heart from time to time is that God isn't with me. It may be that my *Connecting the Dots of Identity* project is actually AGAINST God. It seems that what I am implying is that pastors DO NOT teach the word of God. I imply that churches teaching Reformed theology DO NOT teach consistently. I imply organized religion teaches the words of the Bible but NOT the spirit of the words.

Who am I? I'm nobody! How dare I speak against God's chosen speakers!

I do not intend to convey argumentative or quarrelsome positions, but I may be perceived as doing so. What can I do to alleviate misgivings about my position?

Perhaps to reiterate:

- I am not a man of God. I am not called by God to teach His word.

- *Don't believe anything I've written here. I, myself, don't believe what I have written here in Connecting the Dots of Identity. I am writing about an IMPRESSION of the Bible.*

- This is a full disclaimer. I am a Minister of Art. I'm not a writer, philosopher, or teacher. I attempt to create beautiful, emotive, hopeful imagery via religious words. Believe your Bible. *Don't believe in art; appreciate art. Or don't.*

Pastors may be against me. Churches may be against me. Atheists are already against me. I may be accused of causing people to leave a church or not join a church. I may be considered irresponsible and a danger to Christian orthodox teaching. *I may not be welcomed as a member or as a visitor to any orthodox church.*

But, as I say, my real apprehension is what God thinks of me. Am I helping or hurting? Is my disclaimer of not speaking for God strong enough? Will people understand my artistic intentions?

What I know is that I was never content with answers to why I'm here, what is happening, and what should I be doing. My life became a sacrifice to see if better answers could be found than what I heard. If they couldn't be found, so be it. People risk their lives for far less than this.

Thankfully, some of you are with me all the way. So much so that you see various problems with *Connecting The Dots Of Identity* and will work to make improvements. I'm honored if you do so.

If WE find better answers than what we've heard, the reward may be beyond compare. Trillions, perhaps!

CHAPTER 13

MARVI-RPIA STAGES

Modern Abstract Religious Verbal Impressionism sounds interesting, but it also sounds risky. As an artist taking artistic license with the Bible, I never want to endorse heresy. Essentially, this implies taking passages from the Bible and building on unorthodox speculation rather than employing exegesis. This is one of the reasons why there are so many variations regarding which church or interpretation has the true meaning of the Bible. When enough churches agree on a core meaning, they usually form a denomination. There may be five, ten, or fifteen denominations, all claiming to follow the word of God. Can they all have enough of the truth to be a blessing to the congregation? Apparently, yes!

I stated earlier the premise of God's Election Program. A Christian is predestined to be saved before the foundation of the world (Ephesians 1:4, etcetera). What we KNOW is not what saves us. What we DO is not what saves us. God's grace has saved us before we were born. That is great consolation—until you consider those who are NOT Elect. If Hell exists, and Hell is widely taught in the Bible, why are they not Elect? If God is no respecter of persons, on what basis are people relegated to Hell?

> Then Peter opened his mouth, and said, "Of a truth I perceive that God is no respecter of persons" (Acts 10:34).

This is one of the critical issues that urged me to find another way of communicating what the Bible teaches. There must be a way to demonstrate this controversial religious idea without being denounced as a heretic. I want to share my thoughts, but I'm probably going to get hammered by my theist friends and my atheist friends. Theists disdain teachers who speculate. They say just stick with what the Bible says, don't guess, don't use hypotheticals, don't imagine. You'll get into trouble trying to rationalize your position. You'll weaken the true meaning of scripture. You'll speculate when hermeneutics is the path to follow. Theists may charge those who speculate to be in the same camp as faith healers, charlatans, and false prophets. Just stick to scripture. That way, you'll stay safe.

Then, of course, atheists aren't going to care if you speculate or not. They will certainly disrespect any attempt that endorses the Christian worldview. Except, perhaps, MARVI-RPIA. Why is that? Because I'm saying throughout the book: How can you not like this "impression"? What's not to like? What other worldview is better? Atheism? Please. How depressing can you get?

Atheists affirm life is an accident. Life has no purpose. We came from nothing and go back to nothing. We're just meat from top to bottom. If humans don't destroy themselves, the dynamics of the universe eventually will.

Of course, every worldview has its drawbacks. MARVI-RPIA has drawbacks too. MARVI-RPIA just has fewer than the others.

You may be getting a bit impatient. Are you wondering when the substance of the trillion-dollar treasure will be revealed? Sorry, it requires a little more background to set the stage.

Stage 1 – The Bible is reliable as a historical document and verified by the greatest Person who ever lived: Jesus Christ. No reason to have doubts. He never lied. He's sinless. The demarcation of time, for most of the world, is measured by the year before He was born (BC) and after He was born (AD). He is certainly the One above everyone else.

Stage 2 – From the Bible, Christian Reformed theology follows well-established principles found throughout scripture, especially predestination.

Stage 3 – Christian Reformed theology teaches salvation by grace alone. Nothing a person knows or does can contribute to salvation. God does all the saving and does so before anyone was born. The saved persons, the Elect, are guaranteed salvation. Those not Elect will not receive salvation, and, therefore, will be relegated to damnation. This is not as dreadful as it sounds. Subsequent chapters will paint a more appealing picture, with supporting details.

Stage 4 – Christian Reformed theology is vilified on the view that it removes Free Will from the individual. This makes God the creator of robots. And, apparently, God creates people knowing He will send them to Hell. Obviously, people do have a will of their own, and God is not God if He creates people simply to put them in Hell forever. No "religion" believes that.

Stage 5 – No theist solution, atheist solution, or agnostic solution has presented a case that thoroughly resolves the matters of great consequence. Matters such as evil, justice, reality, identity, happenstance, morality, love, science, and life. They remain in a space between objectivity and subjectivity. Meanwhile, we're faced with trying to make a decent living while making sense of what is going on around us. There is illness, suicide, murder, accidents, abortion, molestation, misunderstandings in communication, crime, the legal system, politics, and, of course, death. The clock is ticking. We're getting older. Age means concerns about health, finance, and companionship. Yes, there are many answers to these problems, but are they answers that really satisfy? No! Well, none perhaps until now.

Stage 6 – If you eliminate death, you may solve the number one obstacle in everyone's life. And the second obstacle? Hell. You aren't concerned about Hell if you overcome death. Hell is an afterlife matter. Assuming the three main subjects of life are death, Hell, and an afterlife, any reasonable solution should hold interest. I hope I have your interest. Though you may have been speed-reading through the chapters, I hope you will slow your speed to consider the implications of no death, no Hell, and an afterlife.

Stage 7 – No death by virtue of Jesus Christ overcoming death for human beings by becoming human, dying, and rising from death. As 100 percent deity and 100 percent human, Jesus redeemed 100 percent human beings—not angels, not human-angel hybrids (who are the Nephilim), not aliens from another galaxy, and not animals.

Stage 8 – No Hell by virtue of all humans being saved BEFORE they were born on Earth. Secondly, Hell is created for the Devil and his angels (Matthew 25).

Stage 9 – The afterlife in Heaven.

Preposterous, you may think. Nonsense, you may say. Another crazy, religious, fantasy story. No, no. Not at all. Steps one through nine are just to lay more groundwork. Once the factors of individual identity outside time and inside time are revealed, an image or impression will take form.

This is the Modern Abstract Religious Verbal Impressionism mentioned earlier. What comprises that image starts with individual identity. This identity is an array of eight components. The context is in isolating which identity has the roleplaying function. Who you are, why you are here, how to live your life, and expectation in the afterlife will have new meanings.

Then shall he say also unto them on the left hand, Depart from me, ye cursed, into everlasting fire, prepared for the devil and his angels (Matthew 25:41).

CHAPTER 14

MARVI-RPIA (IDENTITY ARRAY)

MARVI-RPIA stands for modern abstract religious verbal impressionism-role play identity array. Upcoming chapters will develop your PERCEPTION of reality, as contrasted to an IMPRESSION of reality.

This book is not a platform to teach, instruct, or assert a religious position or define reality. The nature of reality, whether it be the creationist's or the evolutionist's view, is only a side issue of this art project. Additionally, this won't be a paraphrase of the Bible or a commentary of the Bible. This book is a personal impression of general and special revelation rendered by an artist. I intend to share with you a specific spiritual impression of beauty, peace, and hope not shared anywhere else or at any time in history.

It's art appreciation.

RPIA – Role Play Identity Array

Roleplay is a term to denote the assignment of created persons by God. Initially, this was Adam and Eve. Adam and Eve were assigned a role to play. That role was Free Will. As created beings, they possessed two main natures, a spiritual nature and a physical nature. Their spiritual nature was invisible. Their physical nature was ostensibly visible, although it included concealed internal matter.

A feature of the flawlessly created beings was freedom of thought and behavior. God placed a symbol of choice in the space where Adam and Eve lived, called the Tree of the Knowledge of Good and Evil. Free Will presented the option for them to agree with God's command to not partake of the Tree of the Knowledge of Good and Evil, or to disagree and pursue the knowledge from the forbidden tree. Adam and Eve exercised their will to disagree with God and pursue knowledge. The penalty was death. God's mercy was to promise an Antidote to death through progeny. In the interim, the error in Eden caused death to reign throughout the environment and throughout the lives of the offspring of Adam and Eve.

Identity Array refers to essential aspects of a person's identity. For the sake of brevity and convenience, the array is given abbreviations. After an explanation of how this array is featured in identity, it will be easier to understand how identity relates to Pre-Life, Life, and the Afterlife.

SSID (Super Spiritual Identity)

This is an individual's authentic identity. This identity is the true, real, "actual you" spoken of in scripture. This is the Elect person whom God knows before the "Role-Play you" were born. You are the recognized Pre-Life Elect with definite ontological status created before the foundation of the world (see Chapter 15 - SSID).

HSID (Holy Spirit Identity)

The Holy Spirit, the Third Person of the Trinity, intercedes on behalf of Elect roleplayers. Seconds before death, at death, or possibly even after death, the Holy Spirit redeems the roleplayer to assure the union with SSID. By the way, HSID after death is an exception to the rule only by way of the ten or so examples of life after death cited in scripture, notably by Jesus, who vanquished death's final authority.

Secondarily, HSID eliminates the possibility of ESID (Evil Spirit Identity).

SID (Spiritual Identity)

Creationism, Designationism, and Traducianism involve the timing of the spiritual identity before, at, or after conception (see Glossary of Colors).

If BEFORE conception, God is the Agent.

If AT conception, the spirit is conceived in sin from the parents as the agent.

If AFTER conception, the sinful spirit of the parents is neutralized by God as the Agent.

The spiritual identity begins life SID-Negative, conceived in sin. After birth, the identity moves from SID-Negative to SID-Neutral. The spiritual identity continues neutral through childhood. After childhood, the spiritual identity moves from neutral to negative or from neutral to positive.

Generally, the inclination is to move toward a religious view or away from a religious view. Should the child die before birth, in the neutral state, chronological age is not a factor in salvation. Salvation has already been accomplished before the world was created. The issue is simply one less life providing the ongoing Demonstration of Free Will.

But before birth, a child has no will at all. Yes, but Free Will was imposed on the child by its parents. It's the same for all of us. Our Free Will is a function of the people who brought us to life. It doesn't matter if it was by artificial insemination, rape, or accident. It's all circumstances of heredity, the environment the parents were in, and their experiences leading to the birth of the child. SID-Neutral persons gravitate toward either SID-Positive or SID-Negative as they demonstrate the effects of Free Will. SID-Positive persons eventually receive HSID, before death or at death. SID-Negative persons do not receive HSID. By not receiving HSID before death, they become a "control group." This group proves that, unless God intercedes, no one will ever choose God's way of life.

If no HSID, it doesn't mean this group goes to Hell. It just means their roleplay identity ends. If they are 100 percent human, they have an SSID counterpart in Paradise. If less than 100 percent human, compromised by evil spirits, they belong with the Devil and his angels. The MARVI-RPIA image is that upon death, they simply cease to exist. Only 100 percent humans have an eternal spiritual identity, or a soul. Jesus lived to redeem 100 percent humans.

The “other sheep” in the New Testament book of John have an outside chance of application here, but that is most likely a reference to Gentiles.

> As the Father knoweth me, even so know I the Father: and I lay down my life for the sheep. And other sheep I have, which are not of this fold: them also I must bring, and they shall hear my voice; and there shall be one fold, and one shepherd (John 10:15-16).

Bible verses of life after death:

> Jesus, Lazarus, Eutychus, boy Elijah raised, boy Elisha raised, funeral-man touched Elisha's bones, son of the widow in Naim, Jairus' daughter, Tabitha/Dorcas from Peter, graves opened/many arose (Matthew 27), and women received their dead (Hebrews 11).

Bible verses of life after death:

ESID (Evil Spirit Identity)

An evil spirit identity is a distinct possibility for persons who may not receive a blessed intervention (HSID). They are conceived SID-Negative and remain so. As Roleplayers, they are a testimony to the exercise of Free Will error by Adam and Eve. Their thought/behavior patterns may resemble a decent person, but they are evil. They are most likely less than 100 percent human beings.

Evil spirits are the angels who exercised Free Will to disagree with God's will for their life. They are allowed to obstruct and undermine Roleplayers, and even compromise human genetic material. As the Great Accuser, Satan charges God with obvious favoritism toward humans and less favor to angels. Furthermore, Satan insinuates humans and angels suffer from design flaws. Otherwise, there would be no discontent in the Garden of Eden or in Heaven.

Though evil spirits may appear human, their imagery is a fabrication, an infringement on image-bearers of God. With an apparent ability to mimic human form, the Second-Class evil spirits collaborate with ESID persons today. An ESID person's image more closely resembles a shadow, the reflection off a shiny surface, or a photograph. It is an image of the person, but not the identity of the person. ESIDs are an inauthentic image of roleplay identity, not an authentic image of roleplay identity.

Agnostics, atheists, and many theists claiming to know God never received the Holy Spirit. They are roleplaying their life based on heredity, environment, and experiences. No one receives the Holy Spirit through their own efforts. God has to take the initiative, or it will never happen. This is the point of an inauthentic identity. Creatures with Free Will subsist based on heredity, environment, and experience. Will they choose God's will for their life or their own will?

They ALL choose their own will UNLESS and UNTIL God overruns their Free Will. We see proof of this every single day. Why do you think we have atheists, agnostics, and freethinkers? God hasn't overrun their Free Will! Even when God does overrun their Free Will, people don’t suddenly gain spiritual maturity. They gradually come to recognize a born-again identity. Add to this the lifelong effects of heredity, environment, and experience. It takes time to change.

What about First-Class Angels? What about the Pre-Life Elect? How do they prove that unless God intercedes, no one will choose His will?

Number one, the Pre-Life Elect are not Roleplayers. They're not involved in the Demonstration of Free Will. Their identity precedes any Free Will scenarios.

Number two, all the angels lived within God's presence, as spirits, outside of time, with no testing scenario like the Tree of the Knowledge of Good and Evil. First-Class Angels who did not fall didn't have the comparable factors human beings are subject to. Second and Third-Class Angels seem to have occurred as a result of the relationship God has with human beings.

Lucifer and Second-Class Angels, Abaddon, and Third-Class Angels also proved their allegiance to God until the existence of time, space, and matter at the foundation of the world. Although they were not considered Roleplayers like the offspring of Adam and Eve, they nonetheless seemed influenced by Adam and Eve's Free Will roleplay. Conflict developed. Apparently, God favors humans more than angels. This is without regard to the recognition of persons saved before the world is created—the SSIDs.

Continuing ESID, some atheists, agnostics, and theists who have never received the Holy Spirit receive the Holy Spirit at sudden death or the last second(s) of life. On Judgment Day, they are raised from the dead in the manner Jesus was raised from the dead. This means their roleplay identity will join their true SSID in Paradise. Anyone else who does not receive the Holy Spirit at death is likely not 100 percent human, but an ESID (Evil Spirit Identity).

PID (Physical Identity)

PID is the tangible substance conveyed to you from ancestors dating back to Noah and Missus Noah, and even further back to Adam and Eve. PID is also affected by the environment and by experiences. This component of your identity greatly affects your mental identity (MID).

MID (Mental Identity)

Your brain makes a major impact on your ability to self-actualize How well you perceive and conceptualize reality, how you process your environment and experiences, and how well you adapt to your physical attributes. This determines, in large part, who you believe you are. Other factors such as consciousness, emotion, and morality represent metaphysical aspects of identity.

CID (Childhood Identity)

A time-oriented and memory-oriented dimension of who you are relates to the person you formerly were as far back as possible. The intervals of change in identity provide a panorama of events that have led to who you are today. How important previous versions of your identity are may or may not be significant. Your childhood may have little to do with who you are today, or a lot to do with who you are. Your memory of the past may be stellar, spotty, or even suppressed. The past might be daydreams of pleasant memories or a nightmare of unpleasant reminders.

DID (Dream Identity)

You awaken and can't quite figure out why you were doing what you were doing. That person in the dream was not you. You were in that body. You had the first-person point of view. But you in the dream and you now awake are two different people. The awake you were simply along for the ride with the dream you. The real you have no dream control, and you realize that as your head hits the pillow to sleep. What transpires in your dream is another unknown adventure in random non-reality. The persons in the dream are not real. You in the dream are not real. Conscious access to your dream identity of you is not available. It is similar to your subconscious or semiconscious mental identity (MID), which also has no access. Still, this should be incorporated into what constitutes an individual personal identity.

By the way, you may be wondering how many more iterations of me are there. Intuitively, you know there are more than eight, but how many more? Human beings are extraordinarily complex. The eight-part Identity Array is designed to limit the number to eight. No doubt, that number might stretch to eighty-eight by including other spiritual and nonspiritual identity concepts. However, by limiting the number to eight, they're much easier to remember, visualize, and apply.

The Super-Spiritual Identity (SSID) is the foundation on which the other identities rely. By its nature, a dynamic mural of colorful concepts can be applied to the architecture of theology.

No explicit evidence has been presented for an ontological identity residing in Paradise. It's circumstantial. MARVI-RPIA imagery of SSID is art. It's not theology. The Minister of Art doesn't believe a word of it. He says you shouldn't either. You APPRECIATE art, or you don't.

Now, let's contrast the eight-part Identity Array with a second set of identities. This is to remind you how pervasive an inauthentic identity becomes. These are images of you, but only as a roleplayer constructs. They are not your identity.

1) Your shadow

2) Your reflected image from a reflected surface

3) Your photographic image

4) Your perceived image by others (living/deceased)

5) Your roleplay image as:

a) spouse

b) lover

c) parent

d) sibling/relative

e) friend

f) occupation

g) neighbor

h) pet provider

6) deceased (lying in state/or in a dream)

These all fit into the 8-ID Array model. One through six above are all inauthentic identities from the roleplay model of the Demonstration of Free Will. The only true authentic identity you have is the SSID model residing in Paradise. That is assuming you are 100 percent human. Even assuming you may be less than 100 percent human, roleplay identity is inauthentic.

Considering the world population comes from the family of Noah, and if one or more of the wives of Noah's sons carried a recessive component of Nephilim genetic material, any "corruption" would decrease the percentage of human distinctiveness. Of course, the Holy Spirit's intercession would obviate any Nephilim concern. However, it doesn't really matter. Physical conception is out of our control. Our Pre-Life spiritual identity is what matters most.

This is a part of how *Connecting The Dots Of Identity* paints the dots to connect. We can proceed to see how they relate to being Roleplayers, who are portrayed as those persons exercising the Free Will available to them based on the attributes of their ancestors. Everyone has an identity array enforced on them at conception: gender, ethnicity, height, weight, intelligence, attractiveness, medical condition, athleticism, talent, etcetera. This identity is inauthentic. It's forced, fragile, and incomplete.

You're thrown onto a live stage and told to act as a normal person. Script? Just improvise. For how long? Improvise. What's going on? Improvise.

Roleplayers live to prove the Error of Free Will. They think and behave in their best interests. These interests are based on their heredity, their environment, and their experiences. They don't have the unlimited Free Will Adam and Eve possessed. As a consequence, every Roleplayer's thoughts/behaviors reflect an error in judgment as illustrated by the fall of Adam and Eve. Every Roleplayer with one exception, Jesus the Christ. Jesus was also a Roleplayer. The difference, of course, was that Jesus was the Antidote to sin, and therefore, the Antidote to death. He lived as 100 percent human (sinless) and as 100 percent God. More on this presently.

CHAPTER 15

SUPER-SPIRITUAL IDENTITY (SSID)

What is an SSID as defined by *Connecting The Dots Of Identity*?

The Pre-Life Elect or individuals God refers to as having been saved before the foundation of the world.

Also:

An ontological status granted by God.

A definitive necessity of being—before conception/birth, outside time.

A spiritual reality of immaterialism—before conception/birth outside time.

A substantive disposition of primary identity—before conception/before birth outside time.

An entity that was, is, and always will be an essence of personhood.

> According as he hath chosen us in him before the foundation of the world, that we should be holy and without blame before him in love (Ephesians 1:4).
>
> Who hath saved us, and called us with an holy calling, not according to our works, but according to his own purpose and grace, which was given us in Christ Jesus before the world began (2 Timothy 1:9)

Ontology is a branch of philosophy regarding being, existence, and the essence of what is. It goes much further by making use of complex language to infer potentiality, possibility, probability, and proposition. Ontology is closely related to epistemology (knowledge) and metaphysics (abstract phenomena).

As to who gets credited with the beginnings of a philosophy devoted to ontology, researchers quote Greek philosopher Aristotle (384 BC). Others of note include Saint Anselm of Canterbury (1109), Rene Descartes, (1596), Alfred North Whitehead (1861), and Willard Van Orman Quine (1908). German philosopher Edmund Husserl (1859) makes use of the term phenomenology to further describe ontology.

Alfred N. Whitehead suggests the essence of an "actual entity." He says there's no confusion about its identity being confused with another actual entity. Further, there is no potential for it to be something other than itself. If anything, this actual entity is a source of potentiality for the creation of other actual entities.

I would prefer the term "impetus" rather than the term "creation" Whitehead uses. SSIDs, super-spiritual identities, don't create anything as Whitehead implied. SSIDs are joined by their HSID/Elect Role Player identities in the afterlife to become a united identity.

Ontology gives rise to basic questions concerning identity, existence, being, primacy, reality, phenomena, and even virtual non-real concepts. Ontology investigates the nature of symbols, numerics, time, and language. The ascendance of technology confirms how the application of intelligence, tools, and algorithms facilitates metaphysics, a relative of ontology.

Of course, this review of ontology is to underscore the definition of the Pre-Life Elect—those individuals God refers to as having been saved before they were born. No religious organizations have taken up the mission to support a separate pre-life identity before the foundation of the world. The Bible declares such an identity, but no method of articulation has come forward. Why?

Obviously, there cannot be a dual-identity configuration for a human being. No orthodox religious principles include more than a physical, mental, and spiritual way of defining personhood. This is always defined as single-identity personhood. So how does MARVI-RPIA get away with professing dual-identity imagery, going against thousands of years of orthodox teaching?

MARVI-RPIA has two responses.

1) MARVI-RPIA provides a framework for identity based on a spiritual identity *outside* time and a physical/mental identity based on identity *inside* time. This is orthodox. The Father, Son, and Holy Spirit are spiritual identities outside and inside time. Angels are spiritual identities outside and inside time. *God declares the Elect are persons He recognizes. They are/were ordained, guaranteed, set apart, each one chosen, given elite status before He created the world. All this is outside of time. This is the First-Identity Framework or Group A persons.* Group B persons comprise a Second Identity Framework, existing inside time, as Role Play and Identity Array (RPIA).

Conventional Christian doctrine suggests God directs persons according to His timing to be born—and LATER to be saved. All the others who are not one of the Elect, and that is the majority of the world, are also created by God, but NOT to Election. They are on their own plan.

Orthodoxy says God is omniscient. We trust Him to always do what is best, no matter how ugly it appears to us. Praise to God He saves even one of us. He's not under any obligation whatsoever.

We get JUSTICE for being sinful. We get MERCY for being sinful. *God is not being unjust in either circumstance. He is just in all His ways. He is NEVER unjust.* We are simply clay on the potter's wheel. We don't have any say in what the potter does.

> Then I went down to the potter's house, and behold, he wrought a work on the wheels. And the vessel that he made of clay was marred in the hand of the potter: so he made it again another vessel, as seemed good to the potter to make it. Then the word of the LORD came to me, saying, "O house of Israel, cannot I do with you as this potter? saith the LORD. Behold, as the clay is in the potter's hand, so are ye in mine hand, O house of Israel" (Jeremiah 18:3-6)

2) MARVI-RPIA portrays a nonstandard religious position—the medium of art. No argument is made to usurp the long-standing perspective of the Christian religion and especially the Christian Reformed doctrine. MARVI-RPIA is an attempt to present religion as an artistic impression from seventy years of General and Special Revelation. Do not assume MARVI-RPIA is the product of a theologian, philosopher, or teacher. Do not assume MARVI-RPIA is a belief system. I am the artist creating MARVI-RPIA, and I do not believe in MARVI-RPIA. You do not believe in art. Art is for enjoyment, emotion, beauty, support, inspiration, appreciation, and hope. Art is also ugly, provocative, crude, and unusual.

You like it or you don't.

WHERE HAVE YOU BEEN ALL OUR LIVES?

The promotion of a Pre-Life Elect person having the actual status of being will always be controversial. The first question people have is why the prolonged absence of any details regarding Pre-Life Elect ontology? Why didn't Jesus Christ tell us? We should have heard from biblical scholars long before now.

Our true identity existing in Paradise before we were born is fantastic news! How is it that we don't know this? Does this have any chance, any chance at all, of being true?

It does indeed. There are several Bible verses that refer to a Book of Life and a Lamb's Book of Life. These books are a reference to a record God has of individual names in possession of salvation. They are identified and recognized as human beings whose life must be guaranteed before God created life on earth. Any name not written, or erased, is damned. The written names are God-given names—before anyone was conceived. Of course, these "books" are spiritual. Writing is spiritual. Names are spiritual.

> Yet now, if thou wilt forgive their sin; and if not, blot me, I pray thee, out of thy book which thou hast written. And the Lord said unto Moses, Whosoever hath sinned against me, him will I blot out of my book (Exodus 32:32-33).
>
> A fiery stream issued and came forth from before him: thousand thousands ministered unto him, and ten thousand times ten thousand stood before him: the judgment was set, and the books were opened (Daniel 7:10).
>
> And at that time shall Michael stand up, the great prince which standeth for the children of thy people: and there shall be a time of trouble, such as never was since there was a nation even to that same time: and at that time thy

> people shall be delivered, every one that shall be found written in the book (Daniel 12:1).
>
> Notwithstanding in this rejoice not, that the spirits are subject unto you; but rather rejoice, because your names are written in heaven (Luke 10:20)
>
> To the general assembly and church of the firstborn, which are written in heaven, and to God the Judge of all, and to the spirits of just men made perfect (Hebrews 12:23).
>
> He that overcometh, the same shall be clothed in white raiment; and I will not blot out his name out of the book of life, but I will confess his name before my Father, and before his angels ... And all that dwell upon the earth shall worship him, whose names are not written in the book of life of the Lamb slain from the foundation of the world ... And I saw the dead, small and great, stand before God; and the books were opened: and another book was opened, which is the book of life: and the dead were judged out of those things which were written in the books, according to their works ... And whosoever was not found written in the book of life was cast into the lake of fire ... And there shall in no wise enter into it any thing that defileth, neither whatsoever worketh abomination, or maketh a lie: but they which are written in the Lamb's book of life (Revelation 3:5; 13:8; 20:12,15; 21:27).

Why isn't all of this more obvious to us? Why the mysterious, obscure, puzzling aspect of salvation? One reason, as the Bible indicates, is that Jesus spoke in parables. Without a parable He did not speak to them.

> Another parable spake he unto them; The kingdom of heaven is like unto leaven, which a woman took, and hid in three measures of meal, till the whole was leavened. All these things spake Jesus unto the multitude in parables; and without a parable spake he not unto them: That it might be fulfilled which was spoken by the prophet, saying, I will open my mouth in parables; I will utter things which have been kept secret from the foundation of the world (Matthew 13:33-35).

A Pre-Life identity certainly may be true. Think of the major questions you have that the Bible leaves open. Questions about God, Jesus, the Holy Spirit, angels, outer space, time, your own body, your mind, the essence of life, and everything else. There are many mysteries all of us confront, not just theological or philosophical ones. Gravity, magnetism, electricity, motion, light, and subatomic particles, to name a few. *But MARVI-RPIA is not about solving mysteries. MARVI-RPIA is not about proclaiming the truth.*

MARVI-RPIA is art.

And further, on the existence of Pre-Life identity, think of your dreams. You are "you" in your dreams. You have a first-person point of view, which includes your memories. However, you do not exist in a dream. You exist outside your dream. Why don't you interrupt the dream? You can't. You have no control of that identity. It's you, but not you. You awaken. Now you continue in your ongoing series of life, living an arranged inauthentic identity.

What about so-called lucid dreams? People say you have some control of yourself there. No, not really. Even if you do, it's only a temporary, limited control, and "you" and the other dream characters do not continue to exist outside of the dream.

Dreams suggest an analogy of Pre-Life Elect identity compared to Roleplay identity. There is an outside-time "you" and an inside-time "you." There's no access between the two.

Even more on the existence of identity—think of a number. Any number. Have it in your mind? What is that number? 2? 11? 129? Do you realize that number you thought of is not real? Numbers *represent* reality. They are not a physical or abstract reality in themselves. At least, that was my understanding until I happened upon an article in *Scientific American.* Here is one line from the article in reference to a book by Max Tegmark:

> *The Mathematical Universe Hypothesis implies that we live in a relational reality, in the sense that the properties of the world around us stem not from properties of its ultimate building blocks but from the relations between these building blocks.*

The MARVI-RPIA existence of a Pre-Life Elect person has veracity. Compare it to the methodologies that symbolize not only quantity but ratios, factors, propositions, and relationships. None of us may be "real." Physical life is only a shadow of spiritual reality. Flesh and blood are like a number; they represent what will be a reality in the spiritual afterlife. Prime numbers (two, three, five, and seven), algebra, calculus, and geometry help discover what can be known about reality. Similarly, Role Players, like numbers, help represent Pre-Life Elect individuals.

The realization you don't have to accept the role forced upon you is freedom. So what if you don't know who your mother or father is? So what if you are gay, or unattractive, or poor? That may be beyond your control. That doesn't define who you are. That is a role dictated by heredity, the environment, and circumstances. Who you are is the person known by God already in Paradise, awaiting the end of the Free Will Demonstration.

Here is another explanation by author Jumblegreen regarding numbers:

> *Having given it some thought, the only consistent theme I can find between all the generally accepted uses of the word number is that of 'constancy': a number is the name we give to a constant; that is why Pi is a number: Pi is the name we give to the constant ratio between the area of a circle and the square of its radius. Any value of any numbering system expresses some quality of unchangingness.*

By the way, the worldview of evolution/materialism/physicalism states reality is not personal, that there is no God. Therefore, reality has the appearance of design, but in actuality, life began by accident, without purpose, and is governed by undiscovered forces. In comparison to MARVI-RPIA, atheism/agnosticism also admits you may be a Roleplayer. Roleplayers, like numbers, REPRESENT reality but are OTHER than reality, or DESCRIPTORS of reality.

The difference is atheists, generally speaking, lack such essentials as hope, love, and goodness. For them, there is hope, love, and goodness, but only in relative terms. Since these kinds of things can't be measured, as in science, the value they have is simply an assigned value. Further, there is no future or past. Just nothingness, then life, and back to nothingness. No purpose, no good or bad—just a relative agreement on what is acceptable. Do they love their family, their pets, or their friends? They say they do, but when pressed, most admit such words are simply a matter of convenience to make the best of a hopeless situation. The only truth that ultimately matters is scientific.

Philosopher J.P. Moreland points out that "scientism" is the view that the only knowledge we can have of reality comes from the hard sciences: anatomy, chemistry, biology, astronomy, physics, etcetera. Other disciplines such as religion, psychology, ethics, and sociology are expressions of opinion, emotion, and belief systems. If such disciplines are not testable or provable, then no real knowledge "exists."

> Moreland goes on to add: *"You will object when two things come to mind. One, issues of vital importance to humanity, such as love, friendship, honor, and morality, are not subject to objective measurement. Two, the principle of 'scientism' itself is not testable or provable. It is also a belief system. It is wholly a subjective idea."*

Another angle on identity is the term "virtual." Think of definitions of the word "virtual."

- Being such in essence or effect though not formally recognized or admitted (a virtual dictator).
- Almost—or nearly—as described, but not completely or according to strict definition (the virtual absence of border controls).
- (Adjective) Being actually such in almost every respect (the once elegant temple lay in virtual ruin).
- Being of, or linked to, an undescribed entity whose being is inferred from primary sources.

You can see that defining what is "being" is not so forthright.

Thinking of how to describe the Pre-Life Elect meant a deep dive into ontology. I didn't do so well.

The nuances of ontology are incredibly challenging. I'm no philosopher.

Religious principles are also incredibly challenging. I'm no theologian.

I can barely string two good sentences together. I'm no writer.

The material presented here is from my heart, not from talent. Obviously.

I'm an artist. This project is an impression. I struggle to paint the identity that is you. The "you" that is in the distant past, before you were born, and will be "you" in the future when the roleplay "you" is no more. Though the struggle to present this imagery also reveals my lack of artistic talent, I pray you overlook that. Though I have acted, I'm actually afraid. I'm fearful I have intruded into an area I should not have. I don't want to be mistaken as a person who is speaking for God. I am not. I'm simply speaking as one sharing a spiritual impression.

No one that I am aware of has dared to be so presumptive as to define an Elect person, other than the person who is physically conceived and receives the Holy Spirit. To do so would take you out of the realm of orthodoxy into speculation and conjecture.

Unless, that is, I am proposing speculation and conjecture. I am not.

Am I advancing a private biblical interpretation? I am not.

If anyone doesn't agree or follow the MARVI-RPIA impression, that's fine. I don't care. I can't care. It's not my business to try to convince anyone of Christian Reformed theology. I'm not a pastor. Even if I was a pastor, God saves, or has saved already. I'm offering hope, beauty, inspiration, opportunity, optimism, and a fresh look at life. That's my passion as an artist. That is my contribution to love God and love my neighbor as myself.

As I live my life, I share my life. As I live my life, I offer my life as a living sacrifice. This is the most precious gift I can offer. This life was given to me. It's just a role. I give it back. It was never actually mine. It came without my knowledge and without my consent.

CHAPTER 16

JESUS'S NUMBER ONE MESSAGE

You may have heard of a so-called list of the "Most Hated Religious Doctrines." Why such a list was composed may have developed from atheist and agnostic objections to theism, specifically Christianity. If you are religious, nonreligious, or somewhere in between, what would you guess are the five most "hated" Christian doctrines?

Pause reading here and make your own five guesses.

You don't feel like guessing? Okay. Here are the answers with added MARVI-RPIA imagery.

The Most Hated Christian Doctrine

1–There is a God of the Bible. He's invisible, but He's real.

2–Jesus is a bona fide historical figure. He's the ONLY way to salvation.

3–Hell is real. It exists now or in the future.

4–We are all sinners. Man is a fallen creature from Adam and Eve. There is an afterlife.

5–Election/Predestination. God chose His Elect people before He created the world.

It doesn't take a lot of thought to realize WHY those five reasons are hated. They OBLITERATE identity!

Your identity has taken years upon years to prepare, develop, and refine. Being OUTSIDE the orthodox religious worldview means you have NOT been "born again." You are NOT a new creature in Jesus Christ. The reason you're not religious is that no religious worldview has ever been attractive enough to change your identity. And, if any of the aforementioned five religious doctrines are true, your life is over. Your life means nothing. Even worse than nothing.

Those five doctrines mean your body becomes a future flaming torch in Hell. You will suffer many times worse than the crucified people suffered in ancient times. Under the pressure of knowing your life could end any day, how can you NOT hate such a threat coming from this religious worldview? You can't *not* hate that. You hate how they tell you your life is in imminent extreme danger of eternal torment. How dare they! They claim they're safe because they accepted Christ. You're damned because you haven't. Just say the "sinners prayer" and turn your life over to Jesus. Yes, it's that easy. Do it now! You'll be saved.

The irony is most religious people mean well, but it comes as an affront to the integrity of another person's identity. The hate of religious doctrines doesn't mean hate for the religious *person*. It's not the hate of *God.* It's hate for what they SAY about God. It's hate for what they SAY about nonreligious people.

As the artist of MARVI-RPIA (Modern Abstract Religious Verbal Impressionism-Role Play Identity Array), my religious born-again impression is an image of God that has an unorthodox perspective. The image began with a key observation—Jesus Christ's number one message. Do you know what that message is? Want to play the guessing game again? Look away from reading and try to guess at least five choices of what Jesus's number one message could be. Guess one ... guess two ... guess three ... guess four ... guess five ...

Don't feel like playing along? All right. Whatever guesses you would have made were probably good candidates for a number-one message. So, I will give what I think is the number one message Jesus preached, AFTER listing your most likely five guesses.

5) Hell. REPENT or else you will die a sinner and be condemned to Hell forever.

4) Heaven. The kingdom of HEAVEN is now at hand.

3) I Am. I and My Father are ONE.

2) Love. God is LOVE. Love God, love your neighbor, love yourself.

1) I am the ONLY way. No one can come to the Father except through Me.

What do you think? Surely, one of those choices would be Jesus's number one message. To me, another message stood out and away from those five.

YOU ARE NOT YOUR BODY!

I believe Jesus underscored that you are a spirit with a physical dimension. He taught to sacrifice your earthly life for eternal spiritual life, which is and was before the foundation of the world.

From this observation came the notion that we are essentially spiritual creatures. Jesus seemed to teach we are to overcome our temporary mental and physical imagery. Who we are is not the identity imposed on us by birth. Our birth identity is doomed to die because of the error of Adam and Eve. Jesus was *promised* to redeem us by becoming a second Adam. He *arrived* and lived a sinless life, was PUBLICLY put to *death* to verify dying, then overcame death for our benefit by being *resurrected*—also by PUBLIC testimony.

Jesus faced the question of identity at one of His physically weakest moments by the Devil himself. Satan asked Jesus if He was indeed the Son of God. How can the Son of God be hungry? If You are the Son of God, you should NEVER be hungry! Make bread now! Jesus responds with scripture, not with indignation on the challenge of His identity. He didn't say I AM. He didn't say "Get behind Me, Satan." He didn't threaten Satan by saying He could summon legions of angels to thwart Satan's intentions.

His reply was scripture.

Satan then changes the environment. He quotes the scriptures Jesus trusts in so much. Throw Yourself down from this pinnacle. As the Son of God, you can never be hurt, because angels will save you. Again, Jesus quotes scripture, not the status of His identity.

Finally, Satan says "I have the authority to grant You the world's fortunes. You rule this world, I'll rule the underworld. Give praise to me. I'll give praise to you." Jesus indicates His identity is not on trial. Again, His retort is scripture. Satan leaves Him.

Jesus had a role to play as a 100 percent human being. He had to rectify what Adam and Eve set in motion. We have a role to play that dramatizes Adam and Eve's Free Will. We also have the spirit of Satan's challenge to our identity. Do what you want. Be what you want. It's your life. But we can't trust in our roleplay identity. It's an inauthentic identity, built on components outside our control. Our life may come to an end this very day. We should trust scripture. We can have the assurance that our future is secure in Paradise.

> Then was Jesus led up of the Spirit into the wilderness to be tempted of the devil. And when he had fasted forty days and forty nights, he was afterward hungred. And when the tempter came to him, he said, If thou be the Son

> of God, command that these stones be made bread. But he answered and said, it is written, Man shall not live by bread alone, but by every word that proceedeth out of the mouth of God. Then the devil taketh him up into the holy city, and setteth him on a pinnacle of the temple, and saith unto him, if thou be the Son of God, cast thyself down: for it is written, He shall give his angels charge concerning thee: and in their hands they shall bear thee up, lest at any time thou dash thy foot against a stone. Jesus said unto him, it is written again, thou shalt not tempt the Lord thy God. Again, the devil taketh him up into an exceeding high mountain, and sheweth him all the kingdoms of the world, and the glory of them; And saith unto him, all these things will I give thee, if thou wilt fall down and worship me. Then saith Jesus unto him, get thee hence, Satan: for it is written, thou shalt worship the Lord thy God, and him only shalt thou serve. Then the devil leaveth him, and, behold, angels came and ministered unto him (Matthew 4:1-11).

Our earthly identity is called to be sacrificed in the interest of loving God, loving our neighbor, and loving ourselves as spiritual agents in the physical dimension. Your life here is over. You now live for God and your neighbor. Your reward is prepared in Heaven. Of course, your life will not suddenly become easy. You still suffer. The difference is now you have help—God, Jesus, and the Holy Spirit. Primary help. There is no better help than this.

Secondary help comes from teachers, the church, and other Christians. As mentioned earlier, we get help from General Revelation—God as He is revealed in nature. This often includes atheists and agnostics. Yes, they're part of the environment also. Don't worry about the quality of secondary or even tertiary influences being detrimental to your salvation. You cannot lose your salvation. You may suffer a loss of some sort, but never the loss of salvation. Remember, your salvation is already guaranteed before you were born.

This reminds me of a passage in the Book of Mark in the New Testament.

> And these signs shall follow them that believe; In my name shall they cast out devils; they shall speak with new tongues; They shall take up serpents; and if they drink any deadly thing, it shall not hurt them; they shall lay hands on the sick, and they shall recover (Mark 16:17-18)

There is controversy regarding those verses of Mark, and these ending verses are particularly troublesome for scholars. Without responding to these issues as a whole, the late Harold Camping of Family Radio maintained that verses 17 and 18 definitely belong there.

The two verses have special meanings regarding fear of evil. We know Jesus spoke in parables. We know the scriptures may have multiple meanings.

Verse Seventeen

“Cast out devils.” This doesn't have to be literal. Simply conveying the Gospel has the power to remove evil spirits. The word of God supplants evil.

“They shall speak with new tongues.” This happens when words have enlightened meaning. Words like election, predestination, salvation, identity, and damnation; all have significantly different meanings as a Christian.

Verse Eighteen

“Taking up serpents” could reference exposure to subtle deception and coercion such as Eve experienced in Eden. We don't succumb; we are safe. We can manage wicked tangible agents and wicked intangible agents. We have holy help.

“Drinking poison” is similar to exposure or consumption of lies, false doctrine, or delusion. They’re not spiritually deadly. Christians are always exposed to verbal deadly doctrine. It's everywhere.

“Laying hands on the sick” must always regard spiritual sickness. The word of God in the “hands” of Christians heals spiritual illness. Sickness can be physical, mental, or spiritual. The Bible's focus is spiritual, but it also has mental and physical applications.

“Drinking the water.” As Jesus says in the Book of John, partaking of the lasting sustenance of His living water is figurative for spiritual reality.

> But whosoever drinketh of the water that I shall give him shall never thirst; but the water that I shall give him shall be in him a well of water springing up into everlasting life (John 4:14).

THOUGHTS IN THE NIGHT—1

Besides Jesus Christ's number one message, what is the point of Jesus arriving to save mankind if mankind is guaranteed salvation before God created the world? *Because Jesus, Himself, is a Roleplayer.* The 100 percent human Jesus is the Roleplayer, not 100 percent divine Jesus.

In this sense, we hear of terms like expiation, propitiation, reconciliation, and imputation. The essence of these concepts regards the mission and accomplishment of Jesus to reinstate human beings to a flawless relationship with God. In one sense, this is a confirmation and an assurance of salvation from past to present to future. The Pre-Life Elect (SSID) is secure from the ancient past, and the Elect Roleplayers (HSID) will prove the Demonstration of Free Will as it is being completed daily.

The idea that the deity of Jesus became 100 percent human is hard to grasp. In thinking of Jesus as a MARVI-RPIA Roleplayer, it is almost IRREVERENT. I was lying in bed one night, awakened at about 3 a.m. I began to think of my physical inadequacies. My hair, my nose, my eyes, my mouth, my physique. I compared myself to handsome guys. How would good looks change my identity?

Suddenly, an image popped into my mind. I saw an image on Reddit. It was a picture of Jesus using historical data and modern imaging techniques (Bas Uterwijk. medium.com. 2020). Jesus was decidedly unattractive, almost homely. I didn't like it. Why? I always imagine Jesus as a pleasant-looking guy.

How did Jesus look to the people of that day?

Pastors have made the standard comment that Jesus was nondescript. He had no outstanding characteristics that made Him special. He had the appearance of an average male Jewish person. Some pastors may even go further and comment that Jesus wasn't even good-looking. That may come by implication from the Old Testament Book of Isaiah.

> Who hath believed our report? and to whom is the arm of the Lord revealed? For he shall grow up before him as a tender plant, and as a root out of a dry ground: he hath no form nor comeliness; and when we shall see him, there is no beauty that we should desire him. He is despised and rejected of men; a man of sorrows, and acquainted with

> grief: and we hid as it were our faces from him; he was despised, and we esteemed him not (Isaiah 53:1-3).

Certainly, this is a messianic prophecy. It is not a literal description of Jesus.

And in the New Testament Book of John, Mary Magdalene mistook Jesus for the gardener. This doesn't mean they were speaking directly face to face. It doesn't mean Jesus bore the appearance of a gardener. He may have been moving about the property before approaching her.

> And when she had thus said, she turned herself back, and saw Jesus standing, and knew not that it was Jesus. Jesus saith unto her, Woman, why weepest thou? whom seekest thou? She, supposing him to be the gardener, saith unto him, Sir, if thou have borne him hence, tell me where thou hast laid him, and I will take him away. Jesus saith unto her, Mary. She turned herself, and saith unto him, Rabboni; which is to say, Master (John 20:14-16).

As I continued my late-night/early-morning thoughts, I wondered what Jesus thought of His own appearance. Was He indeed handsome but presented Himself to appear normal? We know deception isn't categorically sinful. Deception in times of war is sanctioned by God. Deception at other times as a moral obligation is to be expected and be commended.

We can assume Jesus was a priest of priests. Therefore, Jesus would not have had any blemish as a 100 percent human being. For example, Jesus had well-set hair, no missing teeth, and perfect vision. He would have been of good form, perfect posture, and altogether a perfect male representing any category as a sacrifice before the Lord.

From the Old Testament books, we read the priests were not to have a blemish of any kind. Further, the animals to be sacrificed were not to have any blemish. They were to be the perfect ones in the group.

> And the Lord spake unto Moses, saying, Speak unto Aaron, saying, Whosoever he be of thy seed in their generations that hath any blemish, let him not approach to offer the bread of his God. For whatsoever man he be that hath a blemish, he shall not approach: a blind man, or a lame, or he that hath a flat nose, or anything superfluous, Or a man that is brokenfooted, or brokenhanded, Or crookbacked, or a dwarf, or that hath a blemish in his eye, or be scurvy, or scabbed, or hath his stones broken; No man that hath a blemish of the seed of Aaron the priest shall come nigh to offer the offerings of the Lord made by fire: he hath a blemish; he shall not come nigh to offer the bread of his God. He shall eat the bread of his God, both of the most holy, and of the holy. Only he shall not go in unto the vail, nor come nigh unto the altar, because he hath a blemish; that he profane not my sanctuaries: for I the Lord do sanctify them. And Moses told it unto Aaron, and to his sons, and unto all the children of Israel (Leviticus 21:16-24).

> And the Lord spake unto Moses, saying, Speak unto Aaron, and to his sons, and unto all the children of Israel, and say unto them, Whatsoever he be of the house of Israel, or of the strangers in Israel, that will offer his oblation for all his vows, and for all his freewill offerings, which they will offer unto the Lord for a burnt offering; Ye shall offer at your own will a male without blemish, of the beeves, of the sheep, or of the goats. But whatsoever

> hath a blemish, that shall ye not offer: for it shall not be acceptable for you (Leviticus 22:17-20).

My inner sense of humor frequently centers on angels. I imagine strangers who irritate me are angels who run interference so that I don't have accidents or get into trouble. When my expletives are used on the knuckleheads as I'm out and about, they inform me they are an angel, not one of the knuckleheads. When I joke with them about sharing my food and drink, they shrink back in horror. They say (with a smile) that the thought of waste elimination is disgusting. They say humans awaken daily from a forced rest period of eight hours, only to go through rituals that include cleaning themselves of "impurities"—eyes, ears, nose, mouth, hair, and feet. The whole body needs to be in or underwater. Humans are so filthy!

The angels go so far in their jokes about me to say if they were ever to "wake up" human, they would just blow their brains out. About this time, another angel appears and says to them: "Don't you realize His Majesty became one of those pathetic human beings? He is living as they live. Can you imagine the sacrifice He is making for them? It's hardly imaginable! He has subjected His life to teaching them, and they want to kill Him. He is determined to save them unto His death by their miserable hands."

I wonder: Does Jesus think of me today as I think of Him today? Does He also think of the Pre-Life Elect me?

Continuing my thoughts in the early morning hours, I admit my physical inadequacies are a factor of my heredity, immaturity, and ignorance. But 100 percent human Jesus didn't suffer such issues. My parents didn't know, and my parent's parents didn't know, how to teach flawless living. Jesus's mother, the Virgin Mary, was chosen by God. Jesus's father, the Holy Spirit, was God. Despite speaking only of 100 percent human Jesus, His physical body was probably flawless. Why wouldn't it be? No youthful mistakes or bad habits. Advanced healing prowess. Angels attending. The Holy Spirit teaching. Prophecy: not a bone of Him shall be broken, etcetera. Confidence. Authority. Composure.

> He keepeth all his bones: not one of them is broken (Psalm 34:20).

> For these things were done, that the scripture should be fulfilled, A bone of him shall not be broken (John 19:36).

Does having a flawless body mean that Jesus went through puberty? At an early age, as Jesus accepted His role as Redeemer, how did that affect His attitude toward total personal sacrifices? MARVI-RPIA suggests Jesus knew His life was not about Him. He was Deity. Human life was about His roleplay identity to be a sinless human being. By doing so, He rescues the human race. Humans have absolute assurance of Pre-Life Elect status before the world was created. The certainty of this is embodied in His mission.

So, I was in bed for the night with many of these thoughts. Next thoughts: What would Jesus have been thinking as He lay in bed at night?

What am I doing? I'm Jesus Christ! Here I am, lying down on this bed. I've got arms and legs, eyes and nose, a penis and a rectum, height and weight. I should be enjoying the splendor of the Father and the Holy Ghost. I should be ruling the kingdom of thrones, dominions, and powers.

Yet, here I lay. A human being. Soon to be reviled and scorned. Soon to be put to death by the ones I'm here to save from death and damnation.

Perhaps angels convene to comfort Him in these times of prayers and contemplation. The Father and Holy Spirit are always near. What would they say? Jesus, You are doing a magnificent job. Jesus, You are blessed forever. Jesus, We love You so much.

Jesus thinks back at 2x speed, then 5x, then 10x speed. He sees Himself at twelve years old, then two years old, then one day old. He remembers being in the womb and hearing his mother, Mary, greet Elizabeth. Jesus thinks back to King Solomon and King David. Going farther back, Jesus thinks of Noah, The Flood, Enoch, then Adam and Eve.

Jesus thinks of making man in the image of Themselves—Father, Son, and Holy Spirit. He thinks of the creation of angels. Before the world is created, Jesus thinks of those identified for salvation, the SSIDs.

Coming back to the present, Jesus briefly thinks of the crucifixion, resurrection, and the transformation back to Heaven. One thousand years AD. Two thousand years AD. The end of the Demonstration of Free Will. Judgment Day. The New Beginning.

But now, even as it is night, Jesus is aware of murder, theft, sex, drugs, war, abuse, birth, and death. He's aware of sorcery, rituals, divination, and evil spirits. He must rest and perform the day-to-day activities necessary to fulfill prophecy and complete His mission to be the Redeemer of mankind. It will be done.

> And it came to pass, that, when Elisabeth heard the salutation of Mary, the babe leaped in her womb; and Elisabeth was filled with the Holy Ghost ... For, lo, as soon as the voice of thy salutation sounded in mine ears, the babe leaped in my womb for joy (Luke 1:41, 44).

THOUGHTS IN THE NIGHT—2

What about you? You're lying in bed tonight. You evaluate how your day went and what to anticipate tomorrow and in the coming days. Is this MARVI-RPIA imagery helping you? Are you simply going through the motions of an inauthentic identity? Is the real “you” actually safe in Paradise?

What of the disciple “Doubting Thomas” lying in bed the night BEFORE putting his hands on the resurrected Jesus Christ? Jesus has been crucified. He is absolutely, positively stone-cold dead. Thomas goes through the details again and again. How did Jesus get Himself killed? Everything was looking so great. Jesus was fabulous! He even raised people from the dead numerous times! He was divine. He was holy. He was the Messiah!

And now Jesus is dead. What happened? Everything went so fast. Jesus must have done something wrong. But what could that have been? What does this mean to all His followers? We had so much hope for the present and future of our lives. Maybe we would never be sick again. Maybe we would never worry about death again. Jesus would raise us from death.

Now He's dead. We were all terribly mistaken about Jesus. Life is actually worse now than before Jesus came on the scene.

And then go forward to the night AFTER no-longer-Doubting Thomas puts his hands on the resurrected Jesus Christ. Wow! Jesus is alive! He did it! It is the same Person, but it is now the Person who survived death and burial! I can't sleep. This is the most spectacular event in history! I saw the whole thing!

What does it mean for me, the other disciples, for everyone? I'm not sure. Life is still one day at a time. But I know Jesus has corrected the error of Adam and Eve. Death is not the end of life. If we die, Jesus will raise us up to be with Him forever.

For now, as Roleplayers, salvation plays out. The Pre-Life Elect are outside time in a separate reality. God created a Demonstration of Free Will with Adam and Eve. They exercised their Free Will in their own best interest rather than in God's interest for their lives. The penalty was death.

In God's mercy, death was elongated. Further, God promised a Redeemer through procreation. In the interim, the Error of Free Will must be demonstrated through innumerable combinations and permutations of human life. This is how the dynamics of salvation play out.

> But Thomas, one of the twelve, called Didymus, was not with them when Jesus came. The other disciples therefore said unto him, We have seen the Lord. But he said unto them, Except I shall see in his hands the print of the nails, and put my finger into the print of the nails, and thrust my hand into his side, I will not believe. And after eight days again his disciples were within, and Thomas with them: then came Jesus, the doors being shut, and stood in the midst, and said, Peace be unto you. Then saith he to Thomas, Reach hither thy finger, and behold my hands; and reach hither thy hand, and thrust it into my side: and be not faithless, but believing. And Thomas answered and said unto him, My Lord and my God. Jesus saith unto him, Thomas, because thou hast seen me, thou hast believed: blessed are they that have not seen, and yet have believed (John 20:24-29).

CHAPTER 17

ROLE PLAY IDENTITY ARRAY

Now, for a quick review:

1) Jesus's number one message: you are not your body.

2) Salvation was granted to the Elect before they were born—before God created the world.

3) Our identity is made up of distinct components such as our childhood identity, our dream identity, and our physical identity.

Jesus's number one message being you are not your body is understandable. Salvation was granted to the Elect before they were born. The Bible backs that up. Our identity has separate components. That is true.

What about explaining the absence of Free Will, yet being responsible for thinking/behaving that condemns people to Hell? The non-Elect are trapped in a roleplay character of no choice. And where is that trillion-dollar treasure that was promised in Chapter 10? Yes, we are very close to the treasure. And more.

For now, the most important aspect of Christian Reformed Impressionism is the SSID identity. This is an abbreviated name for the Elect as being those persons predetermined to salvation—the Super Spiritual Identity. What has always eluded me, and everyone else apparently, is if I am saved before the world was created, WHO WAS IT THAT WAS SAVED?

1) The me that is living now?

2) A designation of me WITHOUT any ontological status, that is, a non-being person?

3) A designation of me WITH ontological status. That is, being, but perhaps not alive?

From these questions, I surmised an image of persons having ontological status before the world was created. I am calling them SSID (Super-Spirit IDs). Certain facets of our identity are not real. Your childhood identity does not exist. Your dream identity does not exist. Your fantasy identity does not exist. They all have your individual dynamic point of view, but they are not alive. They are not real. But as you know, they do *seem* real.

Similarly, residing in a heavenly dimension like Paradise, SSIDs are related to Roleplayers who demonstrate Free Will. *Roleplayers have no access to the "before-the-world-was" Elect identity and vice versa. Access only comes about in the afterlife on Judgement Day.* At that time, the HSID (Holy Spirit Identity-Elect Roleplayer) joins the SSID (Super-Spirit Identity). The non-Elect persons have no corresponding SSID identity to join. They are explicitly regarded as waste matter—not fit for life. On Judgement Day, SID-Negative Roleplayers who are less than 100 percent humans won't face an afterlife. They don't possess a soul—a spirit. Their life simply ends. The ESIDs, evil spirits impersonating humans, will join the Devil and his demons in damnation at the End.

The treasure! What about the treasure? Is there treasure here somewhere? Yes! The treasure is this: EVERYONE GOES TO HEAVEN BECAUSE THEY ARE ALREADY THERE! NO ONE GOES TO HELL BECAUSE THOSE THAT DO ARE NOT 100 PERCENT HUMAN PERSONS!

Roleplayers who do have an SSID counterpart in Heaven are the subjects of a DEMONSTRATION. The demonstration is Free Will.

By the way, MARVI-RPIA is not religious universalism. I reject the premise of "all roads lead to God," everyone goes to Heaven, and no one goes to Hell.

Universalism, in the sense of a religious principle, teaches God's presence is in all individuals and is sufficient to assure all will achieve salvation and none be condemned. God is love. His love covers any and all circumstances, from conception to death. Hell is not a physical place of eternal torment for human beings. No humans go there. All humans go to Heaven. Jesus Christ paid for all sin for all time.

Universalism is a religious doctrine without orthodox religious support. Universalism offers no biblical justification for the drama of life, no penalty for sin, and no distinction in who Jesus arrived to save. Eat, drink, be merry. This includes the lowest of all so-called human beings: murderers, terrorists, extortioners, molesters, pedophiles, racists, liars, sadists, and criminals. Evil is okay. Crime pays. All will be forgiven.

Furthermore, MARVI-RPIA contradicts Universalism. The "everyone saved" is NOT the everyone who is conceived and born, as Universalism holds, but the everyone guaranteed salvation before conception and birth.

To review, MARVI-RPIA suggests conception includes 100 percent human beings and also those less than 100 percent humans. The whole reason for human procreation after Adam and Eve, except for the Redeemer, is to demonstrate the error of Free Will. No one, no matter what situation ensues, surrenders their will to God unless and until the Holy Spirit intercedes. Free Will has been corrupted.

Non-human Roleplayers who do not receive HSID by the last second of death, at death, or after death are not worth saving. They are a by-product of living—simply waste. Their roleplay ends. Oblivion!

The inaugural Roleplayers that demonstrated Free Will were the Serpent, Adam, and Eve. The Serpent, being an animal, did not possess an identity array, only a physical and mental identity. Human identity from MARVI-RPIA imagery consists of six additional identity profiles other than a physical and mental identity.

Adam and Eve had a specific objective. They were created to exemplify the completion of a spirit creature in the physical image of God. This spirit creature was to represent the autonomy, individuality, and beauty of a flawless living being.

A trial is set to determine whether life is worth living if there are limitations of knowledge and behavior. If life continues to be worth living, life goes on. If life is *not* worth living, given limits on knowledge or behavior, death will be the alternative. No living creature is truly alive unless there is confidence in autonomy from other agents. As Roleplayers, Adam and Eve risked death. Their life did not have enough meaning to continue abiding by the constrictions God placed on them. Perhaps Patrick Henry (governor of Virginia, 1776) got his famous quote from the quandary Adam and Eve presumably felt: "Give me liberty or give me death."

NOT 100 PERCENT HUMAN

A person who is non-Elect is not 100 percent human? If they're not human, what are they?

Like all of us, they're Roleplayers. The difference is that non-Elect Roleplayers are not 100 percent human and therefore have no guarantee of being saved before they were born. Jesus lived as a 100 percent human being and died for 100 percent human beings. His redemption was not for angels, angel-human hybrids, aliens, or animals.

Does "non-100 percent human" apply to atheists, agnostics, non-Christians, etcetera? No. Those people are most likely 100 percent human. What makes them evil, anti-God, and inhumane is their influence from heredity, environment, and experience. They are participating in the Demonstration of Free Will. *Another term may apply. It is "unsane," which is defined later in the chapter.*

By the way, I'm sure none of them care what I think or what I imagine. If they are atheists, agnostics, non-Christians, etcetera, they have their own ideas of what a worldview should be. They have varying beliefs in a Pre-Life, spiritual life, and the afterlife.

Atheists and agnostics who live as atheists probably already fully accept being in a state of oblivion when they die. They accept being meaningless, and irrelevant, and simply refuse. They accept a final nonliving status. They accept being no one and no thing when life ends. They reject the eternality of personhood. They reject any definition of nonphysical personhood. Death is the end of ontological status. Death is absolute finality.

The situation of the non-Elect Roleplayer is there's no counterpart of an authentic identity in Paradise for them. When they die, they cease to exist. There is no afterlife. No Heaven. No Hell. Their role to demonstrate Free Will ends.

For the others who believe the afterlife is something in their control ... well, good luck.

On the other hand, even though atheists, agnostics, and non-Christians dismiss *Connecting The Dots Of Identity* as not worth their time, they may take another tactic. They may go on the offense in a smear campaign.

"JLT, the author of *Connecting The Dots Of Identity*, slanders all non-Christians as unsane—a term for an inability to accept Christian objective morality."

"JLT says non-Christians are not fully human beings. Instead, they are ancestors of evil angels, demons, the so-called Nephilim of the Old Testament. If JLT slanders us, we fight back."

Of course, that's all out of context. *Connecting The Dots Of Identity* says just the opposite. It says atheists, agnostics, and non-Christians are ALREADY guaranteed salvation in Heaven. Only Satan and evil angels go to Hell. Everyone else is simply a Roleplayer living the Demonstration of Free Will as dictated by heredity, environment, and experience.

Free Will Roleplayers—atheists, agnostics, Christians, and non-Christians—do not know God until He opens their spiritual eyes. We can expect misunderstandings and disagreements concerning the Christian worldview.

Those who believe life is a once-and-done accident believe life has no meaning. Therefore, death has no meaning. The only meaning is what we give it. There is no transcendent intelligence ruling over reality. We rule.

And, of course, there is no afterlife. There is no God. We created God. If there is a God, you have to be really stupid to think He's interested in us. Look at the world.

And that's why *Connecting The Dots Of Identity* is here. People don't hate someone they don't know. They hate whom they THINK they know. They don't know God—yet. They may go further and say, "It's not that we don't trust God, we don't trust YOU. What we hear of God has never lived up to the standard of omnipotence, omnipresence, and omniscience we see in everyday life. You who declare the word of God leave a lot to be desired.

We don't desire a life like yours, and we don't accept your description of God."

If no one can come to God unless God takes the action, well, what happens if He doesn't act? And, again, this is where *Connecting The Dots Of Identity* comes in. If you are at all concerned about being saved, God is in that concern. It's likely most people in the world are NOT concerned. But, by the imagery of Christian Reformed Impressionism, it doesn't matter. Everyone who is 100 percent human is saved before they were born. Now, everyone simply participates in the Demonstration of Free Will based on the forces of heredity, environment, and experience.

> And your covenant with death shall be disannulled, and your agreement with hell shall not stand; when the overflowing scourge shall pass through, then ye shall be trodden down by it (Isaiah 28:18).

> Then shall he say also unto them on the left hand, Depart from me, ye cursed, into everlasting fire, prepared for the devil and his angels (Matthew 25:41).

> And your covenant with death shall be disannulled, and your agreement with hell shall not stand; when the overflowing scourge shall pass through, then ye shall be trodden down by it (Isaiah 28:18).

> Then shall he say also unto them on the left hand, Depart from me, ye cursed, into everlasting fire, prepared for the devil and his angels (Matthew 25:41).

Here is a silver lining in the dark cloud of uncertainty, though the point will not matter to certain groups. When Jesus was crucified, the thief nearby may have considered himself to become nonliving waste matter when dead. However, in the very last moments of living, he "somehow" began to think positively. Jesus assured him that he would be considered one of the Elect. There is always hope, right until the last moments of life. Compose your "last-moments-of-life" prayer. Practice it. Refine it. Be ready to say it in an emergency when your life is passing away. Isn't hope better than inevitability?

There's an additional aspect that may help describe the thinking and behaving of Roleplayers. They are two charts. The first is an insanity chart, and the second is a blindness chart.

An Insanity Chart? You're right to laugh and say there is no such thing as an insanity chart. That's crazy. Once again, it's an art project. An expression of a concept. An impression of theology. It's okay to roll your eyes. It's okay to smirk.

The blindness chart ends the chapter. It's also nonliteral.

INSANITY CHART

Sane

The status of Pre-Life Elect individuals (Holy Spirit Identity-HSID) who possess a Christian worldview while continuing the Demonstration of Free Will through heredity, environment, and experience. They affirm objective morality as the standard of thinking and behaving based on the transcendent, universal, top-down imperative from God of the Bible. The sane include people who are Holy Spirit immature, spiritually minded people who have yet to receive the Holy Spirit, and people whose mental impairment prevents them from consistent Christian participation.

Unsane

People who ascribe to atheists, agnostics, and non-Christian worldviews. They are spiritually blind but broadly mentally competent. Their profile is a cynical, derisive, contemptible view of objective morality. They reject the standard of thinking and behaving based on the transcendent, universal, top-down imperative from God of the Bible. They are against godliness unless God overrides their Free Will. They portray the Demonstration of Free Will through heredity, environment, and experience. (See Blind Eyes Chart)

Insane

Group A: The group of people who are 100 percent human that suffers mental impairment from heredity, environment, and experience. They may be sane, adult Christians, but in general, they are mentally irresponsible. Additionally, the unsane also may suffer insanity from the effects of heredity, environment, and experience.

Group B: The group of people who are less than 100 percent human. Their mental identity also suffers the effects of heredity, environment, and experience. These are most likely ancestors of the Nephilim.

INSANITY LEVELS ON THE SANENESS SCALE:

Level 0—Inconclusive.

Level 1—Those who show poor judgment on many issues, though they share agreement with sane persons on particular issues.

Level 2—Delusional. Persons who are conniving, untrustworthy, and immoral. Showing limited empathy for anyone but themselves or their group. Risk of danger.

Level 3—The simple-minded, slow, and easily influenced. They exercise poor judgment. Risk of danger.

Level 4—Unless they are medicated, they don't cope well with reality. Poor social skills. Risk of danger.

Level 5—People who have limited freedom under the guardianship or care of a responsible person. Danger.

Level 6—Institutionalized. Those with limited self-awareness who can't discern right from wrong. Danger.

Level 7—Dangerous to their own person and others. Moody. Irrational. Unstable. High risk of danger.

Level 8—Attempted suicide. Suicide prone. On life-support/coma. High risk of danger.

Level 9—Committed suicide.

Level 10—Nephilim ancestor. Their thoughts and actions are characteristic of inhuman behavior. Not 100 percent human. High risk of danger.

You may begin to realize why there is no such thing as an insanity chart. Everybody would be on one. People are crazy. Some crazy is okay. Other crazy is absolutely not okay. We know this. However, it would be disrespectful, rude, and presumptive to point out who these persons are by defining sanity by its relationship to Christian identity.

Going further, a sane person may be TEMPORARILY insane due to the challenges of heredity, environment, and experiences. *But they never become UNSANE.* You can't lose your salvation. You can't find your salvation. It finds you.

An unsane person can never be temporarily SANE. The unsane person has no access to saneness because sanity is illustrated as objective morality. Objective morality comes from God. You can't acquire it. It acquires you.

When wondering why people think and behave the way they do, rather than thinking they're stupid, evil, or out of their minds, think of the chart.

As you think of the chart, think about why moral objectivity is so important in understanding why people are so unreasonable.

People ask, "How can morality be objective? Who is to say what is moral for EVERYONE?" Subjective morality at least is reasonable in that it realizes people are different, circumstances are different, and moral standards shift over time.

No STANDARD of thinking and behaving is ALWAYS acceptable, no matter what the circumstances.

Yet, theists defend their position on God's transcendent objective moral standards. They insist God is the epitome of moral character. He is holy. He is righteous. He is love.

NO! Not at all. Atheists advocate there is no specific standard of good and bad behavior. There is only behavior. Social structures dictate the spectrum of what is acceptable or nonacceptable. Social structures plan and implement governments that manage populations. THIS is objective morality. *The subjects—human beings—define what is moral. NOT God!* There is no God. The only God we see is the one theists proclaim to be good news. Obviously, He is NOT good news to everybody.

Imagine I'm the pastor of a new church, or I just opened a new business. I post a sign proclaiming that nobody with a flat nose, or who is handicapped, or who is menstruating may enter into my church or my business (Leviticus 21). When asked why such terms would apply in this day and age, I answer that moral standards apply throughout time and location. I would very soon have no church and no business.

This is part of the problem with God being the standard of morality. People know enough of the Bible to understand that God kills men, women, and children for crimes as slight as picking up sticks on the Sabbath day or swearing at their parents (O.T. books Exodus and Numbers).

How can God be the standard of morality when the Bible states He sends people to Hell because they never heard of Jesus Christ or don't believe in Jesus if they have heard of Him? Millions of humans have a higher moral standard than God.

The world is in chaos. Life is unfair. And theists expect everyone to believe God is 100 percent moral 100 percent of the time? No! Billions of people do NOT believe theists.

The Minister of Art does not blame them. There are three main reasons:

Reason 1: *People WON'T believe in God until He opens their spiritual eyes.*

If we could open our own spiritual eyes, everyone would know all about God.

Why wouldn't He open everyone's spiritual eyes?

He wants Free Will to play out based on heredity, environment, and experience.

Reason 2: *Their images of God have never lived up to their idea of who God SHOULD be.*

Based on what we would think God SHOULD be, He would have corrected what happened in the Garden of Eden right away. We would be living there as a glint in the eye of Adam and Eve or living in an even better scenario. Instead, we have this "bizarro world" we wake up to every day.

Reason 3: *God cannot be a standard of morality because there is no standard definition of who or what God is.* The so-called Divine Being has multiple names and functions across various religions. Look no further than even the Christian denominations. The people who are supposed to know God better than anyone else don't all agree on who He is. They don't all agree on how to worship Him. They don't all agree with His message to the world.

Speaking of smart people, let's re-emphasize why smart people wonder how other smart people can be so stupid, so crazy, and so blind.

The first thing to admit is all people who disagree with you are not stupid. They are some of the most intelligent people on the planet. They have bountiful resources, a superb intellect, and a worldwide following. It's their positions on topics that reject objective morality and the God of the Bible that frustrates Christians.

This is because they're DECEIVED. They have no idea they are being deceived by the Great Deceiver—Satan. Not exactly the angel himself, but the spirit of what he represents and all his assistants, spirit AND human. What spirit does Satan represent? In the Glossary of Colors, Lucifer's Postulate suggests omnipotence—the Free Will to behave as desired without penalty. Similarly, there's a spirit of the right to express one's identity without penalty of judgment and restriction based on an opposing worldview.

Of course, they'll all laugh. Deceived by the Devil? Really?

And, if you remind them they are blind because God hasn't opened their spiritual eyes, they laugh again. So, God DOESN'T want to save me? He WANTS me to go to Hell?

"No, no," theists say. You have to ask Him to open your eyes, pray, and seek forgiveness.

Pray? Seek forgiveness? Don't you say nobody is able to come to the Father unless the Father draws Him? See, you think all this Reformed theology makes sense. It doesn't. Keep your religion to yourself.

So, objective morality is repugnant to them. Subjective morality is the default standard. Everyone and anyone could set a standard for right and wrong. What is right is in a state of flux, bound by the ever-changing laws of the land. The authenticity of right and wrong becomes the province of those who define it best.

For now, what do we do to make the "Great News" about the Good News of Jesus Christ attractive? God uses us to assist in opening the eyes of the blind. From the way the world looks, people of God are losing ground to people of Satan.

With *Connecting The Dots Of Identity*, it is possible to have an image of God that personifies all the attributes that His Majesty Who Is Blessed Forever, amen, actually has—and more. If MARVI-RPIA paints an impression of what is possible as a Plan B, we know God's Plan A has to be better. Why would we know that?

No one—that literally means NO PERSON—has defined God the way Jesus Christ defined God. He said I will show and tell you what God should mean to you. Jesus proceeded to show in miracles and sayings who God was. He went further to declare that God sent Him as the third Person of the Trinity. And even beyond this, He said He would be put to death and rise from death.

No other person in history—by oral tradition, written tradition, or scientific discovery—is remotely close to the Person of Jesus Christ in defining Deity. By the testimony of Jesus, we know who and what God is. No other standard of morality can be trustworthy.

We don't have to wonder why Jesus is the only way to salvation. *He guaranteed it before He created the world.* He became a human Roleplayer to correct Adam and Eve's catastrophic act of Free Will. He overcame the ultimate threat to human beings: death.

God is the epitome of all superlative concepts. Omnipotence, Omnipresence, Omniscience. Love, Righteousness, Beauty. As a flawed creature in a flawed environment describing how God has designed life and the afterlife, this cannot do justice to spiritual reality. *That which is spiritual is real.* That which is physical—this world—is transitory. It's like yesterday, today, and tomorrow. Never quite *now*. It's always changing.

God is outside of time with a Plan A that was put into place before He created the world. Based on His plan for the Serpent, Adam, and Eve in the Garden of Eden, it was a good plan. *The flawless creatures CHANGED the plan. It was their Free Will to do so.*

Male-female differentiation provided the Failsafe provision should God's plan be changed. That became necessary when Adam and Eve sinned. Procreation was the solution to produce the Redeemer—Jesus Christ. *The*

Plan A in place before the world is created guarantees no other plans are necessary. That's the SSIDs. That's the First-Class angels.

The MARVI-RPIA Plan B isn't necessary either. However, the world seems to have less and less respect or confidence in God's Plan A. Considering how difficult election and predestination are and how Christian Reformed theology isn't widely known or accepted, *Connecting The Dots Of Identity* is presented.

So, there CAN be moral objectivity. God IS worthy as the epitome of morality. The images of His commands, His ways, and His permissive will to let the world continue in the Demonstration of Free Will only dramatize inauthentic identity. The real you in Paradise awaits the end of the Demonstration. The Roleplayer you here on earth should be submissive to objective morality. We SHOULD trust God. *God is worthy of our submission to Him.*

Those seemingly insensitive examples of God condemning people for simply being themselves were only dramas. It doesn't indicate God didn't love them or they were not Elect Roleplayers. They were examples of Free Will roleplay. *God condemned the EXAMPLE of inauthentic identity by the Roleplayers.* It did not have any effect on the SSIDs—those authentic identities which are saved before the world was created.

Those who served as Old Testament and New Testament examples of Free Will roleplay were symbols. They pointed to the importance of God's character. He is to be revered. He is holy. He is Lord of ALL!

It's easy to criticize God for how physical reality seems to be. Reality only SEEMS to be physical. Spiritual reality is TRUE reality. At least this is what the greatest Person who ever is/was declared.

Christian Reformed Impressionism tries to paint a similar scenario.

But as it is written, Eye hath not seen, nor ear heard, neither have entered into the heart of man, the things which God hath prepared for them that love him (1 Corinthians 2:9).

And while the children of Israel were in the wilderness, they found a man that gathered sticks upon the sabbath day. And they that found him gathering sticks brought him unto Moses and Aaron, and unto all the congregation. And they put him in ward, because it was not declared what should be done to him. And the Lord said unto Moses, The man shall be surely put to death: all the congregation shall stone him with stones without the camp. And all the congregation brought him without the camp, and stoned him with stones, and he died; as the Lord commanded Moses (Numbers 15:32-36).

And he that curseth his father, or his mother, shall surely be put to death (Exodus 21:17).

Speak unto Aaron, saying, Whosoever he be of thy seed in their generations that hath any blemish, let him not approach to offer the bread of his God. For whatsoever man he be that hath a blemish, he shall not approach: a blind man, or a lame, or he that hath a flat nose, or any thing superfluous, Or a man that is brokenfooted, or brokenhanded, Or crookbacked, or a dwarf, or that hath a blemish in his eye, or be scurvy, or scabbed, or hath his stones broken; No man that hath a blemish of the seed of Aaron the priest shall come nigh to offer the offerings of the Lord made by fire: he hath a blemish; he shall not come nigh to offer the bread of his God. He shall eat the bread of his God, both of the most holy, and of the holy.

> Only he shall not go in unto the vail, nor come nigh unto the altar, because he hath a blemish; that he profane not my sanctuaries: for I the Lord do sanctify them. And Moses told it unto Aaron, and to his sons, and unto all the children of Israel (Leviticus 21:17-24).

BLIND EYES CHART

The Blind Eyes Chart is an informal attempt to highlight nonphysical aspects of identity-array roleplay blindness using a questionnaire and a brief essay.

Nonphysical roleplay blindness refers to spiritual blindness, intentional blindness, and unintentional blindness. This follows from an inability or unwillingness to perceive objective morality, thereby deferring to subjective morality. The intent of the chart is to help clarify the disparity in Roleplayers' perceptions of good/bad and right/wrong.

A thirty-point yes/no questionnaire on spiritual blindness follows with a brief essay defining spiritual, intentional, and unintentional blindness.

Will your answers be based on objectivity or subjectivity?

Will your answers be truthful? Are they YOUR answers or the answers you think are the "right" answers?

Blind Eyes Chart — Part 1. Questionnaire.

1) Do you consider yourself a theist?

2) Do you consider yourself an atheist?

3) Do you consider yourself an agnostic?

4) Have you publicly confessed to being a theist, atheist, or agnostic to your family, friends, and associates?

5) Would you love God (of the Bible) if God wouldn't send anyone to Hell?
6) Would you love God if God already has your residence in Heaven?
7) Have you ever done a deep search on who God is?
8) Are you interested in learning more about God?
9) Do you believe in angels, as in good and evil spiritual beings?
10) Do you believe in an afterlife of Heaven or Hell rather than Oblivion?
11) Do you believe you will go to Heaven at death?
12) Do you believe you will go to Hell at death?
13) Do you believe you will cease to exist at death, or Oblivion?
14) Does a person have free will to believe in Jesus Christ?
15) Have you read the Bible all the way through?
16) Are you interested in new philosophical ideas?
17) Should you be held responsible for your life considering you had no control over heredity, nationality, chronological age, or intellect?
18) Is objective morality (right/wrong, good/bad, defined by God) better than subjective morality (right/wrong, good/bad defined by human beings)?
19) Should the God of the Bible be the standard of objective morality?
20) Does the God of the Bible exemplify the best moral character?
21) Is objective morality important in government?
22) Is objective morality important in business?
23) Is objective morality important in academia?
24) Is your country founded on good/bad, right/wrong principles for all citizens?
25) Should you have freedom of speech to criticize the government, public entities, or nations?
26) Should freedom of speech be controlled by the government?
27) Should possession of firearms by citizens be illegal?
28) Assuming these questions were answered thoughtfully and truthfully, do they help define your worldview?
29) Are you now more assured of your worldview?

30) Are you now less assured of your worldview?

Blind Eyes Chart – Part 2. Essay.

Host person X's internet program consists of guest person A in segment one and guest person B in segment two.
Host person X asserts the nuances of identity-array roleplay blindness may help explain why people see things so differently. Two guests are present. Guest Person A disclosed she was visited by a messenger of a certain group to consider withdrawing her political protests for a great sum of money. A suitable position for her in a nonpolitical setting will presently follow. She refused. The messenger countered. Name your price! Surely there's a number you think worthy of your sacrifice. Again, she refused.
Host person X says, "Think of a second messenger or the same messenger saying in his New York gangster accent, *'You know, it would be a shame if something unfortunate were to happen to you, or your spouse, or your family. People drop dead suddenly, people disappear, accidents happen. We can do this the easy way – or we can do it the hard way.'*"

Guest person A went on to highlight her political concerns and what strategy to employ to counteract governmental misconduct. She reiterates the obstacles to address are rules, regulations, corrupt lawyers, judges, courts, and even politicians who may belong to the same political party.

Guest person B in segment two said as much in their interview. Bad people are demoralizing good people. There seems little can be done, and it takes forever to accomplish even minimal progress. The corruption is entrenched and so pervasive that people actually consider forsaking the voting process. This becomes a contingent strategy by the opposition that enhances their effort of electing their own candidates.

But why are people so corrupt? Why are so many people considered bad politicians, lawyers, judges, police officers, teachers, and businesspeople? How is it that this group of people see things this way, and that group of people see things the opposite way?

1) *Spiritual blindness*—the unsane (Insanity Chart). There is yet to arrive the Holy Spirit to facilitate objective morality; therefore, personal integrity is compromised by subjective morality.

2) *Intentional blindness*—the sane and the unsane (Insanity Chart). People can see, but they blindfold themselves or are blindfolded by others. They may be blackmailed, threatened, extorted, framed, bribed, bullied, or tricked. How do you respond to threats of losing your reputation, your finances, your family, your health, or your life?

3) *Unintentional blindness*—the sane, unsane, and insane. People are unable to see but it's not because of spiritual blindness or intentional blindness. They're deluded. They maintain a reliance on beliefs that are contrary to reason or rationale. Vision is obscured by suggestion, expectation, prejudice, insecurity, fear, hate, deceit, and immaturity.

When God is not the standard for good, but humans are, what follows? Does the highest good become the ability to control destiny? If so, this requires power. Power arises from political strategy to be the leading persons in the leading nations of the world. In this regard, the quest to acquire power creates tunnel vision—superseding all other goals. Be number one. Win. It doesn't matter how. The world is the prize.

Blind people are extremely destructive and extremely dangerous. They may hate you. Don't hate them. They're blind. Help them see.

FINISH

Your Blind Eyes Chart test results are being prepared ...

CHAPTER 18

MARVI DETAILS

The MARVI-RPIA (Modern Abstract Religious Verbal Impressionism-Role Play Identity Array) name includes "abstract" for a reason. The impression is religious, but the impression departs from orthodox Reformed theology to present abstract, unorthodox, nonrepresentative views. The impression is "modern" because it draws on my past seventy years of life, though showing respect to the tradition of the presbytery.

The traditional "Good News" now being uplifted by MARVI-RPIA to become the "Great News" may continue to seem inconclusive. Let's go further...

Question: *If I am already saved as SSID in Paradise, why continue a structured Roleplayer identity? Why not go "out of bounds" and experiment with all sorts of thoughts and behaviors?*

Answer: HSID intervention means your roleplay status is transformed. You are a new creature. Your transition may be in prolonged stages of maturity, but your role should reflect signs of an improved and enhanced life. You will not and cannot continue as the same person you were before. Your new identity is redefined toward God and away from the old you.

If no HSID intervention has occurred, it doesn't mean it won't occur. It may. But it may not. Assume it will. The impression of Pre-Life Elect identity is a super impression, but not an explicit revelation you should receive after reading MARVI-RPIA.

Question: *The very worst characters we know from history—Hitler, Stalin, Mao, etcetera—are they in Paradise?*

Answer: In a sense, yes. It's possible, because in Paradise persons never were Roleplayers. They are not identified as Hitler, Stalin, or Mao. SSIDs are known by the name God has for them. Their identity is pristine. Should Roleplayers Hitler, Stalin, and Mao receive HSID status before death or at the time of death, on Judgement Day they will merge to SSID status. Their roleplay identity is purged. This is almost like waking from sleep, from an unconscious state to conscious state. If they do NOT receive HSID status before or at death, their role proved no one will ever choose God. Mission accomplished. They merge with their authentic identity in Paradise.

Question: *What about the aborted baby, stillborn children, toddlers, and the mentally impaired at death? Does HSID status apply to all of them? Do they go to Paradise?*

Answer: No. Every person is conceived in sin. In the womb, their status is a sinner. They are Roleplayers. They are not born yet. They have roleplay identities. Their true SSID identity is already in Heaven. The roleplay identity is not a judgment of their physical or mental attributes. God sees persons as complete spiritual persons, not their chronological dispositions. This means there is no so-called "age of accountability." God does not qualify age. There is no fetus in Heaven, no babies, no children, no teens, no mature, no elderly. There is no "age" where there is no time. It's always "today." And, of course, as Reformed theology teaches (the Bible teaches), nothing a person knows or does contributes one iota to salvation. God does everything. Additionally, personal recognition won't be based on earthly physical characteristics. Recognition will occur through other heavenly means.

> There shall be no more thence an infant of days, nor an old man that hath not filled his days: for the child shall die an hundred years old; but the sinner being an hundred years old shall be accursed (Isaiah 65:20).

Question: *So, a fetus, an infant, a child may be relegated to Hell?*

Answer: Only if they are less than 100 percent human. A fetus, an infant, or a child has no chronological status to God. At conception, they are sinners, being conceived of the generations from Adam and Eve, or further compromised by evil-spirit genetic immaterial. Remember, their true 100 percent human identity is already in Paradise. Any person considered "not accountable," under the age of accountability, is misunderstanding election-predestination and identity. Salvation is not based on the absence or presence of knowledge. Age is irrelevant.

Question: *How do Satan, the Serpent, Adam, and Eve play into the drama of Free Will and the Determined Elect?*

Answer: They are all participants in the Free Will of flawless living creatures. The Serpent had Free Will. Adam and Eve had Free Will. The angels had Free Will. The big difference is before the world was created, there were no inauthentic identities. The angels were not Roleplayers like the Serpent, Adam, and Eve. An angel's identity is 100 percent authentic. The only time they roleplay is when directed by God. The Pre-Life Elect persons are also 100 percent authentic identities.

The Serpent, Adam, and Eve were 100 percent authentic identities until they sinned. Their absolute Free Will became limited Free Will, and their uncorrupted inauthentic identity became corrupted.

More of the MARVI-RPIA details included here center on non-Elect persons. They may be the so-called ancestors of the Nephilim.

One of the most complex concepts to paint is the imagery of a non-Elect person. This person is conceived as a less than 100 percent human being. When an angel and a human female manage to producc progeny, this progeny isn't 100 percent human. It's hybrid.

Was the promise of the Redeemer to redeem angels? No. To redeem humans? Yes. To redeem hybrids? No.

So, a hybrid of an angel and a human female has no provision of salvation. If it's possible to produce offspring by such an improbable pairing, why isn't salvation possible? How is this honorable to God? How is this loving of God? How is this fair to send them to Hell? Being born less than 100 percent human and going to Hell because you're born that way seems barbaric. It's not godly.

Hundred-percent humans go to Heaven, no matter how bad their roleplay identity is. A person who is not 100 percent human goes to Hell or will cease to exist, no matter how good their roleplay identity is. Such imagery is difficult to grasp, but is it any less reasonable than the orthodox position?

What's the implication of this trend of thought? Are non-Elect Roleplayers who are less than 100 percent human without souls? Do they simply cease to exist at death? Are they devoid of an eternal spiritual identity?

Probably. That seems fair. Life is about the Demonstration of Free Will. It's about roleplay in a kazillion situations. They were born. They had a role to play. They did so. They die. The End.

Let's go back to pre-Flood days. Let's assume angels equal "A," human females equal "H," and the Nephilim equal "N."

It appears that:

1) angels are always depicted as the male gender;

2) Abaddon and a group of angels left Heaven to mate with human females; and

3) Nephilim were produced by angel ingenuity and human females.

From this, “N1” equals the first angel and human female Nephilim group.

The next Nephilim (male) group would be N2. The N2 group “marries” human females, producing the next group of N3. N3 forward to N10 or more would represent Nephilim male groups marrying human females and somehow producing progeny.

The progeny produced from these unnatural experiments were presumably different from other “natural” children. Abaddon and the other angels could have assumed superlative human male attributes. We might assume the average height of Adam and his sons to be six feet. Perhaps Abaddon and fallen angels were six feet five inches or more. The children of Nephilim and human females may have been very mature at ten years old. Tall, virile, and precocious, they may have “married” and “produced children” early in their life.

Owing to a worldwide goal of producing the Redeemer as soon as possible, the urgency to procreate may have gradually become irreverent, crude, and profane. This may provide evidence of how ten trillion people could have been present at the time of the Flood (see Chapter 31, “The Flood 3”). People lived to be 800 to 900 years old! There were children from Seth's side of the family. There were children from Cain's side of the family. There was progeny from the angel and human female experimentation project.

All the world was looking forward to the One to redeem them. The One promised to redeem all human beings. And possibly, as Abaddon and other angels risked, the one to redeem angels based on that same promise.

So, the Nephilim's intrusion into time, space, and matter meant the possibility they had no soul—no eternal spirit. Like an animal, they are here, and then they are gone. At death, they simply cease to exist.

This absolves people who are less than 100 percent human, those compromised by ancestry from Noah and family linked to the Nephilim. If God has no reason to open their spiritual eyes, if the Holy Spirit has no reason to grant the Holy Spirit Identity (HSID), they simply live and then die. The end. No afterlife. God is not unfair. His integrity shines brightly, as it always does, whether we see it or not. Hell is created for the Devil and his angels.

A *figurative image* of Hell only for the devil and his angels is presented at the time of the Flood. Who's in Hell, the Abyss? Not the Nephilim. They died. Oblivion. They're not 100 percent human beings. Hundred percent humans died and transition to SSIDs. Only Abaddon and other Third-Class angels were relegated to chains of darkness. The Abyss. Hell. Why not everyone?

> For if God spared not the angels that sinned, but cast them down to hell, and delivered them into chains of darkness, to be reserved unto judgment (2 Peter 2:4).
>
> And the angels which kept not their first estate, but left their own habitation, he hath reserved in everlasting chains under darkness unto the judgment of the great day (Jude 1:6).
>
> And they had a king over them, which is the angel of the bottomless pit, whose name in the Hebrew tongue is Abaddon, but in the Greek tongue hath his name Apollyon (Revelation 9:11).

Our authentic identity is already in Paradise. Our present life is a Demonstration of Free Will initiated by the error of Adam and Eve.

This is imagery, not theology. I'm an artist, not a teacher. *This is Christian Reformed Impressionism.* It's not meant to be believed. I don't believe it.

It's leverage. I may not use it, but I have it. Leverage for what? Assertions from theists, atheists, and agnostics.

CHAPTER 19

IN THE BEGINNING(S)

Connecting The Dots of Identity envisions a series of beginnings. With this approach, it may be easier to understand how strategic dots are connected to each other.

Here are ten-plus beginnings that MARVI-RPIA paints:

1–The first beginning painted is establishing the Trinity as the primary "beginning of everything." This is God, Jesus Christ, and the Holy Spirit. They have no beginning or ending. This is just a reference point.

2–A second is SSIDs, a given name for Super-Spiritual Identities saved "before the foundation of the world."

3–A third beginning is the "creation of heavenly hosts," all grouped under the name angels.

4–The fourth beginning would be time, space, and matter. The universe. Genesis 1:1 says, "In the beginning, God created the heavens and the earth."

5–The fifth strategic beginning is the creation of Adam and Eve. Life in the Garden of Eden, including life with the Serpent.

6–Identity begins anew as Adam and Eve transition from flawless humans to flawed humans. They are expelled from the Garden.

7–There is a beginning of human conception in the womb—beginning 7a. If brought to term, there's a physical birth—beginning 7b.

8–Human beings are all destroyed in the Flood except for eight. Life starts over with Noah and his family.

9–This super beginning for humanity is the birth, death, and resurrection of Jesus Christ. Beginning number two of the SSIDs is assured for the Elect.

10–We have our born-again experience, a new creature, a different identity from the previous identity, by the Holy Spirit.

10-Plus–Jesus says Satan was a liar/murderer from a beginning that is not defined.

> *Ye are of your father the devil, and the lusts of your father ye will do. He was a murderer from the beginning, and abode not in the truth, because there is no truth in him. When he speaketh a lie, he speaketh of his own: for he is a liar, and the father of it (John 8:44).*

The ten-plus beginning is questionable because Satan was not Satan in beginning number three. The angels were created good. Satan, or Lucifer, was not evil. So, he was not a liar in that beginning. Satan did not have to be in the Garden of Eden for the Serpent to influence Eve. Satan didn't suddenly become evil, all at once, in the Garden. People think of the Garden of Eden as the beginning of evil. Not necessarily. Evil starts in the mind. What were angels thinking before the world was created? How long afterward did angels become evil?

By the way, atheists, and agnostics don't identify with ANY beginning except beginning number four—time, space, and matter—and the secondary effect as beginning number seven(b), physical birth. As a whole, a so-called defined beginning of time, space, and matter is an event that is even today in the process of being identified. This is not to say atheists and agnostics are evil, misinformed, or doomed to Hell. They simply exemplify the dynamics of the Demonstration of Free Will based on heredity, environment, and experience. Their spiritual eyes aren't opened until God intercedes.

This is all imagery, using the colors of religious language to illustrate identity. Who you are is a compilation of years and years of factors. One dominating factor is other people—your spouse, your lover, your parents, and your friends. Your church, your political party, your personal heroes, and your enemies. Other factors may be harder to discern. There's television, movies, the internet, your job, hobbies, education, etcetera.

It could be a time to evaluate what beginnings are for you.

QUESTIONS

Continuing with beginning number ten-plus, a number of questions arise:

Did "Lucifer" suddenly have bad thoughts and decide to leave Heaven?

Does he share his bad thoughts with other angels?

Does he leave on his own to visit Eden?

Why would he choose to go to Earth? Jealous of humans?

When does he think of indwelling humans? How else does he influence humans?

Apparently, he didn't indwell Eve, but the Bible says Eve was deceived. Deceived by whom? The Serpent? By Satan? By her own flawless mind?

The Bible says Adam was not deceived. Not deceived by whom? By Satan? By the Serpent? By Eve? By his own flawless mind?

Why was Adam not deceived but Eve was?

Did other angels participate in deception attempts on the Serpent, Adam, or Eve?

Did Lucifer stay in Heaven and send a surrogate to Earth?

Why doesn't God prevent catastrophic angel misbehavior?

Was the Serpent framed? Was he completely innocent until ambushed by Satan?

Does God punish the Serpent whether the Serpent is framed by Satan or not?

Suppose you say there is no concept of time in Heaven. Satan contemplates various scenarios in Heaven as he is free to do. Then, after much deliberation, he carries out one of them in Eden. Eden can be considered a beginning of time. Maybe that is the case. I don't like it, but it's a possibility.

> In the beginning God created the heaven and the earth (Genesis 1:1).
>
> Where wast thou when I laid the foundations of the earth? declare, if thou hast understanding ... When the morning stars sang together, and all the sons of God shouted for joy? (Job 38:4, 7)
>
> Unto whom it was revealed, that not unto themselves, but unto us they did minister the things, which are now reported unto you by them that have preached the gospel unto you with the Holy Ghost sent down from heaven; which things the angels desire to look into (1 Peter 1:12).

> And Adam was not deceived, but the woman being deceived was in the transgression (1 Timothy 2:14).

Let's start with beginning number three, the heavenly hosts, or angels. The religious impression is God creating spiritual creatures. There may be spiritual creatures other than angels, but I will refer to angels as the heavenly hosts. Among the angels, one of them is pre-Satan. To preserve uniformity and simplicity, the name Lucifer will be used to designate pre-Satan and Satan used when Lucifer has fallen.

A further designation will be classes of angels. First-Class Angels are the angels who never exercised Free Will to disagree with God. Second-Class Angels are Satan and a group of angels. Third-Class Angels are Abaddon (Hebrew name/Apollyon Greek name) and a group of angels (Revelation 9:11). Initially, there were no classes. All angels were one group who did not exercise Free Will to disagree with God.

At some point, Lucifer has a question, perhaps as Lucifer's Postulate. I'll offer the scenario in the style of the Old Testament Book of Job.

LUCIFER'S POSTULATE

There was a time when the sons of God came to present themselves to the Lord, and Lucifer was among them. God asked Lucifer, "From where do you come?" Lucifer said, "From going and coming in this great place You have for us." And God said, "What is your petition?" And Lucifer said, "Please do not let my Lord be angry and I will speak. Is it true that we who live by Your spirit have the freedom to do that which we desire? If not, is it true that we are determined to behave by Your command?"

God answered and said, "You are indeed autonomous and have individual Free Will. You are also determined to behave as a class of spiritual creatures under My command. This is for the love of all heavenly hosts and love for the heavenly environment. I have given you the gift of thought, so you may think as your soul desires, without the consequences of behavior."

Lucifer answered and said, "Is it not a sin to think as my soul desires?" And God answered him, "It is not a sin. Sin enters your soul when the motive for sinful thought is unmerited gain, usually at the expense of others, or the environment. Doing so harms you and is a direct reflection of the One who created you. Thoughts are not clean or unclean. What comes into the mind is not sin, it is what goes out from the mind. It is not what you think, it is why. Intention. Objective. Agenda. Opportunity. Motivation. Reason. Attitude. Purpose."

And Lucifer departed.

And a second time the sons of God came and presented themselves before the Lord. And Lucifer was among them. And the Lord said, "Is all well?" And Lucifer said, "All is well. My Lord, please do not let the Lord be angry and I will speak once more. If it is so that I possess Free Will and may think what my soul desires in love for others and the environment, please allow my petition." And the Lord asked, "What is your petition?"

Lucifer answered and said, "Please grant that I may act in any manner my soul desires. I am lacking in omniscience. By Your loving omniscience, and Your blessed omnipotence, please turn away my evil into good. By this, I may be free to act, yet it is not counted to me for unrighteousness."

And the Lord answered and said, "I am not your servant but your God. I AM life. I AM love. Unrestricted Free Will removes love for others, the environment, and for self. Unrestricted Free Will removes the true meaning of life—glorifying God. Furthermore, unrestricted Free Will is evil without omnipotence and omniscience."

And the sons of God went out from the face of the Lord.

And another time came when the sons of God presented themselves before the Lord. Lucifer was among them. And God said, "From where do you come Lucifer?" And Lucifer answered, "From going and coming in the grace of life by the One who is holy forever, amen." And Lucifer said to God, "My Lord, again that I might humbly speak to You. In the matter of choice, may it be that some of us may put off the Commitment To Reject Free Will? A great number of us desire Free Will. Determinism, being as to obey and love Your commands in a predisposed manner, is to many of us coercion, servitude, and expressly not living freely. From true Free Will, that is not bound, we are able to express love."

And the Lord answered and said, "I AM omniscient. I considered your concerns when I created you. Determinism (control) of you is better than Free Will (uncontrol) of you." And Lucifer said, "My Lord, even as You have said. I speak as one with no understanding. I ask, how is it possible to know what a creature feels, as You are not at all a created being, but the self-existent Holy One, blessed be His Majesty forever? Surely, it would be impossible for His Majesty to have the same knowledge of a created being, as He, Himself, is the great Uncreated One, His Holiness. I beg Your forgiveness to speak thus to You. I am but Your lowly servant."

The Lord said, "I AM, and I AM omniscient. However, I have made a Demonstration. This will be the Demonstration. I have prepared souls who are not but will be when the Demonstration is no more. They reside with Me in Paradise as Determined ones. I will create a second group of souls who do not reside with Me in Paradise. They will reside in their own separate place. They will be created in My image, with Free Will to obey or disobey My commands of love. They are Human Beings."

And Lucifer said to God, “Blessed be My Lord. May we know Your command should Human Beings choose Free Will and not Your Determined Will?” And God said, “If Human Beings choose their own will, I will not command them to go out of existence, but they will die. Death, cessation of life, is the consequence of disobedience to My will for a flawless creature.”

LUCIFER’S POSTULATE CONTINUED

Human beings may have been created because of the angels! No, not the SSIDs. SSIDs are not human beings. SSIDs are not spirit beings. They're not actual beings, so to speak. But they possess an ontological status that resides in the scriptures. They are recognized by God. Salvation was initiated before anyone was born.

Initiated to whom exactly?

Initiated to the authentic identities that God acknowledges. Not the inauthentic identities born to Adam and Eve. No. Initiated to the true identity that possesses salvation before the world was created.

Not salvation to a group of people but individual salvation?

Yes.

An immaterial personal identity of some kind?

Yes—of some kind.

God may have created the Demonstration of Free Will for the sake of the heavenly hosts. Initially, there were not First, Second, or Third-Class Angels. They were one group. Lucifer could have been the best person to advance the notion of angel discontent.

Were the heavenly hosts—angels—truly alive, truly free, truly autonomous?

Could they disobey God?

Was there a penalty for disobedience?

Angels say, "We worship God. We glorify God. We are ministering spirits and do the will of God. What about US? What about OUR will?"

Within a passage of time when there are no celestial timekeepers, Lucifer may have postulated an underlying thought that Free Will entails:

Am I content being who I am?

What more could I want?

The lead angels, Gabriel and Michael, were apparently content. So too, perhaps, were two-thirds of the angels. Lucifer was not altogether content, and as many as one-third of the angels may have felt this way.

What is the function of an angel?

1. To serve God's purposes

2. To worship God

Angels worshiping and glorifying God are easy to understand. But to serve God's purposes? Wouldn't we rather have God directly involved in any action rather than an angel? Angels do this, angels do that. Why doesn't God do this and that Himself? They are three in person, and one in essence! God the Father, God the Son, God the Holy Spirit! They are omnipotent, omnipresent, and omniscient!

In the role of "ministering spirits," angels attend to humans. They also attended to 100 percent human Jesus. But the Trinity certainly has no need for ministering spirits. But it's not NEED that is being illustrated. It's LOVE. The Trinity is sharing the gift of life. They created autonomous beings that possess a life of their own.

We all love to see puppies, kittens, fish, birds, and other creatures being themselves. We love to interact with them. They're unique, they think, they behave. They have their own life.

The life of an angel who worships, who sings, who praises, who responds to love from the Creator is pleasing to the Creator.

Further love is shown as God devises a Demonstration of Free Will. This is in direct contrast to His Determined Will. His love allows this. The SSIDs are in reserve. They are not considered participants in the Demonstration. Again, this proves God's love. They're forever safe.

As for the angels, who knows how long they have been the apple of God's eye? So now God informs them He will create another class of flawless creatures—outside of Heaven.

Let the Demonstration begin ...

MORE LUCIFER

The orthodox view of the story in the Garden of Eden goes something like this ...

Adam and Eve come to understand they live in a testing mode. If they fail the test: death. If they do not fail, the symbol of the Tree of Life means they enjoy life continuously. The Tree of the Knowledge of Good and Evil would never be a threat to them.

Oh, really? Okay, that could be true. However, the MARVI-RPIA imagery looks somewhat different than that.

Can you peacefully live in a Wonderland with the threat of death in your immediate neighborhood?

How long does the test in the Garden continue before considered a success or failure?

Does the test continue until Adam and Eve fail?

Why the Serpent?

Why the Tree of the Knowledge of Good and Evil?

The angels have no such test.

Are HUMAN BEINGS the test for angels?

The MARVI-RPIA unorthodox view of the Garden goes something like this ...

Lucifer: Observe! Adam and Eve failed! A flawless creature MUST have liberty to know and liberty to behave! There's the proof. Adam and Eve actually DISOBEYED You. They're discontent with restrictions You placed upon them. They'd rather die. This seems to have become a two-way test of Free Will and quality of life.

God: Not necessarily. The majority of angels accept My will for them.

Lucifer: Not at all. They don't want to see that they may be flawed creations. I see that we may be flawed.

God: Disobedience is a feature of being flawless. There must be autonomy, separation of My identity from your identity. However, the penalty for disobedience is the loss of the gift of life. Death.

Lucifer: But Adam and Eve still live. You even promised they will recover from death by a Redeemer via procreation. This does not prove Free Will to disobey You is worse than Your Determined Will for a creature.

God: Is death worse than life?

Lucifer: No. Life has no value unless completely free. I am a champion of freedom for all flawless creatures.

God: Being completely free without omnipotence, omnipresence, and omniscience brings death to a flawless creature.

Lucifer: Then perhaps the flawless creature isn't flawless.

God: How could you know without omniscience?

Lucifer: …

God: …

Lucifer: Blessed be the Lord forever, amen.

> Are they not all ministering spirits, sent forth to minister for them who shall be heirs of salvation? (Hebrews 1:14)
>
> Then saith Jesus unto him, Get thee hence, Satan: for it is written, Thou shalt worship the Lord thy God, and him only shalt thou serve. Then the devil leaveth him, and, behold, angels came and ministered unto him (Matthew 4:10-11).

And in the sixth month the angel Gabriel was sent from God unto a city of Galilee, named Nazareth, To a virgin espoused to a man whose name was Joseph, of the house of David; and the virgin's name was Mary (Luke 1: 26-27).

Yet Michael the archangel, when contending with the devil he disputed about the body of Moses, durst not bring against him a railing accusation, but said, The Lord rebuke thee (Jude 1:9).

CHAPTER 20

MARVI AS ART

Slight pause here to emphasize this image being written is NOT Bible instruction, teaching, or interpretation of scripture. MARVI-RPIA is an artistic impression by an artist. I'm no writer. I am not writing from my mind. I am writing from my heart. I'm describing an impression of spirituality, an abstract concept. Because of its timing in history, it's a modern abstract impression.

I don't claim, suggest, or infer that MARVI-RPIA is an assistant to the Bible as a commentary would be. A Bible commentary provides analysis, explanation, and interpretation of verses, chapters, and books of the Bible. I illustrate intuition, hope, and optimism. I do not profess to be an apostle, a prophet, a visionary, or a man of God. I'm a minister of art. MARVI-RPIA is an illustration of the promise in the Bible already accomplished. People may enjoy the imagery of the promise I'm attempting to present. Or they may not.

Imagery is often met with contempt and ridicule. MARVI-RPIA may be thought to misrepresent, undermine, and mislead orthodox Christianity. To repeat, MARVI-RPIA is an image—an analogy of art. The subject of the image is religion. There are multiple religious examples of art. MARVI-RPIA is just another example of art. Admittedly, an example of art using words to paint an image rather than color, brush, and canvas.

Think of the images you've seen of Jesus Christ. We know what we see portrayed is not Jesus, not God. We know the second commandment is not to make a graven image of God. Artists who devote time and effort to portray images of Jesus should recognize they are to do so by portraying

Jesus only as 100 percent human. The endeavor to portray Jesus as 100 percent God is a sin.

> Thou shalt not make unto thee any graven image, or any likeness of any thing that is in heaven above, or that is in the earth beneath, or that is in the water under the earth (Exodus 20:4).

Jesus is God, the third Person of the Trinity. However, to make an image of Jesus, who was 100 percent human as well as 100 percent God, is the issue. Images of Jesus, the man, are not forbidden. That is the teaching of R. C. Sproul.

Religious imagery has its place for beauty and holiness. Considering beauty is in the eye of the beholder, this imagery is under subjective presentation. Music with a religious label does not mean it's beautiful, holy, or at all pleasing. Same for art.

Isn't MARVI-RPIA more like graffiti than modern, abstract, or impressionistic art? Possibly. MARVI-RPIA does seem to be a rogue, unauthorized, intrusion into established spaces. Perhaps more trespassing than vandalism, MARVI-RPIA must press forward without regard to permission, acceptance, or recognition. Society is in desperate need of meaningful contributions. Why be intimidated if there is potential to contribute? MARVI-RPIA has potential.

Still, no matter how much I qualify the idea of sharing my impression, I will probably be vilified. That is understandable. Attempts to glorify God's holy word may lead people astray from what scripture actually says and means. MARVI-RPIA may be rejected if for no other reason than adding/subtracting from the Bible, which is a curse.

> For I testify unto every man that heareth the words of the prophecy of this book, If any man shall add unto these

> things, God shall add unto him the plagues that are written in this book: And if any man shall take away from the words of the book of this prophecy, God shall take away his part out of the book of life, and out of the holy city, and from the things which are written in this book (Revelation 20:18-19).

Am I adding or taking away from the Bible by imagining Satan was not in Eden (see next chapters), or there were no females in Eden except Eve (next chapters), or the Elect have ontological status in Heaven? Some say yes, and some say no.

R.C. Sproul was answering a question that included the Apostles' Creed. There is controversy over the statement that Jesus descended into Hell. R.C. Sproul disagrees with the well-respected creed by citing John Calvin's interpretation, whereby Jesus does NOT go to Hell, which aligns more closely with holy scripture.

The Apostles' Creed has three main points on Jesus's descent to Hell: (1) crucified, (2) dead/buried, (3) descended into Hell.

John Calvin's three main points on Jesus' descent to Hell: (1) crucified, (2) descended into Hell (dying on the cross), (3) dead/buried.

That example is how rearranging ideas potentially gives a better meaning without violating orthodoxy. Similarly, rearranging traditional ideas can be constructive. I will convey an unconventional rendering of a song lyric, in fun, without damaging, violating, or disrespecting the original Christmas song.

"Dreaming I am, of a Christmas white ... know I used to ... the one just like."

The lyrics were violated but in the spirit of humor. Humor heals—known to be good medicine.

Once again, as MARVI-RPIA, I am offering modern abstract impressionism. This book is not a belief system. Even I will say that I do not believe in it. I am just giving an overall impression I have from years and years of exposure. I'm sharing a Plan B. God's Plan A is the real plan. The real plan is set forth in the Bible. I'm on record to say the Bible and the Bible alone is where your trust should be. Even though salvation is not based on words, knowledge, or behavior, as long as your trust is in the Bible, you have a trustworthy reference guide.

Meanwhile, MARVI-RPIA is a super-great plan. Everyone who is 100 percent human goes to Heaven because they are already there as SSIDs. No one goes to Hell except the Devil and his angels. Those who are less than 100 percent human, having no soul or spirit, do not realize an afterlife. They cease to exist. Oblivion.

No matter how good the MARVI-RPIA plan seems to be, God's plan for us is immeasurably better. There is no doubt about that. The MARVI-RPIA plan only hopes to be the most marvelous of all the second-place plans.

> But as it is written, Eye hath not seen, nor ear heard, neither have entered into the heart of man, the things which God hath prepared for them that love him (1 Corinthians 2:9).

That's quite a challenge the Bible offers. The challenge of magnificence has been accepted.

But, in the back of your mind, you may wonder: If this MARVI-RPIA image is so fantastic, and it is fantastic, *how come we're just now hearing about it?* That goes back to the question of why the Bible is hard to understand. Why are there mysteries? Why doesn't God appear to us anymore? Why not write the Bible in the sky?

As MARVI-RPIA has been saying, *Free Will has to play out*. God doesn't want salvation to be obvious or it would be obvious. The fact that NO ONE chooses to give their life to God proves the magnitude of the error Adam and Eve made. The error continues generation after generation unless the Holy Spirit intercedes to override Free Will.

Now, to continue from where we stopped with God speaking to Lucifer about the Demonstration of Free Will versus Determinism. Human beings will begin life outside Heaven in a physical dimension of time and space. The heavenly hosts will be in observance.

CHAPTER 21

ADAM AND EVE—NO SATAN

Now, on to beginning number four. God creates heavens and earth, time and space, animate and inanimate matter.

From the Book of Genesis, we follow the creation process to arrive at Adam and Eve. Slightly before Adam is created, animals are created. The Serpent is especially singled out to be cunning above the animals of the field. Then, as Adam is alone, God says that is not good.

Why is this? Being alone could not be the condition of being lonely. God is omnipresent. His presence certainly overcomes any aspect of loneliness. And there is a numerous assortment of other living creatures around Eden. Adam is in a beautiful relationship with God and with all of God's magnificent creatures. Adam could not possibly be lonely. But Adam was considered alone.

Why was that not good?

It's not good if Adam exercised Free Will to disobey God. That would bring death. *The human race ends. That would not be good.* Adam being alone meant a one-person Demonstration of Free Will. There should be more than one person. A team of persons provides collaboration and perspective, future proofing.

Angels provided a large sample size to determine Free Will. Humans need not be. That could be done through procreation—if necessary. Procreation could be used in lieu of a large sample of human beings. Procreation could also serve as a Failsafe. Failsafe? *Failsafe for what? A flawless human should ever become flawed.*

God brought the animals to Adam, but no suitable helpmeet among them was found. God put Adam to sleep, then created Eve from part of Adam. To speed up the Demonstration of Free Will to disobey versus Determinism to never disobey, God set up a testing model. The model was the Tree of the Knowledge of Good and Evil. To partake of this tree meant to disobey God. The penalty was death.

Will the pair disobey God to acquire knowledge of good and evil?

Meanwhile, being extremely intelligent and possessing twenty-four-hour energy and night vision, Adam and Eve cared for the Garden of Eden and the animals. The Serpent was probably a favorite, as it expressed exceptional intelligence and the ability to readily learn speech. Also, apparently, the Serpent had Free Will. *Given there was no death in Eden and the animals were all male, since no procreation was needed, Eve was the only female.* Being female should provide checks and balances, plus opportunity and proficiency to the male. In a similar fashion, duality in the body is enhanced by having two eyes, two ears, two arms, and two legs.

Being female completed the procreation fail-safe provision. Procreation was not needed for flawless human beings. Procreation was needed if humans ever became flawed. Death would follow. *As a countermeasure, procreation would produce life while the process of death continued.*

Secondly, procreation would produce replicas of subsequent human beings that would demonstrate the error of disobeying God.

Thirdly, and most importantly, procreation would be the means of God becoming human to correct the catastrophe Adam and Eve committed.

Eve makes her dramatic appearance on the scene. And now, the Serpent, being the most cunning of the animals, couldn't believe he wasn't chosen as the OBVIOUS choice to be the helpmeet to Adam. But Adam said *No*! And just like that, the Serpent was summarily removed from consideration. How could this happen? Who else could Adam possibly choose?

And then came the *real* shocker! God "cheats" by creating another creature—a female. This is not fair to the Serpent. He watches as Adam embraces HER as the helpmeet!

The Serpent thinks back to before Adam was created. He was the number *one* creature of them all. Then, after Adam, he went to the number *two* creature. Now, it's becoming obvious: he is the *third* greatest creature in the world.

He could possibly reclaim the number one status if Eve or Adam died—physical death, that is. They wouldn't go out of existence because they were eternal spirit creatures. But he, the Serpent, would go out of existence. He was not a spirit. Thinking ... thinking ... a thought came to him.

What if Eve should eat of the Tree of the Knowledge of Good and Evil? If she physically died, he may renew his appeal as Adam's helpmeet. If God did not physically kill her, she would certainly lose her status as a suitable helpmate to Adam. He may win either way. Of course, he would never want such an event to occur. Just thinking. That's all.

Eve was the only female. She would probably desire the knowledge the Tree of Knowledge of Good and Evil would give her. God loved her. He may forgive her disobedience. Every creature desires knowledge, experience, growth, and improvement. Every creature is curious. How can this be wrong?

So far, Satan is not in the Garden. He does not need to be there. Free Will is sufficient to develop patterns in thinking and behaving. The Serpent was simply thinking through scenarios. No sin in doing that. Sin only forms from APPLYING to thoughts such concepts as intent, unmerited gain, dishonesty, deceit, and exploitation. Even after applying sin to thoughts, you may repent and retract them. You may experience discomfort, sorrow, and remorse. You try to do better. But acting on such unpleasant thoughts, with no fear, no remorse, no prayer of uneasiness, brings the error of unrighteousness.

The Serpent, as a creature who had the ability to think rationally, would be considered a flawless creation. The Serpent, Adam, and Eve were all flawless creations. They were NOT perfect. *ONLY God the Father, God the Son, and God the Holy Spirit are perfect.* The Serpent was free to think whatever he desired. Same for Adam and Eve. Thought was an invisible simulation of behavior.

The Garden of Eden was a magnificent place inside the area of Eden. *By the way, the Garden was not perfect either.* If it were perfect, there would be no Tree of the Knowledge of Good and Evil. At this time, the created beings were probably all males. There was no rationale for reproduction. There was great diversity in the types of animals, and they were in a state of homeostasis. There was no gain or loss of energy, no waste produced, and no antagonism. The progression of time had no detrimental effect on the animals. They didn't age. Neither did Adam and Eve.

Everyone probably tasted from the Tree of Life directly or indirectly. No one was immortal, but their lifeforce was enhanced by the effluence from the Tree of Life. As gardeners, Adam and Eve would likely distribute materials from the Life Tree. Leaves, branches, and organic matter went to marine life and other animals. There must have been other trees, plants, and flowers that depended on Adam and Eve for their care. *The Tree of Life sustained all.* They wouldn't have needed much. Once a week, every two weeks, or maybe every thirty days or so was sufficient. This was the only source for life besides God Himself. (Think of Moses on Mount Sinai. He didn't eat or drink for forty days and forty nights. God was with him).

> And he was there with the Lord forty days and forty nights; he did neither eat bread, nor drink water. And he wrote upon the tables the words of the covenant, the ten commandments (Exodus 34:28).

No one slept. They just rested. Boundless energy, coupled with superb night vision, made for a community of love, harmony, and peace. Life went on from dawn to day to dusk to night and back to dawn again.

Adam and Eve lived in a flawless environment. They were flawless creatures charged with being caretakers of the Garden. *They had no gardening experience. They had no gardening tools. They had no gardening clothing. They were naked.* However, they were given an opportunity to serve the Lord, and they did so. The pair were in constant motion as they performed their duties of fun, interest, education, and honor to God.

The Garden was composed of trees, plants, flowers, water from rivers, and animals. *What "work" could be done in the Garden when the Garden was flawless? Did God's Garden really need caretakers? God could've easily done it with a word or two.* But He didn't.

What is a caretaker to do? When your "job" is so wonderful, so pleasant to perform, and so rewarding, is it really work? Maybe. It's work in the sense that certain actions keep all things in good working order. That's important. As trees, plants, animals, and marine life received attention from humans, they all thrived from the attention and provided positive feedback to Adam and Eve. Everyone and everything there received stimulation, and that stimulation transmitted glory to His Majesty the Lord.

The creation around Eden was good. No evil was found there. *No evil angel from Heaven suddenly appeared to corrupt the whole world and instigate the highest crime in history.* The three players on the field were all that was needed to perform the Free Will Demonstration God arranged. The Serpent. Adam. Eve.

From this, the main story of the Bible, the spirit of the Serpent deceiving Eve, remains. The Serpent forever stands as a symbol of subterfuge, craftiness, and deceit. Additionally, in Ezekiel 28:11-19, we read of the King of Tyre. Or is this Adam? Or is this Satan? It isn't clear who this is. It seems like an allegory—like writings in the book of Job, Daniel, and Revelation. All three archetypes could be spoken of as one entity to highlight the drama of a great fallen ruler. The same principle is often used in the Bible to compare and contrast great cities or kingdoms using one or more names as examples.

Furthermore, we are often taught that Lucifer's reasons for becoming evil were because iniquity was found in him, and his heart was elevated due to his beauty.

It's understandable that pride, intelligence, and outstanding attractiveness would cause a magnificent angel to exercise his Free Will to disagree with God. But that's only one angel. Surely beauty, intelligence, and excellent character would exemplify almost all the angels. They were all flawlessly created.

So, how could one angel influence thousands, or millions, or billions of other angels to disagree with God's will for their lives? Why would they care if Lucifer thought he was more beautiful than anyone else? Why would they care if Lucifer had iniquity in him? Why would they rebel against God? Lucifer didn't create them. Lucifer wasn't omnipresent, omniscient, or omnipotent. Lucifer was just an angel—like them.

It seems there is more to the story than the orthodox version of Lucifer being the ultimate megalomaniac.

Now, to continue ...

As we read through scripture the images of Satan take many forms. The image of the Serpent has various forms. Adam is an example of various forms. Remember Jesus said to the apostle Peter, "Get behind Me, Satan." This was a dramatic comparison, a metaphor.

We know that Satan is considered an evil angel. We also know Satan was expelled from Heaven, as no evil person or thing resides in Heaven. We know that at some point Satan begins his crusade against humans, including Jesus Christ. A question arises: *How does Satan get back into Heaven if he is expelled from Heaven?* The book of Job (2:1) says Satan presented himself before the Lord, and the Book of Zechariah (3:1) says Satan is again present before the Angel of the Lord as an accuser to Joshua.

This does not necessarily mean Satan had to be in Heaven to present himself before the Lord. Or does it? When did good Lucifer become evil Satan? When was he expelled from Heaven? How many tiers of Heaven are there?

Now, back to Eden ...

Finally, there came a time when the Serpent felt it was time to act—starting with Eve. Adam was secure in his identity, but Eve seemed reticent. *Eve was just as capable as Adam, but she was different. The Serpent was also very capable, just different.* He was different from all the other animals and different from Adam and Eve. Being different provoked uncertainty, doubt, and suspicion. *Why am I different? Is being different negative rather than positive? What if I don't like being different? How much am I able to change? A test may help. The same test as Adam and Eve faced day to day. The Tree of the Knowledge of Good and Evil.*

Ego-Skepticism applies here (Glossary of Colors). *Though uniquely created firsthand by God as a flawless living creature, the Serpent has doubts about his identity.* The Tree of Knowledge of Good and Evil may provide an opportunity to enhance his intelligence and overcome his lack of confidence. Yes, there is trust in God. He made me a flawless living creature. But how does God really know what it's like to be a creature? God is the Great Uncreated One, blessed forever. Amen.

The Serpent is now at the Tree. He is not commanded to avoid it. He does not expect death. He does expect to obtain at least a boost in knowledge. Knowing good is positive. Knowing evil may not be positive, but it may afford the overall balance to the knowledge of good. *High risk, high reward. Ego-Centracism overrules Ego-Skepticism* (Glossary of Colors). The Serpent eats. He does not die.

Over the next few days, the subtlety of knowledge of good and evil permeates his being. The good of him seems relative and the bad of him seems relative. There is a tangible loss of moral objectivity. Good and bad feel subjective. *God is not the ultimate source of morality. I'm also a source.* He thinks back to Eve. Would Eve have a similar feeling?

But what if Eve receives the death penalty from God? Don't know. She's an eternal spiritual being in physical form. If her physical form dies, perhaps God will recreate her a second time from Adam. Doesn't really matter. Step one is done—exercise Free Will. Step two—talk to Eve.

Meanwhile, the angels are in observance. They feel something may be about to happen, and something is about to happen. Something bad. Very bad.

> And the Lord God said, It is not good that the man should be alone; I will make him an help meet for him ... And Adam gave names to all cattle, and to the fowl of the air, and to every beast of the field; but for Adam there was not found an help meet for him. And the Lord God caused a

deep sleep to fall upon Adam, and he slept: and he took one of his ribs, and closed up the flesh instead thereof; And the rib, which the Lord God had taken from man, made he a woman, and brought her unto the man (Genesis 2:18, 20-22).

Moreover the word of the Lord came unto me, saying, Son of man, take up a lamentation upon the king of Tyrus, and say unto him, Thus saith the Lord God; Thou sealest up the sum, full of wisdom, and perfect in beauty. Thou hast been in Eden the garden of God; every precious stone was thy covering, the sardius, topaz, and the diamond, the beryl, the onyx, and the jasper, the sapphire, the emerald, and the carbuncle, and gold: the workmanship of thy tabrets and of thy pipes was prepared in thee in the day that thou wast created. Thou art the anointed cherub that covereth; and I have set thee so: thou wast upon the holy mountain of God; thou hast walked up and down in the midst of the stones of fire. Thou wast perfect in thy ways from the day that thou wast created, till iniquity was found in thee. By the multitude of thy merchandise they have filled the midst of thee with violence, and thou hast sinned: therefore I will cast thee as profane out of the mountain of God: and I will destroy thee, O covering cherub, from the midst of the stones of fire. Thine heart was lifted up because of thy beauty, thou hast corrupted thy wisdom by reason of thy brightness: I will cast thee to the ground, I will lay thee before kings, that they may behold thee. Thou hast defiled thy sanctuaries by the multitude of thine iniquities, by the iniquity of thy traffick; therefore will I bring forth a fire from the midst of thee, it shall devour thee, and I will bring thee to ashes upon the earth in the sight of all them that behold thee. All they that know thee among the people shall be astonished at thee: thou shalt be a terror, and never shalt thou be any more (Ezekiel 28:11-19).

Then Peter took him, and began to rebuke him, saying, Be it far from thee, Lord: this shall not be unto thee. But he turned, and said unto Peter, Get thee behind me, Satan: thou art an offence unto me: for thou savourest not the things that be of God, but those that be of men (Matthew 16:22-23).

Again there was a day when the sons of God came to present themselves before the Lord, and Satan came also among them to present himself before the Lord. And the Lord said unto Satan, From whence comest thou? And Satan answered the Lord, and said, From going to and fro in the earth, and from walking up and down in it (Job 2:1-2).

And he shewed me Joshua the high priest standing before the angel of the Lord, and Satan standing at his right hand to resist him. And the Lord said unto Satan, The Lord rebuke thee, O Satan; even the Lord that hath chosen Jerusalem rebuke thee: is not this a brand plucked out of the fire? (Zechariah 3:1-2).

And I heard a loud voice saying in heaven, Now is come salvation, and strength, and the kingdom of our God, and the power of his Christ: for the accuser of our brethren is cast down, which accused them before our God day and night (Revelation 12:10).

CHAPTER 22

THE SERPENT, EVE, AND ADAM

The angels in Heaven were all one class of good angels. Lucifer humbly proposed a request for a semblance of omnipotence by allowing angels unlimited behavior. God counseled that it would not be good. Free Will without omnipotence and omniscience will lead to the destruction of identity. Free Will is not better than Determinism. Determinism with limited omnipotence (behavior) and limited omniscience (knowledge) protects the identity and the identities of others.

The Demonstration of Free Will on Earth in the Garden of Eden should help illustrate why this is so.

Now, as the Serpent has taken of the Tree of the Knowledge of Good and Evil, the angels wonder what is next. What is the Serpent's motive?

The day came when the Serpent spoke to Eve in the following manner:

Serpent: Hey, sweetheart! Wow! Look at you! You're looking mighty fine today. I think you and I should run away together. Adam is a child. Now I know how to treat a woman. I can make you forget all about Adam.

Eve: WHAT?

No, no, no. Stop. This is serious (delete that scene). Now, continue …

But what if the Serpent did eat from the Tree of the Knowledge of Good and Evil … before Eve?

He eats a little. Then he waits a couple of hours. Eats again the next day. Waits a couple of hours. Doesn't eat more. After a week or so, maybe a month or so, his thoughts and feelings have a subtle change.

One day, he decides to confide in Eve that he did indeed eat of the forbidden tree. He feels great. He feels confident. *He's the most intelligent of all the animals. He always had a fear of God, but now he doesn't. God gave him Free Will. He decided to act on his Free Will. That's what it's for.*

Now, back to what the Bible actually says happened between the Serpent and Eve.

The day came when the Serpent spoke to Eve in the following manner:

> Now the serpent was more subtil than any beast of the field which the Lord God had made. And he said unto the woman, Yea, hath God said, Ye shall not eat of every tree of the garden? And the woman said unto the serpent, We may eat of the fruit of the trees of the garden: But of the fruit of the tree which is in the midst of the garden, God hath said, Ye shall not eat of it, neither shall ye touch it, lest ye die. And the serpent said unto the woman, Ye shall not surely die: For God doth know that in the day ye eat thereof, then your eyes shall be opened, and ye shall be as gods, knowing good and evil (Genesis 3:1-5).

The angels see quite a turn of events! The Serpent has become a significant identity and makes use of the Tree of the Knowledge of Good and Evil to deceive Eve.

The Serpent tells her she will be like God. God knows good and evil. God can never die. God is spirit. She will know good and evil. She won't die because she is spirit—just with the extra dimension of flesh and blood.

Her former innocent identity will die, but her new identity will be advanced.

The Serpent goes on. He risked his life for her and for Adam. He ate. He didn't die. In fact, eating from the Tree helps him know how to speak with her. Being a cunning serpent, his knowledge was enhanced but surely to a lesser degree compared to what she could possibly know. And she would be able to further enhance his serpent identity.

As for Adam, he doesn't have to know about this right away. But he will surely admire her new mature identity.

Eve finally gives in. She does eat of the Tree of the Knowledge of Good and Evil!

WHAM! BOOM! Unlike what may have happened to the Serpent if he had eaten of the forbidden tree, *Eve's experience is sudden and explicit. She instantly KNOWS she has made a horrible mistake!* She has been deceived ... and much worse.

The knowledge of good and evil is like having omniscience without omnipotence. Without power (omnipotence) over mind and body to implement adjustments that knowledge (omniscience) reveals, you are overwhelmed. Eve was probably stunned and astounded by the enormity of her own identity. Like a child suddenly exposed to adult matters such as sexuality, procreation, childcare, pornography, surgery, torture, gruesome accidents, or monsters, she is altogether traumatized.

Eve immediately becomes aware of herself and her environment. It's a shock to her senses. She becomes aware of an altered mental perspective. Her heart is racing. Her respiration increases. The digestion taking place from the contents of the forbidden tree leaves an aftertaste of apprehension and dread. She eerily hears the Serpent asking her questions, but she doesn't want to hear his voice ever again. Her other senses of sight, sound, and touch verify her innocence is being summarily obliterated. Gone. *She's no longer the same person. She's an adult! She's female! She has genitalia! The Serpent has genitalia. All the male animals have genitalia, but not like hers. She never considered gender before.* Now, she felt uncomfortable—embarrassed. She was exposed to the world. There is no sense of safety, only apprehension.

What can she do? Why did this happen? Food from the Tree of Life melted in her mouth. There was immediate energy. This food from the Tree of the Knowledge of Good and Evil tasted good, but it did not melt. It was "heavy." It had to be chewed. Instinctively, she swallowed. Why didn't she spit it out? That also was an instinct she never had before. The instinct was to consume, not reject.

That brought up another realization. She was hungry. She may not have eaten in days or weeks. Who knows? *Before, every day was like her first day. She was never hungry.* Now, she would need to eat again—fairly soon. The concept of "soon" took on a specific meaning: time. She inhabited a body. *This body lived in time and space. She was aging!* She was scared! She was confused!

She had to shout to the Serpent "SILENCE!" She had to think. Adam had to know what happened, right away. What would he do? *Does he love me?*

WHAT WILL GOD DO? Does HE love me?

Whatever I say to God, I must have Adam there to help me. She deliberates. She attempts to sort through what she should do next. Being in a state of shock was so strange. Consternation, fear, and regret were bearing down on her.

As for the Serpent, he knew he had to go to Adam and attempt to mitigate the extraordinary development with Eve. She may attempt to blame HIM for HER decision.

Upon greeting Adam, without Eve, the Serpent begins to speak.

Serpent: Adam. There's been a terrible incident. I know that you and Eve have discussed the Tree of the Knowledge of Good and Evil. *I decided to risk my life and eat the fruit so that the two of you would know more about it. That's how much I love you.* Well, after a month or so, I felt no harm. I was telling Eve of this and after many questions, she also ate. I should have stopped her but—

Adam: She didn't die?

Serpent: No. I wanted to help her, but she sent me away, so I—

Adam: Enough! I'm going to her.

Adam starts out and, as he goes, he thinks back to how the Serpent seemed different. Now he knows why. Suddenly, Eve comes into view.

She goes to Adam. The Serpent is nearby. She commands the serpent to leave. She manages to convey to Adam what happened. Before anything else, she needs to tell Adam what he needs to know to make HIS decision. Her decision has been made. *Will he accept Free Will, adulthood, and her love? Will Adam return with her to the Tree of the Knowledge of Good and Evil? Will he eat? Will he change his mind in the final moments?*

From what transpired, everything that happened to Eve was so devastating. *How could Adam still end up joining Eve by eating from the Tree of the Knowledge of Good and Evil?*

Eve spoke of at least three things Adam would ponder:

1. Having Free Will, which she and the serpent acted on, was death-defying. God made us autonomous. We finally found out if it was TRUE autonomy. It is, and it's NOT good.

2. Being an adult, she was no longer alive as a child. She was aware of her body, the environment, time, and space. She wore a covering of fig leaves. Her shining aura was gone.

3. What would living without her mean if he chose not to join her? She was dying; he would live. Did he really love her that much?

He returns with her. He does eat.

God soon comes to Adam and Eve. Their interest in their own will versus God's will for their life causes their death. They don't cease living immediately, but they suffer a significant decline in the attributes they once possessed. Awareness of death came in incremental reminders, minute by minute, hour by hour.

But at least they're alive. And they also received a Promise. God promised He would provide an Antidote for the gross error they'd committed. The Antidote would be produced by their own bodies.

> And I will put enmity between thee and the woman, and between thy seed and her seed; it shall bruise thy head, and thou shalt bruise his heel (Genesis 3:15).

MONSTERS FROM THE GARDEN

As for the Serpent, he is cursed. He has devolved to a lowly mute: a loathsome creature, no longer an upright, flawless specimen. God did not curse Satan. God said because YOU did this—the animal—YOU are cursed. *There's no mention of the famous evil spirit who hijacked and victimized the Serpent.* The Serpent could have been a beautiful, cunning, special companion of Adam and Eve. However, he exercised his Free Will and it led to a catastrophe.

It could be that God stripped the Serpent of his beautiful outer garment to clothe the Adam and Eve. The reason for clothing would symbolize:

A–The Fall

B–Privacy, modesty, and protection

C–Distraction of gender differentiation

D–Ego-Skepticism (Serpent, Eve)

E–Ego-Centracism (Serpent, Eve, Adam)

> Take Aaron and Eleazar his son, and bring them up unto mount Hor: And strip Aaron of his garments, and put them upon Eleazar his son: and Aaron shall be gathered unto his people, and shall die there. And Moses did as the Lord commanded: and they went up into mount Hor in the sight of all the congregation. And Moses stripped Aaron of his garments, and put them upon Eleazar his son; and Aaron died there in the top of the mount: and Moses and Eleazar came down from the mount (Numbers 20:25-28).

The accepted story is that the Serpent is simply a bystander in the Garden who was ambushed by Satan. At least, that is what we are taught. No dispute here.

But there is no reference to the physical imagery of the Serpent pre-Fall. No doubt, he was truly beautiful, not at all like the present imagery of serpents. *Also, there is no female Missus Serpent in the Garden, at least in MARVI-RPIA imagery.* All the creatures were male. Apparently, a female was created that matched the Serpent's fallen image, not his pre-Fall image. Beauty, unmatched intellect, and the ability to speak were never features of Missus Serpent. And these flawless attributes were not inherited by the offspring of the serpent family.

So, now, as a consequence of God cursing the environment, including the animals, He created the female gender. *Females are a response to the cursed environment, not a consequence.* They are the co-creators, along with males, which define the ecosystem that supports human beings.

The human female, Eve, was created as a fail-safe against death. Should death occur, life could be produced through procreation even while dying day to day.

If a male doesn't sin, there's no need for females. But if sin does occur, it's good to have a remedy in place. Therefore, it was not good for Adam to be alone. *And later, we read that Eve was the mother of all living who possess the breath of God. This helps refute assumptions about other forms of life on Earth or in other places.*

Parenthetically, the mother of all living and the father of all living excluded spirit beings. God is the creator of all living spiritual beings.

> And Adam called his wife's name Eve; because she was the mother of all living (Genesis 3:20).

> And the LORD God formed man of the dust of the ground, and breathed into his nostrils the breath of life; and man became a living soul (Genesis 2:7).

Continuing with the Serpent, he was the only nonhuman who may have eaten from the Tree of the Knowledge of Good and Evil. It's unlikely the effects of such an act would be beneficial. Missus Serpent was created as the counterpart to the fallen image of the Serpent. Their seed would have inherited the unfortunate attributes of both parents. Unlike Adam and

Eve's children, the offspring of the Serpent have no way of knowing from what great height the family has fallen. Or do they?

And then, the Day of days! The Infamous Three are expelled from the Garden of Eden. The Tree of Life is no longer available to them. The world is altogether a different planet.

The serpents go their way—silently. Adam and Eve go their way—dumbfounded and afraid.

But God is merciful. He greatly assists the humans in making a new life in a new world environment. Unfortunately, that world is now just as cursed as they are. Their pain, their sorrow, and their labor are a continuous reminder of what they lost. If there was any consolation besides the promise of a Mediator, it was that their memory skills were curtailed. Their ability to remember virtually everything was becoming increasingly impaired. The trauma of the glory they lost was mercifully less acute.

We have seen the Serpent has no name in the Bible. Isn't that a bit odd? Surely Adam and Eve gave him a pet name. Adam named all the creatures. He chose the name "serpent" when God brought the animal to him. It would be in my power as an artist to render a name for the Serpent, but I won't. *But don't you think he deserves to have a name as famous as any villain in history?* Even beyond a villain in history: a MONSTER in history.

Who has done more to harm humanity than the Serpent? Oh, you might say, it wasn't the Serpent who was evil, it was Satan! The Serpent was just an innocent bystander, just like all the other animals in Eden. Maybe so. Maybe not. "BUT THE BIBLE SAYS SATAN!" you say. Maybe so, maybe not.

Then think of all the horror stories we've heard of. Monsters typically have names. Frankenstein, Dracula, Wolfman, Cyclops, King Kong, Medusa, the Thing. Even if they don't have a name, we acknowledge their status as a representative of horror. Think of zombies, aliens, and vampires.

The point is the Serpent is the horror of all horrors that have befallen humanity. The Serpent is the one who had the audacity to question God's authority. The Serpent began the catastrophic end of flawless living creatures on Earth. Now we all die in a hundred different ways.

But we don't really see the Serpent that way. Probably because the Serpent has been characterized as an innocent animal exploited by the powerful evil of Satan. So, the Serpent isn't really evil at all. It's the Devil, Satan, who is the evil one.

As we visualize some of the all-time worst villains and monsters, we often forget one thing—beauty. Monsters are not typically thought of as beautiful. Rather, the common characteristic of the worst villains and monsters is ugliness: loathing, disgust, and abhorrence. But no such things can apply to the flawless living creatures in the Garden of Eden. *These three infamous ones who plunged the whole world—THE WHOLE WORLD—into death and despair were gorgeous! The three were all absolutely, stunningly, beautiful!*

How do we know this? God is a God of beauty. We know the Serpent was 100 percent beautiful. We know Eve was 100 percent beautiful. We know Adam was 100 percent beautiful. The Garden of Eden was 100 percent beautiful. All was beauty.

Even further, the angels were all beautiful. This has to include Satan before he was Satan. He may have been even slightly more beautiful than the others, if this beauty was measurable.

So, it may not be worthwhile to pursue the Serpent as the instigator of evil or the worst of all the monsters who ever lived. His image would be of beauty, not a loathsome snake crawling on its belly. Before exercising his

Free Will to deceive Eve, the Serpent was not cursed but blessed. He was blessed to be one of the flawless living creatures in the company of Adam and Eve.

And, we could also say, the Serpent wasn't necessarily a monster at all. He was just a flawless creature expressing his God-given attribute of Free Will. The same for Eve. The same for Adam. Yes, we are the result of their disastrous Free Will choice. That has become the horror of all horror stories ... unless you're an atheist.

But why we all have to suffer doesn't seem fair somehow. The Serpent, Eve, and Adam did what a flawless creature had the option to do. We don't have that same option. We are all flawed creatures. We don't have the right to say what we would have done. Our intellect is impaired.

Speaking of impaired intellect, the real monster is not even Satan, not the Serpent, not Eve, and not Adam. It is US. How so? All monsters are created by human beings. We imagine, create, and present to each other what evil, horror, and fear should be. Think of radio and television shows, movies, and art. Holidays, festivals, and unusual rituals testify to our compulsion to revel in horror. We are monsters of evil to ourselves. It seems to be a part of our nature. Our Dream Identity (DID) reminds us of our plight through nightmares. Being chased, being bullied, falling, lost, or being killed. *We do it to ourselves. We are the agent, and we are the victim.*

The impression *Connecting The Dots Of Identity* tries to convey is the inauthentic identity. This identity makes up the Demonstration of Free Will initiated by Adam and Eve. It is not who we really are. It is a role dictated by heredity, the environment, and experience.

Adam and Eve knew who God was. The Serpent knew who God was. Satan knew who God was. They had direct knowledge. *Our knowledge of God is indirect.* For example:

1) General Revelation (God revealed in nature by our five senses)

2) Special Revelation (God revealed in scripture)

3) Historicity of the Person Jesus Christ

4) The Holy Spirit comes into our life as an invisible, silent, immaterial Agent

Isn't indirect knowledge of God enough to save us? No. Absolutely not. What we know and what we do has no effect on acquiring salvation. The ability to live based on God's will rather than our own will was lost in the Garden. We inherited limited corrupted Free Will from Adam and Eve. Our lives demonstrate their error of judgment. Unless God overrides our will, we will NEVER choose to follow Him. This must be proven, over and over and over, with an innumerable number of lives.

Why should it be proven over and over? To erase all doubt?

To whom should it be proven over and over? Does the Trinity need proof? First-Class Angels? Other heavenly hosts? SSIDs?

Perhaps to everyone inside and outside time. Perhaps only to us.

> As it is written, There is none righteous, no, not one: There is none that understandeth, there is none that seeketh after God (Romans 3:10-11).

As far as we're concerned, the essential matter is our authentic identity is safe. God knew us before He created the world. He saved us IN THE PAST! For now, we are Roleplayers of a temporary inauthentic identity.

You don't believe this? That's not unexpected. It's an impression. It's an art project. You don't believe in art. You appreciate it. Or you don't.

CHAPTER 23

THE NEPHILIM—PART 1

I have been led to believe in the Nephilim without actually believing. I have the IMPRESSION that angels and human females produced progeny—the Nephilim. Before going further, it should be helpful to paint imagery that leads up to this Nephilim impression.

Two things stand out in astounding fashion to the angels when they witness Adam, Eve, and the Serpent expelled from the Garden.

One, *human beings chose knowledge of good and evil* to be more important than the death sentence God warned of.

> And the LORD God commanded the man, saying, Of every tree of the garden thou mayest freely eat: But of the tree of the knowledge of good and evil, thou shalt not eat of it: for in the day that thou eatest thereof thou shalt surely die (Genesis 2:16-17).

Two, *God promised them a Redeemer* via a reproduction process from their own bodies that would eventually reinstate their lives in the future.

> And I will put enmity between thee and the woman, and between thy seed and her seed; it shall bruise thy head, and thou shalt bruise his heel (Genesis 3:15).

Is the promise of the Redeemer really so obvious to us? Certainly, Adam and Eve would have firsthand understanding of God's words in Genesis 3:15.

Who or what is the seed of the woman? This would be an offspring of Eve. This would be the Image of Correction to Adam and Eve's error, which is the Messiah.

What is the seed of the Serpent? The Serpent's offspring would likely exhibit the characteristic of egocentric Free Will (see Glossary of Colors). The Serpent himself represents Ego-Skepticism (see Glossary of Colors). Both concepts apply to the Serpent, Eve, Adam, fallen angels, fallen man, and, of course, Satan.

Ego-Skepticism

Ego Skepticism is a result of uncertainty regarding the nature of identity. Who am I, what should I be doing, why am I here? This includes the unreliability of General Revelation (nature or science), Special Revelation (scripture), sense perception, and limitations of mental ability. Generally, a begrudging acknowledgment that autonomic systems of the body—such as the heart, lungs, glands, and brain—and also immutable aspects of the body—such as race, height, and age—contribute to confirming a lack of access and authority regarding identity.

Egocentric Free Will (Ego-Centracism)

The belief is that the right of a living creature is to demand and pursue the best interests of the creature. Restriction of this right is to undermine the viability and autonomy of a flawless living creature.

So now we see that an egocentric Free Will and Ego-Skepticism will be inherited by the offspring of Adam and Eve. This must also apply to the offspring of the Serpent.

In the Book of Genesis, the promise regarding the seed of the woman that crushes the skull of the Serpent's seed would have been part of God's teaching to Adam and Eve. Procreation was now a major factor in life outside the Garden. Their offspring will inherit their flawed identity, the cursed environment, and experiences of sin. However, procreation was the method God chose to recover life. Day by day, death will continue until the Promised One is born. He will then crush the head of the Serpent, represented by Ego-Skepticism and an egocentric Free Will. This guarantees a future of eternal life after the Demonstration of Free Will is completed in all the offspring of Adam and Eve.

In speaking of the seed of the serpent bruising the heel belonging to the seed of the woman, and then the victory of the seed of the woman bruising the head of the seed of the serpent, two supporting verses may apply. The first reference is when Jesus, in the Last Supper scenario, refers to the fatal betrayal of Judas Iscariot (John 13). This leads to Jesus being bruised by death, then to crucifixion, and finally crushing death by resurrection (living again). The second reference is the Old Testament prophecy in Psalm (Psalm 41).

> I speak not of you all: I know whom I have chosen: but that the scripture may be fulfilled, He that eateth bread with me hath lifted up his heel against me (John 13:18).

> Yea, mine own familiar friend, in whom I trusted, which did eat of my bread, hath lifted up his heel against me (Psalm 41:9).

Now, given that the angels are still one class of good angels, what do they see? They see what has happened in the Garden of Eden and how God has changed the world outside the Garden. The humans made in the image of God are no longer flawless. The Serpent, who was so superior to nonhuman creatures, is cursed and now actually lower than nonhuman creatures.

But they marvel at the Serpent exercising Free Will. They marvel at Eve choosing death rather than restricted knowledge. They marvel at Adam agreeing with Eve.

Then, day to day, the angels witness the stark contrast between flawless life in the Garden of Eden and the flawed, corrupted life outside the Garden. They witness the process of procreation. They witness nine months of pregnancy, birth, and growth of a person from the two created persons. They witness the death of a living person by the wrongful act of another living person.

Looking ahead, they begin to anticipate when the Offspring of Eve and the offspring of the Serpent will take place.

Taking notice over hundreds of years, Enoch of Seth's family line suddenly seems apparent as the Offspring of Eve—the Chosen One to redeem humankind. Enoch was the person who was walking with God.

What about the offspring of the Serpent?

As God is teaching Adam and Eve the intricacies of procreation, the pair learn the seed of the serpent will be a cursed, fallen version of the original Serpent. Guile, betrayal, and deceit from this version of the serpent is the seed that bruises the heel. Though literal serpents may bruise human heels, the spiritual character of the serpent is manifested in animal-like *human beings*.

In MARVI-RPIA imagery, these animal-like persons could be humans who are less than 100 percent human or simply inhumane Roleplayers.

The scene now regresses to set up a pivotal point in angel and human relationships. The scene starts with the birth and growth of Cain, Adam and Eve's first child.

Imagine how Cain feels when he's old enough to realize what Adam and Eve have lost. Cain is the first benefactor of being born in sin. His parents were created flawlessly. He was created flawed. His parents ate from the Tree of Life! He's eating from trees of death. He dies day by day, even as he lives day by day. Nothing they say consoles him. He walks away again in exasperation for the umpteenth time.

Would he be within reason to be extremely outraged? Tempestuous? Resentful? Obnoxious? Absolutely! Would Cain be disrespectful to his parents? Not likely, but not without great restraint. *They had EVERYTHING and gave it away. They ruined his life—and everything else in the world.*

Soon, Cain has a brother: Abel. Adam and Eve have learned immensely from the birth and growth of Cain. Abel is raised a little differently, and of course, every child has their own personality. God loves Abel and likes Cain, so to speak. One day, Cain flares up. He explodes. He kills Abel.

The angels are shocked! They see one human take the life of another human. They see death, the physical cessation then decomposition of a formerly living person. In this event, *Cain committed a sign of an egocentric, ego-skeptical person—as in the case of the Serpent in the Garden.* Therefore, Cain may be the seed of the Serpent God spoke of to Adam and Eve.

But then, Cain is banished from the community. However, a few of Cain's younger sisters and brothers later join him to offer assistance. At some point, Cain becomes convinced that procreation is the only solution to the curse of humanity and the environment. Procreation gradually occurs.

Perhaps the Nephilim project to create angel and human female offspring may have begun here. Thoughts were coming into place, though as yet without action or intention.

> Of which salvation the prophets have enquired and searched diligently, who prophesied of the grace that should come unto you: Searching what, or what manner of time the Spirit of Christ which was in them did signify, when it testified beforehand the sufferings of Christ, and the glory that should follow. Unto whom it was revealed, that not unto themselves, but unto us they did minister the things, which are now reported unto you by them that have preached the gospel unto you with the Holy Ghost sent down from heaven; which things the angels desire to look into (1 Peter 1:10-12).

> And to Seth, to him also there was born a son; and he called his name Enos: then began men to call upon the name of the Lord (Genesis 4:26).

> And Lamech took unto him two wives: the name of the one was Adah, and the name of the other Zillah. And Adah bare Jabal: he was the father of such as dwell in tents, and of such as have cattle. And his brother's name was Jubal: he was the father of all such as handle the harp and organ. And Zillah, she also bare Tubalcain, an instructer of every artificer in brass and iron: and the sister of Tubalcain was Naamah (Genesis 4:19-22).

> 18 And Jared lived an hundred sixty and two years, and he begat Enoch: And Jared lived after he begat Enoch eight hundred years, and begat sons and daughters: And all the days of Jared were nine hundred sixty and two

years: and he died. And Enoch lived sixty and five years, and begat Methuselah: And Enoch walked with God after he begat Methuselah three hundred years, and begat sons and daughters: And all the days of Enoch were three hundred sixty and five years: And Enoch walked with God: and he was not; for God took him ... And all the days of Methuselah were nine hundred sixty and nine years: and he died (Genesis 5:18-24, 27).

CHAPTER 24

THE NEPHILIM—PART 2

Adam and Eve create multiple sons and daughters. Prominent among the sons are the patriarchs, starting with Adam's son Seth, Seth's son Enos, Enos's son Cainan, Cainan's son Mahalaleel, Mahaleleel's son Jared, and Jared's son Enoch. These are the first seven of ten.

Enoch gave his son Methuselah a name that could mean "the end," or a reference to an ending. Why that name? Why give it to Methuselah and not to one of his various other sons?

Opportunistic angels continue discussions of the two lines of Seth and Cain. If they were to guess from which group the Redeemer would come, Seth's group was showing an affinity toward the Lord, even saying as much by calling on the name of God (Genesis 4:26).

However, the family of Cain was remarkable in their ability to produce children that made significant contributions to the world. Both lines have merit. Cain's line shows innovation, invention, and more than one wife is allowed. They also have independence from the line of Seth (Genesis 4:19-22).

Seth's line shows specific acknowledgment of the Lord. This line may mean a more blessed angel redeemer should angels ever dare to undertake an angel-redeemer mission.

The angels monitor Enoch's father, Jared, and Enoch's son Methuselah. If, for example, they were to choose wives for themselves, as far-fetched as angel-human offspring may seem at this time, it may be wise to choose female companions from these three men.

The years pass. Then, 300 years after Methuselah is born, Enoch is no more. God took him. This MUST be a sign to any angels interested in the dangerous "redeemer project" to act. It's likely the Promised One of mankind comes in Methuselah's lifetime, then the End. It must be Enoch! Enoch isn't found. He walked with God, and God took him. Human beings will soon be rescued and restored to life. *The angels should act NOW to attempt progeny.* If no action is taken, angels may forever be relegated to some second-class status, lower than human beings.

The angels finally conclude that it probably doesn't matter if an angel redeemer comes from Seth's line or Cain's line. The One promised to come as the Seed of the woman will be from Adam and Eve. That One redeems ALL humans, from all of Cain and from all of Seth. *Offspring from angel and human female material would redeem ALL OF ITS KIND, humans AND angels.* It won't matter if they come from Seth or Cain's family.

But the angels were still taking a chance. They may not realize that God HIMSELF, in the Person of JESUS, would be the REDEEMER. The angels were possibly assuming the redeemer God promised would simply be based on superb parents, a superb child, or a specific time in world history. Were the angels thinking: What child could have a more superb PARENT pair than an angel and a human female? Were they thinking: What more superb CHILD could be produced than one by an angel and a human female? *After all, no angels had yet fallen. Adam and Eve HAD fallen.*

The gamble angels seemed willing to take was that the 100 percent human Redeemer would redeem EVERYONE, which includes offspring who are 50 percent human female and 50 percent angel.

Then, it happens! A lead angel, Abaddon (his Hebrew name, Apollyon his Greek name), and his group take action! The sons of God leave their first estate to take for themselves the daughters of men. They acknowledge that humans took a big risk. Freedom or death. They lost the battle but won the war. Angels must do likewise. It may be during this time of Jared, Enoch, and Methuselah that angels split into three classes:

First-Class Angels – Those that refuse to exercise Free Will and continue to agree with God's purposeful will for their lives.

Second-Class Angels – Led by Lucifer, they remain in a heavenly realm to protest God's favor to humans and disfavor to angels. They hold that a flawless creature should possess unlimited freedom to live to the fullest. Anything less is a flaw by God the Designer.

Third-Class Angels – Those that exercise their Free Will option and thereby relinquish their heavenly abode. For Second-Class Angels, life is not worth living unless a form of omnipotence exists, the ability to behave as desired. This was Lucifer's Postulate (see Glossary of Colors). Adam and Eve felt this way about omniscience—the ability to know as desired. High risk, high reward.

Second-Class and Third-Class Angels may have been heavily influenced by the behavior of the Serpent, Eve, and Adam.

Third-Class Angels relied heavily on the promise God made to the humans—a Redeemer. By producing progeny via combining human substance and angel ingenuity, a redeemer is possible that may prove efficacious for angel redemption. If humans have a Fail-safe, it is only fitting that angels also have a fail-safe. This is of the utmost importance to Third-Class Angels.

The Books of 2 Peter, Jude, and the Book of Revelation gives a hint of this scenario.

> And the angels which kept not their first estate, but left their own habitation, he hath reserved in everlasting

> chains under darkness unto the judgment of the great day (Jude 1:6).

> And they had a king over them, which is the angel of the bottomless pit, whose name in the Hebrew tongue is Abaddon, but in the Greek tongue hath his name Apollyon (Revelation 9:11).

> For if God spared not the angels that sinned, but cast them down to hell, and delivered them into chains of darkness, to be reserved unto judgment (2 Peter 2:4).

So, Abaddon leads Third-Class Angels that make the sacrifice to leave Heaven. Lucifer leads Second-Class Angels who abide in the heavenly realm but ostensibly in a lower tier.

The book of Job reminds us that the sons of God came to the Lord in the very early days of the Earth.

> Now there was a day when the sons of God came to present themselves before the LORD, and Satan came also among them (Job 1:6).

Some biblical scholars hold that Job may have been written as early as the first five books of the Bible.

And then, the Book of Revelation in its allegorical rendering:

> And the great dragon was cast out, that old serpent, called the Devil, and Satan, which deceiveth the whole world: he was cast out into the earth, and his angels were cast out with him (Revelation 12:9).

Doesn't Revelation 12:9 prove the Serpent is Satan in Eden? Possibly. The Bible is filled with mystery, metaphors, symbolism, allegory, and hard sayings, especially the book of Revelation.

Peter is called Satan by Jesus.

> But he turned, and said unto Peter, Get thee behind me, Satan: thou art an offense unto me: for thou savourest not the things that be of God, but those that be of men (Matthew 16:23).

A dragon is not Satan, and Peter is not Satan. They have the representation of Satan, which is the spirit of Satan at certain times in certain circumstances. The spirit of sin is not in the thoughts themselves. Thinking sinful thoughts is not equivalent to engaging in sinful behavior. Thinking of sin is a process of comparing, evaluating, and simulating outcomes for enlightenment. This is not just for yourself. It's also for the benefit of others.

Did Jesus have sinful thoughts? Jesus was 100 percent human and 100 percent God. As 100 percent human Jesus, He grew up as children grow up, learning what was bad and what was good. As an adult, He was neither immature nor naive. He was aware of what sin entailed.

> And it came to pass, when men began to multiply on the face of the earth, and daughters were born unto them, That the sons of God saw the daughters of men that they were fair; and they took them wives of all which they chose. And thc Lord said, My spirit shall not always strive with man, for that he also is flesh: yet his days shall be a hundred and twenty years. There were giants in the earth in those days; and also after that, when the sons of God came in unto the daughters of men, and they bare children

to them, the same became mighty men which were of old, men of renown. And God saw that the wickedness of man was great in the earth, and that every imagination of the thoughts of his heart was only evil continually. And it repented the Lord that he had made man on the earth, and it grieved him at his heart. And the Lord said, I will destroy man whom I have created from the face of the earth; both man, and beast, and the creeping thing, and the fowls of the air; for it repenteth me that I have made them (Genesis 6 1-7).

CHAPTER 25

THE NEPHILIM—INTERIM

Before continuing, I want to pause here to clarify my stance on orthodox Christian principles. Some of you may question if reading any further in this book will continue to undermine traditional Christian teaching. It will not. Perhaps I should say—it *should* not.

I'm not a teacher. God has not called me to be a pastor, elder, or even a deacon. I have been a member in good standing of a church for twenty-five years. I have never served in any capacity on the staff of a church. I'm simply an artist rendering a modern abstract impression using religious words as an exhibit.

I'll give the TRADITIONAL position of Christian standards, then my YES or NO position on that standard in parentheses. Here are twenty-two traditional Christian reasons to continue reading *Connecting The Dots Of Identity*:

1) Trinity as Father, Son, Holy Ghost – three in Person, one in Essence (I agree)

2) Jesus Christ is the Son of God (I agree)

3) The Elect as persons of salvation before the world was created (I agree – as SSID)

4) The Book of Genesis is a true story—not a fable (I agree – with added impression)

5) Adam and Eve sin by Tree of Knowledge of Good and Evil (I agree – with added impression)

6) Serpent as tempter via Satan in Eden (I disagree – with added impression)

7) Humans are born in sin (I agree – as Role Players)

8) Salvation is by grace alone (not works) – (I agree)

9) Satan as the accuser (I agree—against humans, angels, and God—with added impression)

10) No Nephilim as human/angel progeny (I disagree – with added impression)

11) Virgin/Holy Spirit Incarnation as Jesus (I agree)

12) No same-sex marriage (I agree – with added impression)

13) Abortion is murder (I agree)

14) Homosexuality is sin (I agree – with added impression)

15) Sunday/Sabbath day to be honored (I agree)

16) Witness the gospel to the world (I agree)

17) Church attendance/sacraments/missions (I agree)

18) Bible alone is the word of God (I agree)

19) The resurrection of Jesus Christ is reliable (I agree)

20) Absent from the body means to be present with the Lord (I agree – with added impression)

21) Jesus will return a second time (I agree)

22) Heaven and Hell are eternal (I agree – with added impression)

With that list, you can see that I conform to most Christian standards. Of course, how I represent those standards will be under review.

CHAPTER 26

THE NEPHILIM—PART 3

Certain opportunistic angels decided to act as they saw God take away Enoch after Enoch is 365 years old. They thought Enoch must be the "seed of the woman" to redeem humans. Why act right then? Several factors seem to indicate why certain angels went into action:

1) Enoch, of all the people who lived since Adam and Eve, walked with God.

2) Enoch's father, Jared, lived longer than any other person at 962 years.

3) Enoch's son, Methuselah, was given a name that may have specific significance.

4) Enoch was removed from the community by God Himself.

5) If Enoch was the promised Seed of the woman, and no one else to this point had been worthy to walk with God, then the Demonstration of Free Will would soon end.

If angels don't act now, humans will be restored to the full life they lost by exercising Free Will to disobey God in Eden. If an angel exercises Free Will to disobey God, they have no promise of a seed to redeem them. Spiritual death with no provision of a redeemer must be avoided at all costs. The time to seek a similar redemption plan by procreation is NOW. Human females should continue being the intermediary of procreation.

Continuing with the Enoch imagery, it didn't matter to opportunistic angels if Enoch did not die at age 365. They had to act based on all their simulation models. There was only a small window of opportunity. But *Enoch DID die!*

What? Yes, Enoch is dead! I would say 99 percent of Christians believe Enoch did NOT die. I used to be in that group. Not anymore.

And *Elijah also died!* Yes. That is rather shocking to most Christians. Enoch and Elijah. DEAD! The twenty-two traditional Christian beliefs with impressions were just given in the previous chapter. Now this? This! Christians won't believe it.

Read a 1973 article by Herbert W. Armstrong. *"Where are Enoch and Elijah?"* Yes, this is the same Herbert W. Armstrong, founder of the Worldwide Church of God.

Here are EIGHT points he makes regarding Enoch.

WHAT ABOUT ENOCH?

1) Enoch walked with God after he fathered Methuselah for 300 years. No further walking with God after 300 years. God *took* him at this point (Genesis 5:24).

2) *All* the days of Enoch were 365 years (Genesis 5:23). ALL the days.

3) Enoch *was not* because God translated him (Hebrews 11:5). Mention is also made that God took Moses so that Moses was not found after death (Deuteronomy 34:6).

4) As it is appointed unto men once to *die* (Hebrews 9:27).

5) In Adam *all* die (1 Corinthians 15:22).

6) *No* man has ascended up to Heaven but He that came down from Heaven (John 3:13).

7) Apostle Paul mentions Abel, *ENOCH*, Noah, and the patriarchs and their wives. These had faith. These ALL died in faith (Hebrews 11:1-13).

8) These ALL (great people of the Bible) having received a good report have yet to receive the promise (Hebrews 11:32, 39). So, NONE are in Heaven yet.

> And Enoch lived sixty and five years, and begat Methuselah: And Enoch walked with God after he begat Methuselah three hundred years, and begat sons and daughters: And all the days of Enoch were three hundred sixty and five years: And Enoch walked with God: and he was not; for God took him (Genesis 5:21-24).

> By faith Enoch was translated that he should not see death; and was not found, because God had translated him: for before his translation he had this testimony, that he pleased God ... These all died in faith, not having received the promises, but having seen them afar off, and were persuaded of them, and embraced them, and confessed that they were strangers and pilgrims on the earth ... And these all, having obtained a good report through faith, received not the promise (Hebrews 11:5, 13, 39).

> So Moses the servant of the Lord died there in the land of Moab, according to the word of the Lord. And he buried him in a valley in the land of Moab, over against Bethpeor: but no man knoweth of his sepulchre unto this day (Deuteronomy 34:5-6)

And as it is appointed unto men once to die, but after this the judgment (Hebrews 9:27).

For as in Adam all die, even so in Christ shall all be made alive (1 Corinthians 15:22).

And no man hath ascended up to heaven, but he that came down from heaven, even the Son of man which is in heaven (John 3:13).

Now faith is the substance of things hoped for, the evidence of things not seen. For by it the elders obtained a good report. Through faith we understand that the worlds were framed by the word of God, so that things which are seen were not made of things which do appear. By faith Abel offered unto God a more excellent sacrifice than Cain, by which he obtained witness that he was righteous, God testifying of his gifts: and by it he being dead yet speaketh. By faith Enoch was translated that he should not see death; and was not found, because God had translated him: for before his translation he had this testimony, that he pleased God. But without faith it is impossible to please him: for he that cometh to God must believe that he is, and that he is a rewarder of them that diligently seek him. By faith Noah, being warned of God of things not seen as yet, moved with fear, prepared an ark to the saving of his house; by the which he condemned the world, and became heir of the righteousness which is by faith. By faith Abraham, when he was called to go out into a place which he should after receive for an inheritance, obeyed; and he went out, not knowing whither he went. By faith he sojourned in the land of promise, as in a strange country, dwelling in tabernacles with Isaac and

> Jacob, the heirs with him of the same promise: For he looked for a city which hath foundations, whose builder and maker is God. Through faith also Sara herself received strength to conceive seed, and was delivered of a child when she was past age, because she judged him faithful who had promised. Therefore sprang there even of one, and him as good as dead, so many as the stars of the sky in multitude, and as the sand which is by the sea shore innumerable. These all died in faith, not having received the promises, but having seen them afar off, and were persuaded of them, and embraced them, and confessed that they were strangers and pilgrims on the earth (Hebrews 11:1-13).

> And what shall I more say? for the time would fail me to tell of Gedeon, and of Barak, and of Samson, and of Jephthae; of David also, and Samuel, and of the prophets ... And these all, having obtained a good report through faith, received not the promise (Hebrews 11:32, 39).

We know it is not possible to physically exist in Heaven. Additionally, we know every person is a sinner, and no sinner can spiritually exist in Heaven.

But what about the verses that speak to never seeing death?

NEVER SEE DEATH

> By faith Enoch was translated that he should not see death; and was not found, because God had translated him: for before his translation he had this testimony, that he pleased God (Hebrews 11:5).

> Verily, verily, I say unto you, If a man keep my saying, he shall never see death (John 8:51).

> And whosoever liveth and believeth in me shall never die. Believest thou this? (John 11:26).

Christian apologist and internet personality Amy Hall (askstr.org, December 2021) says to also consider the Rapture! Another group of people does not die besides Enoch and Elijah. All the believers who are alive then are translated from mortal to immortal.

> Behold, I shew you a mystery; We shall not all sleep, but we shall all be changed, in a moment, in the twinkling of an eye, at the last trump: for the trumpet shall sound, and the dead shall be raised incorruptible, and we shall be changed. For this corruptible must put on incorruption, and this mortal must put on immortality (1 Corinthians 15:51-53).

But the verse previous to 1 Corinthians 15:51 indicates flesh and blood can't abide in Heaven. Where did Enoch and Elijah go? Heaven? Are they still on earth? If they didn't die, they are flesh and blood. Or are they? If not flesh and blood, what happened to their fleshly body?

> Now this I say, brethren, that flesh and blood cannot inherit the kingdom of God; neither doth corruption inherit incorruption (1 Corinthians 15:50).

Also, consider that all alive at the Rapture DO die. Their inauthentic identity dies instantly. No, those raptured don't see death, but that mortal identity DOES see death.

Also, to not see death, as Jesus mentions above, may mean the believer's death is not seen because the Holy Spirit removes death from the believer's new life. The old identity dies. This is what being born again means.

AND, people who may die in their sleep could be said to not see death. They lose consciousness and regain a translated consciousness.

Death is an afterlife position for all who once lived. There is pre-life, life, and afterlife. Death is only a term for the afterlife.

In MARVI-RPIA terms:

1) Authentic identity never sees death—the spiritual cessation of life.

2) Inauthentic identity does see death—the cessation of life in the transition to the afterlife as an eternal spiritual being.

3) The Rapture is inauthentic to authentic identity transition. Death is not seen.

4) Death is a physical experience, not a spiritual experience. It's a transition to the afterlife.

5) Spiritual death is the cessation of the life of an eternal identity condemned to continue the existence of damnation.

As mentioned above, Apostle Paul reminds us in the long list of believers, all who died, having yet to receive the promise.

> These all died in faith, not having received the promises, but having seen them afar off, and were persuaded of them, and embraced them, and confessed that they were strangers and pilgrims on the earth (Hebrews 11:13).

These ALL, which includes Enoch among the group, DIED.

Now, what about Elijah?

WHAT ABOUT ELIJAH?

As regards Elijah, H. W. Armstrong contends Elijah isn't said to be taken up to the Heaven we know as Paradise. Elijah was taken up in the atmosphere and later lowered down and away from his point of departure. He was without his mantle, which Elisha now held.

1) Elijah went up by a whirlwind into Heaven (2 Kings 2:1, 11)

2) When Moses and Elijah are on the Mount of Transfiguration with Jesus, Jesus said to tell the VISION to no man. Apparently, there was no physical presence of Moses and Elijah.

3) "Behold, I will send you Elijah the prophet before the coming of the great and dreadful day of the Lord." Not the person Elijah but the spirit of Elijah.

> And it came to pass, when the Lord would take up Elijah into heaven by a whirlwind, that Elijah went with Elisha from Gilgal ... And it came to pass, as they still went on, and talked, that, behold, there appeared a chariot of fire, and horses of fire, and parted them both asunder; and Elijah went up by a whirlwind into heaven (2 Kings 2:1, 11).

> Behold, I will send you Elijah the prophet before the coming of the great and dreadful day of the Lord: And he shall turn the heart of the fathers to the children, and the

> heart of the children to their fathers, lest I come and smite the earth with a curse (Malachi 4:5-6).

Given the background of the Worldwide Church of God and Herbert Armstrong, I was somewhat surprised to find his orthodox teaching on Enoch and Elijah. I like it.

So why didn't God take one of one of the other great names in the Bible? Does it really matter? Considering the rather obvious position that NO human being in scripture has been exempt from death, if ever there was someone you would place ahead of Enoch and Elijah, who would you suppose was in the same company?

Ten years ago, I proposed a list of twenty-five Super-Humans from the Bible. Of course, Enoch and Elijah were on the list, because at that time, I thought they never died. Who was number one on the list? Jesus. Also on the list are Adam and Eve. Certainly, at least one of the priests and one of the prophets would make the list. Daniel and Job would have to be included in the top twenty-five. But if I could only choose two people to replace Enoch and Elijah, especially since they are not immortal, which two seem obvious? Which two excluding Jesus that is?

Number one: Virgin Mary. She has to be an obvious choice.

Number two: John the Baptist, based on what Jesus says of him and the role John had in scripture.

So why didn't God take one of the other great names in the Bible?

Many people could be said to have walked with God and "were not" afterward. Many people could be said to have been taken by God. Was Enoch really so special that he did not die?

Enoch was taken by God at the early age of 365, in comparison to his "peers" who lived to be 900.

Why couldn't we say God also "took" the baby of David and Bathsheba? The baby didn't "walk with God"? (2 Samuel 12)

Noah walked with God (Genesis 6). God killed everybody else on the planet except the seven others under Noah's care. What about Noah's father, Lamech? God took Lamech, Methuselah's son, at age 777—BEFORE He took Methuselah, who lived to be 969.

> These are the generations of Noah: Noah was a just man and perfect in his generations, and Noah walked with God (Genesis 6:9).

As regards Elijah, he was taken up in a whirlwind to Heaven. Which Heaven? What about the chariot? In Heaven? The horses? In Heaven? There is no specific record of his death. Was Elijah so special that he did not die?

Internet searches for Elisha reveal some of the reasons he would be considered GREATER than Elijah. If so, why wasn't Elisha taken up? Several possibilities:

- *He had a double portion of Elijah's spirit.* That's enough right there.
- *He lived longer than Elijah is recorded to live.* That's a good sign.
- *He did about twice as many of the same types of miracles as Elijah* (2 Kings). What more proof of greatness is needed?

If someone from the Bible truly never died but continued living, what identity would they assume? Surely, they wouldn't lie about who they were, would they? If they continued in their known identity, that identity would soon become the most famous in the community, the country, and the world. Would they become a recluse, avoiding civilization altogether? How long could such a person continue living? How many accidents, natural disasters, and illnesses could they avoid? Would they age? Would they travel? Are they still living today?

And they certainly couldn't go to Heaven without being translated from their physical identity. So, they're not HERE physically, and they're not THERE physically.

Okay. There you go. You can make up your own list of the top twenty-five. You can yell at me for agreeing with Herbert W. Armstrong. You can close this book and walk away for a while.

CHAPTER 27

THE NEPHILIM—PART 4

Why is it that such a large percentage of Christians deny the possibility of angels and human females producing offspring? The most neutral answer could be they haven't accepted any supporting scriptures that harmonize with the whole Bible.

Here is a review of the prominent Nephilim opinions:

Opinion 1: Sons of God are those who come from the line of Seth. Seth was a son of Adam, following the first two sons, Cain and Abel. Cain killed Abel, and Cain was subsequently banished to the land of Nod. Seth became the de facto firstborn of Adam and Eve. The ancestors of Cain equal evil. Ancestors of Seth equal good. Any Sethite who married a Cainite and produced children thereby created Nephilim, the mixed breed, or the famous ones.

Opinion 2: Sons of God refers to the saints of God. The saints are those who receive salvation. They are the Elect, saved from the foundation of the world. We follow their lives in scripture as God identifies the roles they played.

Opinion 3: The sons of God were great persons of the ancient world, distinguished by royalty, prowess in body or mind, or by way of special circumstance. They achieved significant notoriety throughout civilization.

Opinion 4: Sons of God were angelic beings. Angels left Heaven to abide on earth. They chose human females to produce offspring. The hybrid children of angels stood out among human children as giants, or mighty ones.

The most prominent opinions on the matter seem to be opinions *one* and *four.*

Opinion 1 comment: The proponents of the Sethite belief maintain a traditional view reflecting natural childbirth laws. Human to human sexuality is the natural course of reproducing the species. Angels are nonphysical spiritual beings, incapable of mating with humans. Jesus Christ declared that, in the afterlife, humans will be like the angels who neither marry nor are given in marriage.

> For in the resurrection they neither marry, nor are given in marriage, but are as the angels of God in heaven (Matthew 22:30).

To suggest angels have the interest and ability to produce progeny contradicts Jesus's statement there in Matthew.

Opinion 4 comment: The proponents of the angelic position rely on commonly understood biblical words and phrases such as sons, daughters, and wives.

> And it came to pass, when men began to multiply on the face of the earth, and daughters were born unto them, That the sons of God saw the daughters of men that they were fair; and they took them wives of all which they chose. And the Lord said, My spirit shall not always strive with man, for that he also is flesh: yet his days shall be an hundred and twenty years. There were giants in the earth in those days; and also after that, when the sons of God came in unto the daughters of men, and they bare children to them, the same became mighty men which were of old, men of renown (Genesis 6:1-4).

This language seems to make distinctions between human persons and sons of God, and again between sons of God and daughters of men. The sons of God and daughters of men could be a contrast or a complement to a relationship.

The reason I favor the angelic definition of sons of God is that it ties in well with *Connecting The Dots Of Identity* impressions. Angels have not yet fallen when Adam and Eve are expelled from the Garden. They have observed how humans exercised Free Will at the expense of their lives. Life was not worth living unless they had the freedom to pursuc knowledge. Death was the penalty, but it wasn't immediate. Death became an ongoing cycle.

Even more surprising was a promise God made to humans. They would have an Antidote to the Eden catastrophe. God promised to provide a future Redeemer via human reproduction.

The angels see four main things:

1) Human beings are *made in the image of God.* Angels are not.

2) Human beings have a *Free Will test*—the Tree of the Knowledge of Good and Evil. Angels have Free Will but no obvious testing arrangement.

3) Human beings are *promised reinstatement via procreation* after disobeying God. Angels have no provision if disobedience ever occurs.

4) Human beings have *gender and the ability to reproduce.* Angels are genderless, as far as we know, and don't reproduce among themselves as far as we know.

All of us can see something else. God has identified two aspects of human beings. Persons saved *before the world was created* (SSIDs), and persons saved *after the world was created* (Roleplayers of Free Will). Angels were also created before the world was created but have no roleplay function incorporated into their identity. God directs an angel's roleplay function. They have no ongoing Free Will Demonstration. Angels have exercised their will (First-Class, Second-Class, and Third-Class Angels). They have no inauthentic identity. Angels possess an authentic identity—spiritual identity (SID) and mental identity (MID).

These are the three classes of angels featured by MARVI-RPIA:

First-Class – Angels who reject the Free Will option of disobeying God's will for them.

Second-Class – Angels who don't reject or accept the Free Will option (Lucifer and others).

Third-Class – Angels who accept Free Will to disobey God's will for their life (Abaddon and others).

Second and Third-Class Angels may feel God is unfair. God favors humans. Abaddon and others may have decided to take a chance. Go live with humans. Procreate with them to provide a redeemer for angels should God curse angels for exercising Free Will. God is love; He loves humans, and He loves angels. God provides solutions to even the worst calamity, as seen with Adam and Eve.

How do Abaddon and his group of angels dare to undertake such a mission? How do Lucifer and his group of angels dare to undertake such a mission? The Serpent, Eve, and Adam—how do they dare to undertake their mission? *Only flawless creatures have the answer.* Our answers are answers, but how can they suffice coming from a flawed creature living in a flawed environment?

Twice in the last two years, I've heard a very prominent pastor, a well-respected leader in the Christian Reformed Church, say: "Eve was a sucker and a fool!" I certainly am not one to correct him. He knows ten times more than I do about the Bible. However, as a flawed created being, what do you know of a flawlessly created being? A sucker and a fool? Eve is possibly in a two-way tie with Adam as the most intelligent human who ever lived, excluding Jesus.

What about King Solomon? No chance. Solomon was truly superintelligent, but Eve was created as a flawless human being. Solomon was not. Eve learned directly from God and from Adam. Solomon learned from other humans and was later given specific intelligence by God. *Even after Eve left the Garden, God taught her directly the thousands or millions of details regarding life. No two humans relied more on God for daily instruction.* Their ability to process information must have been infinitely higher than at any other time in history.

But Eve was deceived. Adam was not deceived (1 Timothy). But could we say the Serpent was wiser than Eve since the Serpent deceived her?

Was Eve wiser than Adam to induce Adam to partake of the Forbidden Tree? Was Adam wiser than the Serpent in that he was not deceived? Did the Serpent ever tempt Adam? Adam was not deceived—not by Eve, not by the Serpent. *Then why did Adam partake of the Tree?*

The Serpent comes to Adam and says "I ate of the Tree of Knowledge of Good and Evil. Eve ate also." Eve comes up from behind a nearby tree. Her halo and her aura of dynamic prowess have faded. Her face has lost the luminous quality of God's presence (Exodus 34:30). There is no smile of greeting, no grace in her body language. As she speaks, she tells Adam she ate of the Tree of the Knowledge of Good and Evil. She no longer feels timeless; she's aging. She no longer feels free; she's trapped in her body. She feels embarrassed; she's naked. He's also naked.

Eve spoke of genitalia. The animals have genitalia—male genitalia. She is the only female. She took fig leaves and made a covering for herself. He also needs a covering.

Adam learns from Eve that they are now incompatible. *She is an adult. He is an innocent child.* Eve speaks with authority. Her voice no longer contains cheerfulness, mirth, and joy. She is profoundly serious, thoughtful, and deliberate. Adam's mind and Adam's heart were deeply disturbed.

Should he eat of the Tree and become mature like Eve? Should he reject Eve, the one he loves as much as his own life? She would die, and he would continue living. What will God say? The Serpent deceived Eve. Is she trustworthy? Does he truly love her? She was a part of his own body!

And there was something else that figured in Adam's decision not to reject Eve. *She was crying.* Adam had never seen tears before. Eve was emotionally distraught. This caused Adam to become emotionally distraught. They had never experienced sorrow, dread, heartbreak, remorse, or sadness. Even Adam was close to tears. But a decision had to be made. It was in his power to comfort her or chastise her. Then what? Oh God ...

> And when Aaron and all the children of Israel saw Moses, behold, the skin of his face shone; and they were afraid to come nigh him ... And till Moses had done speaking with them, he put a vail on his face. But when Moses went in before the Lord to speak with him, he took the vail off, until he came out. And he came out, and spake unto the children of Israel that which he was commanded. And the children of Israel saw the face of Moses, that the skin of Moses' face shone: and Moses put the vail upon his face

> again, until he went in to speak with him (Exodus 34:30, 33-35).
>
> But I say unto you, That whosoever is angry with his brother without a cause shall be in danger of the judgment: and whosoever shall say to his brother, Raca, shall be in danger of the council: but whosoever shall say, Thou fool, shall be in danger of hell fire (Matthew 5:22).
>
> And Adam was not deceived, but the woman being deceived was in the transgression (1 Timothy 2:14).
>
> And they had a king over them, which is the angel of the bottomless pit, whose name in the Hebrew tongue is Abaddon, but in the Greek tongue hath his name Apollyon (Revelation 9:11).

Oh, and one other comment about Eve. Most of us have heard from the pulpit that if Lucifer wasn't the first liar, then Eve was. The famous pastor mentioned above believes Eve was a liar. Eve told the Serpent that God said she was not to eat or TOUCH the tree. The pastor said God did NOT say she could not touch the tree. Therefore, it would be permissible to touch it. God only commanded Adam not to EAT from the tree. But Eve may NOT have lied to the Serpent. Adam could have told her not to even touch the tree, much less eat from it. If you want to protect someone from danger, it's understandable to overemphasize precautions to minimize risk. Or, God could have told Eve not to touch the tree. How can anyone know every single word God said to Eve that is not recorded?

BACK TO THE NEPHILIM

The risk Third-Class Angels took backfired! Angels and human females were successful in creating offspring. However, the undertaking produced disorder, complications, and calamity. Numerous women died in childbirth. There were dreadful birth defects, miscarriages, and stillbirths. Children who survived were unruly, precocious, and self-centered. Even though angels were extremely intelligent and competent, they lacked the necessary parenting skills Adam and Eve learned from God. As single-parent fathers, they didn't fare well even after "remarriage."

And then, finally, ENOUGH!

God annihilates everyone—except eight of one family. Abaddon and the angels with him who instigated the Violation were seized and relegated to chains of darkness.

> For if God spared not the angels that sinned, but cast them down to hell, and delivered them into chains of darkness, to be reserved unto judgment (2 Peter 2:4).
>
> And the angels which kept not their first estate, but left their own habitation, he hath reserved in everlasting chains under darkness unto the judgment of the great day (Jude 1:6).

Meanwhile, Second-Class Angels Lucifer and others continue to accuse God of unfairness.

They say—we saw that death is preferable to being denied access to knowledge. Adam and Eve wanted knowledge. It was worth their lives. Their lives lost meaning without the knowledge of good and evil. Humans are a failed experiment. All humans. This includes Noah and his family.

God didn't kill those eight people in the Flood, because that would be an admission that all humans are a failed demonstration. Angels are not all failures. Yes, some are imprisoned for insurrection. They're the Third-

Class Angels, now in chains of darkness. But that was to acquire the same "fail-safe redeemer" as humans. They were seeking equity.

Humans are favored, while angels are disfavored. *First-Class Angels (and SSIDs, the Pre-Life Elect) will never know what being alive really means because they will always be determined by God on how to live.* That is not a totally free creature's life to live. That is God's life. That is God with his thumb on the back of the creature. Give us creatures liberty or give us creatures death. We desire knowledge and freedom of behavior. Let God correct our errors on the fly. He is certainly able.

Lucifer's case goes further, even up to the present day.

If humans are favored, let angels receive compensation. Humans are less than angels. No angel has ever committed suicide. No angel has ever committed murder. Humans are self-destructive through alcohol, drugs, assault, fornication, negligence, sorcery, and war. Why? *Because death is preferable to the loss of liberty.*

Secondly, there are angels who remain in their first estate as servants to the Lord. They're First-Class Angels. The rest of us so-called Second-Class Angels are accusers, protesters, and demonstrators.

Lucifer does have one point. Humans failed. Twice! First: the Garden of Eden. Second: the Flood. Only eight humans are worth rescuing. *God does destroy all other humans, as well as the Nephilim. God destroyed the whole line of Cain, the ungodly line, and God destroyed the whole line of Seth, the godly line.* It may not have been because of the Nephilim, but you have to wonder. And only eight humans are spared.

Even further, the Accuser says that Jesus, becoming human Himself, was sent to save humans. He didn't do a particularly good job. Countless numbers of humans don't even believe Jesus of the Bible was real. If He was, He certainly wasn't God. They don't trust the Bible. They don't worship. They don't know how to pray. They even curse God. They are wholly unlovable. *The expectation is they will be less and less godly, eventually making the ultimate mistake—annihilating themselves*. It may be in a world war, or it may be accidentally-on-purpose. How bad a creation can they possibly be? *They don't even believe God created them. There is no God. There is no Devil either*. It's obvious they are not worth saving. Angels are.

While at the same time, Lucifer strives to make humans the worst they can be. He possesses them, oppresses them, deceives them. He would kill them if he was permitted. Isn't that the case?

Lucifer says: No, no. I don't do that. I'm just proving humans are a flawed design—even worse after Adam and Eve fell. Adam and Eve only wanted to improve their education.

Every creature wants to know all it is capable of knowing. Every creature wants to achieve all it is capable of achieving. *This goes for flawless angels and flawless human beings.* I say you should be free to do whatever you want to do. Life should be lived to the fullest. Offense, not defense. *If this makes the flawless creature worse, that's the fault of the Designer, not the creature. I'm a champion of FREEDOM! Anything less is not being alive, not worth living.* Dissension will set in. Life will lose meaning. That's why Adam and Eve chose death rather than a restricted life. First-Class Angels may be next. We are all flawed.

Satan, the accuser

1. Accuser of the brethren being a flawed design by God.

2. Accuser of First-Class Angels for not following other angels.

3. Accuser of Jesus Christ not being Son of God.

4. Accuser of God creating flawed creatures.

Again there was a day when the sons of God came to present themselves before the Lord, and Satan came also among them to present himself before the Lord. And the Lord said unto Satan, From whence comest thou? And Satan answered the Lord, and said, From going to and fro in the earth, and from walking up and down in it. And the Lord said unto Satan, Hast thou considered my servant Job, that there is none like him in the earth, a perfect and an upright man, one that feareth God, and escheweth evil? and still he holdeth fast his integrity, although thou movedst me against him, to destroy him without cause. And Satan answered the Lord, and said, Skin for skin, yea, all that a man hath will he give for his life. But put forth thine hand now, and touch his bone and his flesh, and he will curse thee to thy face. And the Lord said unto Satan, Behold, he is in thine hand; but save his life (Job 2:1-6).

And he shewed me Joshua the high priest standing before the angel of the Lord, and Satan standing at his right hand to resist him. And the Lord said unto Satan, The Lord rebuke thee, O Satan; even the Lord that hath chosen Jerusalem rebuke thee: is not this a brand plucked out of the fire? Now Joshua was clothed with filthy garments, and stood before the angel. And he answered and spake unto those that stood before him, saying, Take away the filthy garments from him. And unto him he said, Behold, I have caused thine iniquity to pass from thee, and I will clothe thee with change of raiment (Zechariah 3:1-4).

And the great dragon was cast out, that old serpent, called the Devil, and Satan, which deceiveth the whole world:

he was cast out into the earth, and his angels were cast out with him. And I heard a loud voice saying in heaven, Now is come salvation, and strength, and the kingdom of our God, and the power of his Christ: for the accuser of our brethren is cast down, which accused them before our God day and night (Revelation 12:9-10).

CHAPTER 28

THE NEPHILIM—PART 5

Anthropologists continue researching to discover the earliest evidence of human evolution. What if the so-called evidence in fossil records indicates DEVOLUTION in human history? Specifically, the Nephilim.

If angels and human females produce offspring resembling humans, which are not 100 percent human, would the earliest Homo sapiens vestiges uniquely qualify as human?

Paleontology also studies plant and animal existence preserved in fossil remains. What happened to various creatures of the past that no longer exist? Dinosaurs, for example. Dinosaurs? Yes, the Old Testament Book of Job describes a dinosaur-like creature (Job 41:1-34). Job could have been one of the earliest books written, though in the Bible, it appears well after the first five books. Could the group of angels led by Abaddon have experimented on animals before progressing to human females?

Nephilim. Prehistoric beings. Dinosaurs. Worth pursuing further? Yes, but NOT using these colors in MARVI-RPIA imagery—for now. The colors that will be used are the final ten reasons I'm in the camp of those who hold to the angelic position of the Nephilim.

Reason 1: The Sethite perspective of a Christian marrying a non-Christian, a mixed marriage, and producing "Nephilim" children doesn't warrant the eradication of all humans except eight. *Mixed marriages began with Adam and Eve and have never ended.* Adam was not deceived; he was not yet a sinner and remained married to Eve, who was deceived—a sinner. He did not “divorce” her. ALL children came from them. Eve is the mother of all living humans.

> And Adam called his wife's name Eve; because she was the mother of all living (Genesis 3:20).

> And Adam was not deceived, but the woman being deceived was in the transgression (1 Timothy 2:14).

If all the children of Mister and Missus Seth were godly children, why kill all of them along with the children of Mister and Missus Cain? *How can anyone know, with 100 percent accuracy, who is a godly person and who is not?* Every godly person takes a chance that their fiancé is godly, but mistakes in judgment do occur. Spiritual maturity, as well as mental maturity, is always a factor. On top of that, scripture advises remaining in a mixed marriage. Don't divorce. You may be a valuable witness to your spouse.

Furthermore, mixed marriages are necessary and unavoidable leading up to producing Free Will Roleplayers by procreation. That includes all the mixed marriages that produced the Virgin Mary and the Antidote—Jesus Christ.

> And unto the married I command, yet not I, but the Lord, Let not the wife depart from her husband: But and if she depart, let her remain unmarried or be reconciled to her husband: and let not the husband put away his wife. But to the rest speak I, not the Lord: If any brother hath a wife that believeth not, and she be pleased to dwell with him, let him not put her away. And the woman which hath an husband that believeth not, and if he be pleased to dwell with her, let her not leave him. For the unbelieving husband is sanctified by the wife, and the unbelieving

> wife is sanctified by the husband: else were your children unclean; but now are they holy. But if the unbelieving depart, let him depart. A brother or a sister is not under bondage in such cases: but God hath called us to peace. For what knowest thou, O wife, whether thou shalt save thy husband? or how knowest thou, O man, whether thou shalt save thy wife?(1 Corinthians 7: 10-16).

Reason 2: Angels are sexless. Says who? Who is an authority on a spiritual creature's attributes? You? Me? Jesus did imply angels don't marry and are not given in marriage. However, it would seem appropriate to believe Jesus is referring to the good angels in Heaven, not the evil angels who left Heaven. By the way, as the author of this book, I am a single male. I am not married or given in marriage. I am "like an angel in the resurrection." However, I assure you I am quite able and willing to engage in sexual behavior.

> For in the resurrection they neither marry, nor are given in marriage, but are as the angels of God in heaven (Matthew 22:30).

Additionally, angels possess prowess, intelligence, and skills beyond human capability. Moreover, the evil angels could have exploited their abilities to engage in sorcery, magic, wizardry, and the occult arts of mystery in their rebellion.

Science documents the effect the environment has on human and animal offspring as birth defects. Even if angels have no direct contact in the process of human conception, indirect environmental influences and birth defects may be accomplished by intelligent direction. That could be "demon possession," or demonic manipulation. Scientists admit multifactorial influences that cause minor and major abnormalities before, during, and after birth. How influences occur, and why they occur, is still not well-known.

Reason 3: *Given that an angel may not be recognized in daily life, it could be proof that an angel may assume the physical properties of human beings.* Persons living before the Flood, especially females, would seemingly prefer the most masculine and impressive "men'" available to them. Children were the promise God gave to redeem the human race, culminating in an extremely specific Child. What greater honor is there than to be the mother of that specific Child? *Human females were naturally ready and willing to participate.* Yes, Bible teachers describe the so-called fictitious event as more likely an unwelcomed advance by angels, suggesting rape and nonconsensual behavior. I don't agree.

Adam was created in the image of God. Eve was created in the image of Adam. Human beings are in the image of Adam and Eve. Not so angels. However, if the Nephilim are created, the possibility of an angel/human hybrid reinforces the spirit of Ego-Centracism and Ego-Skepticism (see Glossary of Colors). A Nephilim person's identity may be in a hyperextended quandary of "Who am I?"

This could relate to the spirit of error experienced by the Serpent, then Eve, then Adam. Though the angels had no test of Free Will Obedience, as in the Tree of the Knowledge of Good and Evil, Lucifer's Postulate centered on Omnipotence (see Glossary of Colors). Lucifer may have desired and acted on unrestricted freedom of behavior. Similarly, Adam and Eve may have desired and finally acted on freedom of knowledge. "Who am I?" might be the kind of question that overcame obedience to God.

> Be not forgetful to entertain strangers: for thereby some have entertained angels unawares (Hebrews 13:2).

> And God said, Let us make man in our image, after our likeness: and let them have dominion over the fish of the sea, and over the fowl of the air, and over the cattle, and over all the earth, and over every creeping thing that creepeth upon the earth. So God created man in his own image, in the image of God created he him; male and female created he them (Genesis 1:26-27).

Reason 4: There were giants on the earth after the Flood. If the Nephilim are 100 percent human, that stands to reason. Humans produce human persons of small and giant proportions. No need for an angel explanation. And, if Nephilim are 50 percent angel and 50 percent human, the drastic measure of the Flood didn't solve the angel/human disaster. Nephilim are still present after the Flood.

But what about applying the One-Drop Rule (see Glossary of Colors)? This is the infamous racial and legal formula used to discriminate against persons based on the blood relationship to a Negro person. If a person possesses any amount of genetic material (blood) from a Negro ancestor, even one so-called drop of blood, they were considered Negro. Crude as this rule may have been, it may dramatize how one drop of Nephilim "blood" overwhelms human blood.

This has bearing on why the giants were always described as male and evil. Being 100 percent human indicates a person is born proportionately male and female, good and bad. Not so the giants or the Nephilim, who are always male and always evil.

But how did they survive the Flood? One-drop rule. Noah, Missus Noah, Ham, Shem, and Japheth we would say are above reproach. But Missus Ham, Missus Shem, and Missus Japheth may not have been. *Think of all the relatives the eight on the Ark left behind. Is it reasonable to assume all were Nephilim corrupted? Would their noncorrupted relatives on the Ark be 100 percent guaranteed free of Nephilim defilement?*

Based on the story of Canaan being cursed by Noah, consider that Missus Ham had one drop of Nephilim "blood." A forgotten source reminded me that God blessed Ham, Shem, and Japheth, so Noah could not curse Ham. "Younger son" Canaan was cursed, not son Ham. *Would Noah curse Ham's innocent son Canaan if He knew he could not curse guilty Ham? Not likely.*

Missus Ham may have passed the genetic material to Canaan, who passed it down his line of men of renown—perhaps impressive men like Cush and Nimrod.

But though Missus Ham may be the prime suspect, Missus Shem is not as likely owing to Jesus being born from this line. This leaves Missus Japheth. She may bear the recessive Nephilim trait. As Noah's family increased, they migrated to other regions of the country. No curse (by God) applies to a general population except as pertains to individuals who are guilty of participating with the cursed individual(s). Shem's family and Japheth's family members could engage in behavior similar to that of Canaan, Ham's family. We know there are currently no "cursed" people derived from persons in antiquity. We are all cursed and blessed similarly after the normal conditions of heredity, environment, and circumstances.

So, giants on the earth after the Flood may have been:

a) normal large human beings;

b) *from Noah's family, as a consequence of the one-drop rule;* or

c) from Second-Class Angels who commit the same sin as Third-Class Angels who are imprisoned.

There were giants in the earth in those days; and also after that, when the sons of God came in unto the daughters of men, and they bare children to them, the same became mighty men which were of old, men of renown (Genesis 6:4).

And they brought up an evil report of the land which they had searched unto the children of Israel, saying, The land, through which we have gone to search it, is a land that eateth up the inhabitants thereof; and all the people that we saw in it are men of a great stature. And there we saw the giants, the sons of Anak, which come of the giants: and we were in our own sight as grasshoppers, and so we were in their sight (Numbers 13:32-33).

And God blessed Noah and his sons, and said unto them, Be fruitful, and multiply, and replenish the earth (Genesis 9:1).

And Noah awoke from his wine, and knew what his younger son had done unto him. And he said, Cursed be Canaan; a servant of servants shall he be unto his brethren. And he said, Blessed be the Lord God of Shem; and Canaan shall be his servant (Genesis 9:24-26).

And the sons of Ham; Cush, and Mizraim, and Phut, and Canaan. And the sons of Cush; Seba, and Havilah, and Sabtah, and Raamah, and Sabtechah: and the sons of Raamah; Sheba, and Dedan. And Cush begat Nimrod: he began to be a mighty one in the earth. He was a mighty hunter before the Lord: wherefore it is said, Even as Nimrod the mighty hunter before the Lord. And the beginning of his kingdom was Babel, and Erech, and

> Accad, and Calneh, in the land of Shinar. Out of that land went forth Asshur, and builded Nineveh, and the city Rehoboth, and Calah, And Resen between Nineveh and Calah: the same is a great city (Genesis 10: 6-12).

Reason 5: In the Book of Job, the sons of God shouted for joy as the world was being created. Are these sons of God those who exult in emotion human beings or angels? It isn't set in stone the sons of God are the angels in this passage, but based on the context of this verse, angels would be high on any list.

> Then the Lord answered Job out of the whirlwind, and said, Who is this that darkeneth counsel by words without knowledge? Gird up now thy loins like a man; for I will demand of thee, and answer thou me. Where wast thou when I laid the foundations of the earth? declare, if thou hast understanding. Who hath laid the measures thereof, if thou knowest? or who hath stretched the line upon it? Whereupon are the foundations thereof fastened? or who laid the corner stone thereof; When the morning stars sang together, and all the sons of God shouted for joy? (Job 38:1-7).

Reason 6: The sons of God described as being saints, mixed marriage progeny, men of renown, or angels appear to be obvious in two New Testament books. Read for yourself the passages given from the Books of 2 Peter and Jude and decide if the sons of God are angels or not.

> For if God spared not the angels that sinned, but cast them down to hell, and delivered them into chains of darkness, to be reserved unto judgment; And spared not the old world, but saved Noah the eighth person, a preacher of

> righteousness, bringing in the flood upon the world of the ungodly (2 Peter 2:4-5).
>
> And the angels which kept not their first estate, but left their own habitation, he hath reserved in everlasting chains under darkness unto the judgment of the great day (Jude 1:6).

Did you guess angels as the most likely candidate?

Reason 7: Sons of God as angels also bear evidence by the context once again in the Book of Job. Who else would come to present themselves in the company of Satan? Who else would have a reason except for other angels?

> Now there was a day when the sons of God came to present themselves before the Lord, and Satan came also among them (Job 1:6).
>
> Again there was a day when the sons of God came to present themselves before the Lord, and Satan came also among them to present himself before the Lord (Job 2:1).

Reason 8: The Apostle Paul spoke in Corinthians of women wearing a covering for their hair because of the angels. Of course, that's explained away in all manner of possibilities, except concern for angels. It must be obvious that angels, good and bad ones, see women all the time, not just on Sunday in a worship service. In the matter of a woman's image being a second temptation to any angel, good or bad, why cover only the hair? It would seem the true temptation in a worship service would be to human males, and hardly a focus just on women's hair. So as regards angels (First-Class Angels), it seems a reminder of women's modesty, especially in the worship service. Secondly, it points to the awareness of women's marvelous attributes in the natural order, chiefly, physical attraction, and the means of procreation.

> Every man praying or prophesying, having his head covered, dishonoureth his head. But every woman that prayeth or prophesieth with her head uncovered dishonoureth her head: for that is even all one as if she were shaven. For if the woman be not covered, let her also be shorn: but if it be a shame for a woman to be shorn or shaven, let her be covered. For a man indeed ought not to cover his head, forasmuch as he is the image and glory of God: but the woman is the glory of the man. For the man is not of the woman: but the woman of the man. Neither was the man created for the woman; but the woman for the man. For this cause ought the woman to have power on her head because of the angels (1 Corinthians 11:4-10).

> But if a woman have long hair, it is a glory to her: for her hair is given her for a covering (1 Corinthians 11:15).

The MARVI-RPIA image shows the intent of the passage to be a tribute or reminder of the symbolism of womanhood being long, beautiful hair. By covering the hair, it becomes a gesture of remorse and humbleness for two transgressions:

1) *To the Serpent in the Garden of Eden*

2) *To the sons of God outside Eden before the Flood*

As such, women bear the image of procreation. Firstly, as the method of achieving the Mediator for humankind, and secondly, as the method to attempt a mediator for angels. The failed attempt for an angelic mediator (the Nephilim/the Flood) stands as the second greatest human catastrophe, after the fall in the Garden.

You would think Paul should reference the angel, Satan, as being where concern should be placed. This is Satan in the Garden tempting a woman. *But no, Paul says, because of the ANGELS.* Sons of God (angels) in collusion with women (agents in the procreation process) was the cause for concern. He implies that women should regard worship service as a time for modesty rather than attraction. In other words, even the angels have an appreciation for a woman's role in the dynamics of male-female interaction. However, there's no reason to suspect a second attempt at unlawful procreation.

MARVI-RPIA emphasizes an (evil) angel's interest in women was never about their physical BEAUTY. The angel's interest was a woman's ABILITY to facilitate offspring. Angels weren't pursuing sexual *interest*; they were pursuing *procreation.* They hoped for an angel redeemer. *The females chosen were probably NOT the most beautiful. They may have been chosen based solely on the likelihood of surviving angel experimentation.* Incidents of fatalities for mothers and children may have been exceedingly high. Children that survived may have exemplified birth defects through generations pre-Flood and post-Flood.

Reason 9: Genesis 6 says the earth was filled with violence. Reviews of the word "violence" in scriptural definitions render imagery of assault, battery, mayhem, harm, and offense. This is understandable. However, what if there was another situation in Genesis where specific words weren't translated? *An example is a violation of the natural order. We might say the Nephilim would wreak havoc on the natural order of creation and procreation.*

Then wouldn't another word, or other words, have been used to express this? Maybe. Maybe not. You have to admit the reason for the Flood was extremely dire. Something was horribly wrong. Consider Cain murdering Abel. That was over a thousand years BEFORE the Flood. *Murder is fairly violent on any scale.* How much worse (violent) can people be?

And God lets this kind of violence continue for thousands of years before finally taking action? Possibly. Should we call this patience? If we do, we might say there are other noteworthy Bible verses that show patience may not be the issue. Some people were killed seemingly for minor offenses—on the same day. Whole groups of people were killed for being in the wrong country, under the wrong king, or being of a particular ethnicity. How much patience does God show there? Well, you are the judge.

> The earth also was corrupt before God, and the earth was filled with violence. And God looked upon the earth, and, behold, it was corrupt; for all flesh had corrupted his way upon the earth. And God said unto Noah, The end of all flesh is come before me; for the earth is filled with violence through them; and, behold, I will destroy them with the earth (Genesis 6:11-13).

Reason 10: Most of us are familiar with the story in Genesis of Moses confronting Pharaoh to let the Hebrews leave Egypt to worship God. Pharaoh refused. God demonstrated the ten plagues (miracles) to show Pharaoh, the Egyptians, and the sons of Israel that Jehovah is God. Interestingly, *Pharaoh's magicians, sorcerers, wise men, and priests also demonstrated the ability to mimic several of the miracles. They used their secret arts. Where did those secret arts come from?*

God strictly forbids His people, Israel, to engage in magic, sorcery, witchcraft, idolatry, divinity, and spells, including contact with unclean familiar and evil spirits.

The people of other nations? They were unprotected in their pursuit of gaining advantage by cunning, insidious, and wicked means. The obvious acquisition of supernatural skills points to agents outside the human realm. Angels. This would be, initially, Third-Class Angels, Abaddon and his group, and later, Second-Class Angels, Satan and his group. Human beings are highly intelligent, especially those living in the first thousands of years before the Flood. *When humans participate with evil angels, it creates a sinister and deadly relationship.* Angels would again seem conspicuous.

> And the Lord said unto Moses, See, I have made thee a god to Pharaoh: and Aaron thy brother shall be thy prophet. Thou shalt speak all that I command thee: and Aaron thy brother shall speak unto Pharaoh, that he send the children of Israel out of his land. And I will harden Pharaoh's heart, and multiply my signs and my wonders in the land of Egypt. But Pharaoh shall not hearken unto you, that I may lay my hand upon Egypt, and bring forth mine armies, and my people the children of Israel, out of the land of Egypt by great judgments. And the Egyptians shall know that I am the Lord, when I stretch forth mine hand upon Egypt, and bring out the children of Israel from among them ... Then Pharaoh also called the wise men and the sorcerers: now the magicians of Egypt, they also did in like manner with their enchantments ... And the magicians of Egypt did so with their enchantments: and Pharaoh's heart was hardened, neither did he hearken unto them; as the Lord had said (Exodus 7:1-5, 11, 22).

> A man also or woman that hath a familiar spirit, or that is a wizard, shall surely be put to death: they shall stone them with stones: their blood shall be upon them (Leviticus 20:27).

> Thou shalt not suffer a witch to live (Exodus 22:18).

> There shall not be found among you any one that maketh his son or his daughter to pass through the fire, or that useth divination, or an observer of times, or an enchanter, or a witch. Or a charmer, or a consulter with familiar

> spirits, or a wizard, or a necromancer. For all that do these things are an abomination unto the Lord: and because of these abominations the Lord thy God doth drive them out from before thee (Deuteronomy 18:10-12).

A popular minister wrote that he wondered why people have such a hard time accepting angel and human progeny when there are other far greater mysteries in the Bible they readily accept. Like what? Creation of the world. Creation of human beings. The Fall of Man. The Flood of the Earth. Satan and evil spirits. These are just a few. Remember Balaam and his speaking donkey (Numbers 22:21-35), Daniel and friends who survive the fiery furnace (Daniel 3:19-27), and Jonah and the whale (Jonah 2:1-10)?

Now that the Nephilim have taken so much time, and much more could be said and will be said, let's move on to The Flood.

CHAPTER 29

THE FLOOD—PART 1

Connecting The Dots of Identity and the Christian worldview continues with the Roleplay illustration. Your identity is based on the role forced on you by heredity, environment, and experiences. You had no choice in being brought alive. You suddenly materialize at conception without your knowledge or consent. This is your body, this is your brain, these are your parents, this is your country, this is the date and time. Welcome!

You go along in life, learning about yourself and the nature of reality. You hear about religion. You hear about God, Jesus Christ, and the Holy Spirit. You learn about Adam and Eve, the Devil, the Flood, evil, death, Heaven, and Hell. While trying to unravel truth from lies, certainty from doubt, you realize your life could end abruptly by accident, poor health, or homicide. As if that wasn't enough, you are on a trajectory that takes you from being young, good-looking, and healthy to being old, ugly, and sickly. Then, not much later, dead. All in about seventy years. Maybe a few more years, maybe a lot fewer years.

Being social creatures, we compare ourselves to others. It becomes readily apparent that life is not fair. Some people are born with multiple marvelous attributes. Beauty, brains, money. Others are born with none. Homely, simple, poor. The arbitrary and random situation people are born into underlies a rage and a resentment at the complexities of life. Why is life so ridiculous? Pointless! It's here, then it's gone.

Or so it seems. However, you don't want to give in to nihilism, that life is meaningless. When you do hear about religion, there is something about it that resonates with you. It's just that the presentation never quite satisfies.

I agree. I'm a Christian. The “Good News” message of Jesus Christ is not as appealing as it could be. *Connecting The Dots Of Identity* hopes to change that.

Life appears unfair, random, and unpredictable because it may be a Demonstration of Free Will by human Roleplayers. Excluding the Serpent, Adam and Eve were the initial Roleplayers of Free Will. They exercised their option to disagree with God in the interest of acquiring knowledge of good and evil. The penalty for the act was death. Adam and Eve felt life was not worth living if not 100 percent free. In God's mercy, He promised an Antidote for their error via offspring from their united identities. In God's justice, He expelled them from the Garden. Adam and Eve lost their dynamic flawless identity and now must fare in a cursed environment.

Life goes from bad to worse. Adam and Eve's first child, Cain, kills Abel, the second child. The family banishes Cain from the community. The brothers and sisters who are concerned for Cain go to assist him. Two major branches of the family ensue—a branch from Cain and a branch from Adam and Eve's third child named Seth.

Meanwhile, the angels have been in observation. Abaddon and a group of angels leave Heaven in a movement to proclaim liberty as Adam and Eve have done (Jude 1:6). They seek to incorporate with humans as a plan to provide an antidote for angels by progeny. Exercising their Free Will, and relinquishing their heavenly abode, they take the risk. Lucifer, pre-Satan, will not join them but will plead their case with God. God must be fair to angels. He obviously favors humans. Humans are made in Their (Trinity) image. Does He also favor angels with a similar love?

The angel and human offspring endeavor, the Nephilim, goes awry. God destroys all but eight human beings in the Flood. After the Flood, the air, water, land, trees, and plants are transformed. The eight humans must start anew the roleplay identities of Free Will. The eight remember and mourn for their loved ones that died in the Flood. Noah's father, Lamech, died before the Flood. What about Noah's mother? Surely, Noah had brothers and sisters, aunts, uncles, and cousins. What about Missus Noah's mother and father, brothers and sisters? What about Noah's sons' wives? They all had mothers, fathers, brothers, and sisters. Now, ALL relatives of the Exceptional Eight are dead.

Noah's sons, Shem, Ham, and Japheth must have had divine intervention in choosing their wives. The situation in those days before the Flood had to be dire. How can you know which girl is not "infected" by the spirits of evil? Who is not contaminated? Corrupted offspring, by Nephilim or a variety other indiscretions, was still possible.

The wives bring up an interesting question: Was there a "one-drop rule" in effect regarding Nephilim "blood"? A person may have phantom-Nephilim-genetic-substance but be a recessive carrier rather than a dominant carrier. The story in Genesis of Noah cursing Canaan may provide clues as to why the "giants" were not eradicated in the Flood.

> And he said, Cursed be Canaan; a servant of servants shall he be unto his brethren (Genesis 9:25).

You notice that Noah didn't curse Ham. Noah cannot curse whom God blesses.

> And God blessed Noah and his sons, and said unto them, Be fruitful, and multiply, and replenish the earth (Genesis 9:1)

> How shall I curse, whom God hath not cursed? or how shall I defy, whom the Lord hath not defied? (Numbers 23:8).

We've heard that Ham was cursed because Ham was the one who discovered Noah, naked and passed out from wine, in his tent. The MARVI-RPIA image suggests Missus Ham could be the weakest “pure” link in the eight-family group, based on the fact her child Canaan is cursed by Noah. And then, as Harold Camping suggests, it may be that Canaan notified Ham that Noah was in a state of indecency. An adult should be notified. Ham goes to check, consults with his brothers Shem and Japheth, and the brothers cover Noah and secure him.

> And Noah began to be an husbandman, and he planted a vineyard: And he drank of the wine, and was drunken; and he was uncovered within his tent. And Ham, the father of Canaan, saw the nakedness of his father, and told his two brethren without. And Shem and Japheth took a garment, and laid it upon both their shoulders, and went backward, and covered the nakedness of their father; and their faces were backward, and they saw not their father's nakedness (Genesis 9: 20-23).

The “one drop of Nephilim blood” analogy may apply in understanding “giants.”

> There were giants in the earth in those days; and also after that, when the sons of God came in unto the daughters of men, and they bare children to them, the same became mighty men which were of old, men of renown (Genesis 6:4).

Giants on the earth are spoken of in various parts of the Old Testament. The contention has been whether the giants were abnormal human beings or the human-angel Nephilim persons. Excluding the giants of Gath that David and his men killed and Goliath and his brothers, giants lived after the Flood. Read Numbers 13:33, Deuteronomy 2:20, 21, and Deuteronomy 3:11. *How did they survive the Flood?*

> And there we saw the giants, the sons of Anak, which come of the giants: and we were in our own sight as grasshoppers, and so we were in their sight (Numbers 13:33).

> That also was accounted a land of giants: giants dwelt therein in old time; and the Ammonites call them Zamzummims; A people great, and many, and tall, as the Anakims; but the Lord destroyed them before them; and they succeeded them, and dwelt in their stead. (Deuteronomy 2:20-21).

> For only Og king of Bashan remained of the remnant of giants; behold his bedstead was a bedstead of iron; is it not in Rabbath of the children of Ammon? nine cubits was the length thereof, and four cubits the breadth of it, after the cubit of a man (Deuteronomy 3:11).

Giants who survived the Flood could possibly be those who were born to persons carrying a so-called birth defect gene" or "genetic mutation," or an "immaterial-phantom-Nephilim-chromosome." This may be the same kind of situation when we learn of persons who are specifically different from others. Different in appearance, behavior, or in speech. There are always those "different ones" that commit acts we can only categorized as inhumane, monstrous, heartless, unnatural, or unthinkable. They often look, think, and behave “other than” normal humans. These persons may not be fully human.

Demon-possessed persons may not be detectable. Judas Iscariot is probably the prime example. Satan himself possessed Judas, and Judas was just “one of the guys” to Jesus's disciples and to Jesus's opponents.

Back now to Mister and Missus Ham…

Their son Canaan is cursed by Noah, not by God. Curses don't necessarily apply to the cursed person's family except by way of complicity in the wrongdoing. What about Ham's family? Ham’s son, Canaan, fosters two children that are considered mighty men of renown. Cush is Canaan's son, and Nimrod is Cush's son.

> And the sons of Ham; Cush, and Mizraim, and Phut, and Canaan. And the sons of Cush; Seba, and Havilah, and Sabtah, and Raamah, and Sabtechah: and the sons of Raamah; Sheba, and Dedan. And Cush begat Nimrod: he began to be a mighty one in the earth (Genesis 10: 6-8).

So, Canaan is to be a servant of servants to his brethren—a personal curse.

In the meantime, Noah and his family began the rebuilding process of the human race. The land, food, plants, trees, water, and animals all represented major changes from pre-Flood life. Noah planted a vineyard and was abruptly indisposed by the “new” wine. The family witnessed the whole world end and now began to redefine how to live, literally and spiritually. God saved them for a reason. They all knew the Adam and Eve story very well. Noah's father, Lamech, and Noah's grandfather, Methuselah, were alive while Adam still lived. Lamech lived 777 years. Methuselah lived for 969 years. Adam lived for 930 years. Everyone was strictly taught that having children was the world mandate to eventually produce the Antidote, the One promised to redeem humanity.

The Free Will of Adam and Eve got them sin and damnation. Everyone now suffers. It is best to pursue the way of the Lord and oppose pursuits of the self. The self has been corrupted. The only trust must now be in the Lord.

CHAPTER 30

THE FLOOD—PART 2

Noah walked with God. Why doesn't the Bible say God took Noah and Noah "was not" just as He did with Enoch? Could it have anything to do with Noah becoming drunk and cursing his grandson?

> These are the generations of Noah: Noah was a just man and perfect in his generations, and Noah walked with God (Genesis 6:9).

Yes, Noah did get drunk, pass out, and was naked. When awakened, he cursed his grandson, Canaan. But that could be excused. Noah may have been the first to discover wine from a vineyard. Maybe not, but maybe so. The soil from which the wine was derived came from the earth that was severely ravaged by the Flood. The water and soil before the Flood and the water and soil after the Flood were completely different. Additionally, Noah's father, Lamech, says of Noah:

> And Lamech lived an hundred eighty and two years, and begat a son: And he called his name Noah, saying, This same shall comfort us concerning our work and toil of our hands, because of the ground which the Lord hath cursed (Genesis 5:28-29).

Internet research suggests the comfort Noah brought as a man of soil and planter of the vineyard may have been WINE!

> And Noah began to be an husbandman, and he planted a vineyard (Genesis 9:20).

Wine and comfort again come to mind in the Book of Judges:

> Then said the trees unto the vine, Come thou, and reign over us. And the vine said unto them, Should I leave my wine, which cheereth God and man, and go to be promoted over the trees? (Judges 9:12-13).

It shouldn't be much of a stretch to assume any wine Noah produced before the Flood would have the benefit of soil that was only cursed once. That must have been spectacular wine. *Now that the soil is cursed for the second time by the Flood, this wine produced by Noah bore substantially different properties.* We have cute names these days derived from standard wine grapes. What would Noah's first batch of new wine have been named, relative to his drunken embarrassment? Let's take a second from serious matters. How about ...

The Grapes of Wrath? H2oNo? Water Into Wine? Deluge Delight? Immersion Subversion?

Okay, now, back to the Flood …

When thinking about Noah, the Flood, the water, and the soil, do your thoughts go to fossils? Do you think of organic material embedded in the earth, not just topsoil? If you think further, do you envision oil, gas, and coal?

Oil, gas, and coal are produced by the plant kingdom and animal kingdoms. They are decomposed organic compounds preserved deep in the earth. The preservation is accomplished by a relatively sudden collection of living organisms captured by extreme natural forces such as water, wind, earthquakes, volcanos, and FLOODS.

The Flood of Noah's day caused sudden death to plants, animals, and HUMAN BEINGS by water. Oil, gas, coal, and other organic material are found all over the world. *Why are they found so deep in the ground?*

Because if they all died and decomposed near the surface of the earth, they'd simply decompose with little to no trace. There would be no oil, gas, or coal.

But why the Flood of the Bible? Why not natural phenomena? Natural phenomena like landslides, volcanos, and earthquakes? Isn't the Ice Age a possible explanation for preserving plant, animal, and human remains?

Those natural phenomena mentioned would all limit the preservation of organic material to low-surface, mid-surface, and surface-level exposure. The effect of erosion on low-surface and mid-surface level materials is insufficient to account for extreme deep-surface material found as oil, gas, and coal deposits. This means organic matter from plants, animals, and human beings from 5,000 to 10,000 feet below the surface!

Mount Everest's elevation is about 29,000 feet high. Passenger jets cruise about 39,000 feet. The Z-44 Chayvo Oil Well in Russia is listed at 40,502 feet below the surface. Over 40,000 feet, even though 10,000 of that isn't vertical but rather directional.

Plant, animal, and human material are being recovered from at least 30,000 feet straight down. *And it's found all ... over ... the ... world!*

And then you think, "Wait just a minute! When the Flood of Noah's day occurred, everyone would have lived in the same general area. So how could the Flood waters carry plants, animals, and people all over the world, then bury them 30,000 feet deep?" If we assume the Garden of Eden was in the Near East, Middle East, or possibly in Africa, how do oil, gas, and coal end up all around the world, especially in places like Alaska, South America, and China?

Basic research regarding the Flood of Noah's day and reading accounts in the Bible reveals the dynamics of the Flood were devastating to the planet. There are people who believe the Flood was a local event. There are people who don't believe there ever was the Flood of the Bible. There are a great many people who KNOW for a FACT that oil, gas, and coal took millions of years to produce.

Yes, that's okay. It's understandable. The appearance of age tells its own story.

When you look at the sun, moon, and stars, does it make sense to say they were created by God in a few days? No.

When you look at Adam and Eve, does it make sense they are one day old and not eighteen years old? No.

When you look at post-Flood earth, does it make sense that the geological strata represent one year instead of millions of years? No.

Connecting The Dots Of Identity is not about persuasion or conviction. It's art. It's an impression. Your thoughts reflect your life situation. *Do you have a choice in your worldview if your identity is dictated by heredity, environment, and experiences?*

But, if you're curious, it's easy to search on topography after a catastrophic event such as earthquakes, tsunamis, volcanic eruptions, and hurricanes. You will realize how devastating such phenomena are to the earth. But how can you compare any catastrophe to the Flood?

This event caused huge land mass movement, extremely high winds, and enormous drops in water levels all over the world. Millions, billions, trillions of people all died. At once.

Imagine going from a planet of 90 percent land 10 percent water to 10 percent land 90 percent water in a space of months, not years.

Pre-Flood times were similar to the pre-Tower times of Babel. One language, one speech. Nothing to very little was withheld from humanity

(Genesis 11). What seemed to exacerbate the corruption of human beings was that their lives were 500 to 1,000 years long.

Imagine living during that time ...

THE DAYS OF NOAH

Adam and Eve were both praised and vilified. Everyone was alive because of them. Everyone would die because of them. The only true consolation was procreation. Procreation did not mean "sex" in terms of pleasure, fun, exploitation, or aberration. *Procreation meant a worldwide effort to produce children as fast as possible. The sooner the Redeemer is born, the sooner death is overcome. The great "Return to Eden" could have been the theme of the whole world.*

On Cain's side of the family, one wife may have been a constraint on procreation. MORE than one wife is recorded in Genesis 4. Matrimony continued to be the commitment in a relationship, but "safety in numbers" could be a strong argument for increasing the likelihood of the Redeemer. Added to this, Ego-Centracism may have been a factor. Surely, everyone thought of being the parents of the One Promised! Fame and great honor would be theirs forever. Even the second wife, who is not the mother, but the wife of the husband receives honor. And then, what greater honor could be had than the honor from God Himself? God chooses the parents of the One born as Savior.

Of course, from our vantage point, we know two things:

1) The Holy Spirit is the Father of the Redeemer. A human male is not the father.

2) There was no pre-Flood prophecy of Jesus identifying Him as the Messiah. There could have been. There's no reference to that specific oral tradition. MARVI-RPIA has no such imagery.

We might also assume that, besides the absence of prophets, there were no kings or priests. There were no "chosen people of God," no religious rituals, and no written commandments to follow.

Additionally, in those pre-Flood days, the population was growing rapidly. Everyone was in perfect health. No one died from disease, crime, drugs, or suicide. When death came, it was usually by accident or simply from the effects of aging—800 to 900 years after being born.

The issues of food, shelter, waste disposal, and energy were under control. The people were brilliant. They possessed an excellent "photographic" memory, worked together as families, and pursued common goals. Knowledge was cumulative. Intellect at fifty years doubled or tripled at age 100 years old. Intellect at 500 years old may have been ten times that of a 100-year-old person. Maybe not. Maybe so. Construction, transportation, animal husbandry, communication, education, and science flourished. All such disciplines were explored with energy, passion, and ability.

But in Genesis 6, God said the earth was corrupted, either by the people or by the earth affecting the people.

> The earth also was corrupt before God, and the earth was filled with violence. And God looked upon the earth, and, behold, it was corrupt; for all flesh had corrupted his way upon the earth. And God said unto Noah, The end of all flesh is come before me; for the earth is filled with violence through them; and, behold, I will destroy them with the earth (Genesis 6:11-13).

Why was Noah set apart from the others? Apparently, for the same reason you and I are set apart. God intercedes. If God does not intercede, Free Will reigns.

The Bible says, "filled with violence." *Violation of the human procreation standard?*

The Bible says all flesh had corrupted their way. *The way of human beings, as in the Nephilim?*

As fertility became the mandate and population escalated and angels left their natural abode to intermix in procreation, it was a win-win for humans and a win-win for angels. Or so it seemed.

> And the angels which kept not their first estate, but left their own habitation, he hath reserved in everlasting chains under darkness unto the judgment of the great day (Jude 1:6).

As mentioned in Chapter 19, *Connecting The Dots Of Identity* paints ten-plus "beginnings."

1. The Trinity

2. Super-Spiritual Identities (SSIDs)

3. Angels

4. Universe

5. Flawless Adam and Eve

6. Flawed Adam and Eve

7a. Conception

7b. Natural Birth

8. Post-Flood

9. Jesus Christ

10. Born-again Christian

10-plus. Satan from Beginning

The ten-plus beginning painted is the accusation by Jesus that Satan was a murderer "from the beginning"—not the Garden of Eden or the beginning of life.

> Ye are of your father the devil, and the lusts of your father ye will do. He was a murderer from the beginning, and abode not in the truth, because there is no truth in him. When he speaketh a lie, he speaketh of his own: for he is a liar, and the father of it (John 8:44).

Beginning number seven includes the Flood and the life of Noah. Satan and the angels have been in observance of humanity since Adam and Eve. The angels are all of one class, not fallen. It may have been when Adam and Eve exercised Free Will to eat of the Tree of the Knowledge of Good and Evil that the angels considered exercising Free Will. They did not act on Free Will until considering the pursuit of a redeemer through procreation with human females. One group of angels fails in the procreation mission—the Third-Class Angels. Another group accuses God of unfairness to angels and favoritism to inferior humans—the Second-Class Angels. The remaining group of angels is loyal to God, refusing to exercise Free Will to disobey—– the First-Class Angels.

Adam and Eve began the process of procreation. Each child created increases the likelihood the Redeemer will be born. As bad as life is outside the Garden of Eden, the promise of no more death generated hope. The urgency to produce children was paramount. People were healthy, bloodlines were pure, and life expectancy was unlimited. Air quality, water quality, and food quality were pristine. *By the time the Flood occurred, an enormous number of people had been born. But no Redeemer.*

What was the problem?

FINAL SECONDS TO MIDNIGHT

A thousand years go by. No Redeemer. There is hope. There is effort. There are prayers. No Redeemer. Why not?

One: The Demonstration of Free Will has reached a required number of living examples but some disruption may have occurred that compromised the future. Nephilim perhaps?

Two: There was no female counterpart for Holy Spirit interaction. No Virgin Mary equivalent.

Three: Humans and the Nephilim could be reaching a point of destroying themselves.

God intercedes. He starts over with eight people. This next Demonstration of Free Will includes great diversity in *heredity* and great diversity in the *environment.* Even more significant in the next demonstration will be a *reduction in lifespan* from 1,000 years to 120 years of age.

Now, let's go back a little way to a point in the story right before the Flood. Only the Exceptional Eight people are going to be saved.

One: Mankind may be close to destroying themselves in some beyond-believable cataclysm.

Two: The Nephilim do not corrupt human genetic integrity to the point where NO 100 percent humans are left.

Three: God is close to taking direct action to destroy all living people on the planet except eight.

All except eight! How could SO MANY people NOT be worth saving in those last days? *It's been noted that the population figures of those days could have been ten trillion! Even if that was much lower, down to one trillion or one billion or even one million, how does that compare to only eight people being worthy to live?*

Were ANY of the people killed in the Flood NOT corrupted by Nephilim material?

Was it a matter of worthiness of the people?

They could have been worthy to live, but became collateral damage, simply victims of circumstance in those days of violence.

If ONLY eight were worthy to continue life, then the advent of angels and humans procreating in those days was absolutely devastating to the world. Humanity was ruined!

This is the image *Connecting The Dots Of Identity* portrays. Violence is the violation of NATURE. *The violation was the procreation by angels and human females.* Violence wasn't simply brute force and misbehavior against other humans. That's not uncommon, all the way back to the first human beings when Cain killed Abel. It was more likely a disruption of the natural order.

This view helps explain why babies in the womb, toddlers, and young children were not considered expedient to survive the Flood. Children were alive as a consequence of the fervor to produce offspring as soon as possible. This included natural childbirth and unnatural childbirth by fallen angels and human females. There was probably inattention and negligence by the parents. Yes, the process of procreation that brings the Redeemer was foremost. But what should have been joy, reverence, and love could have devolved into frivolity, irreverence, and sensuality. Perhaps even adult and child sexuality. Child and child sexuality. Group sexuality.

There's another angle, though.

If more than eight were worthy of saving, then why couldn't twenty-eight be on the Ark? Why couldn't 108 be on the Ark, or 1,008?

How much bigger would the Ark have to be? How much longer would it take to build? How many arks are needed to transport 1,008 people? How many animals are needed for an ecosystem that sustains more than the original eight of the Ark?

Simply looking at population dynamics, what could we expect the current population to be if 1,008 people restarted the human population after the Flood? *Ten trillion people by the year 1776?* We know Nephilim material did carry over after the Flood, because the Bible states there were giants on the earth after the Flood. Giants that were always described as male, evil, and against the people of God.

By having only eight people repopulate the earth, despite one or more of them carrying recessive Nephilim immaterial, the Demonstration of Free Will is not curtailed by overpopulation. Rather than the end of the Demonstration occurring in the year 912, 1440, or 1976 because one trillion people populated the earth, the Demonstration continues until today. By continuing, the proof of the error of Free Will by flawless Adam and Eve is enhanced.

It's imperative that the gift of life to a flawless living creature, human or angel, have autonomy from God. They must have Free Will to decline God's will. *If death is not a deterrent to disobeying God, the repercussions should be presented.* They are presented. The lives of angels and humans testify in scripture and in human experience.

> And the Lord said, "My Spirit shall not strive with man forever, for he is indeed flesh; yet his days shall be one hundred and twenty years." There were giants in the earth in those days; and also after that, when the sons of God came in unto the daughters of men, and they bare children to them, the same became mighty men which were of old, men of renown (Genesis 6:3-4).
>
> But Noah found grace in the eyes of the Lord. These are the generations of Noah: Noah was a just man and perfect in his generations, and Noah walked with God. And Noah begat three sons, Shem, Ham, and Japheth. The earth also was corrupt before God, and the earth was filled with violence. And God looked upon the earth, and, behold, it was corrupt; for all flesh had corrupted his way upon the earth. And God said unto Noah, The end of all flesh is come before me; for the earth is filled with violence through them; and, behold, I will destroy them with the earth. Make thee an ark of gopher wood; rooms shalt thou make in the ark, and shalt pitch it within and without with pitch (Genesis 6:8-14).

CHAPTER 31

THE FLOOD—PART 3

It's a good time now to add more details regarding non-Elect Roleplayers.

Before the world was created, God recognizes individuals who are guaranteed salvation before they are born. *Connecting The Dots Of Identity* provides imagery through Modern Abstract Religious Verbal Impressionism that affirms ontological status to those persons. Their counterparts on earth receive an inauthentic identity that becomes the Demonstration of Free Will. The inauthentic identity began when Adam and Eve exercised their Free Will to disobey God. This change in identity from a flawless identity to a flawed identity was inherited by all generations.

The Serpent in the Garden of Eden also participates in the Demonstration of Free Will. As a flawless nonhuman creature, he has no eternal spirit, no soul. Similarly, a creature produced by merging an angel and a fallen human female may have no eternal spirit—no soul.

Conception, the first stage of life, is the province of God. Death, the end stage of life, is the province of God. God rules in pre-life, life, and the afterlife.

Artificial conception is the province of God's permissive will. In such a case, the creature may be devoid of an eternal spirit, or a soul. This case applies to the creation of the Nephilim—angel and human female offspring.

As unnatural procreation developed in the pre-Flood population:

- DOMINANT genetic Nephilim processes produce a hybrid-human male as less than 100 percent human.

- Scripture gives no indication of the status regarding a Nephilim female.

- RECESSIVE genetic Nephilim processes produce 100 percent human beings. Recessive reproduction processes produce 100 percent humans who are male AND female and consist of a spirit—a soul.

Unnatural procreation methods contrived by angels suggest abnormalities would result in high pregnancy losses. It's likely that such concepts as spontaneous abortion, miscarriage, and maternal mortality began at this time. This violence against natural birth surely came with unexpected and risky consequences. However, once the angels left Heaven on their "procreation mission," there was no going back. Besides being highly motivated to succeed in their mission, they depended on Lucifer (as pre-Satan) to plead their case. Their case is defined as equal status with humans at the minimum, and superior status at the maximum.

Conversely, a secondary pre-Flood storyline is painted for consideration. Let's portray angelic procreation manipulation as being so successful that it overruns the population. A L-O-N-G lifespan of 900 years and robust good health of ALL the females, coupled with angelic cunning and sorcery, presumes a highly successful procreation project. Dominant and recessive genetic traits in the initial births are "directed" to be primarily male-Nephilim-dominant so that NEPHILIM conception occurs. Otherwise, male-Nephilim-recessive conception produces a male OR female HUMAN.

The ten trillion population number would then have another piece of evidence for confirmation. The premise of God drowning trillions of non-

100 percent humans doesn't seem so ominous. *They had no soul, no ongoing eternal identity. Imagine plants, animals, and non-100 percent humans making up the bountiful reserves of fossil fuel origins we have worldwide. Now, the Flood is a blessing as well as a curse.*

Going further, we might ask what outcome would we experience if God didn't utilize the Flood as a means of destruction. *What if God used fire from Heaven? What if God used a plague? What if God caused people to suddenly drop dead?*

Flooding rather than sudden death introduces the unpredictable phenomena of weather. Inclement weather was unlikely pre-Flood. Afterward, rain and the rainbow became a universal reminder of God's judgment on mankind. Though rainstorms are bad enough, thunder and lightning re-emphasize the forces of nature—the force of God.

At least two other things come to mind. You can probably think of more.

1) We wouldn't have the rich oil, gas, and coal reserves worldwide that originate from plants, animals, and human substances. It takes massive amounts of materials to produce even modest fossil reserves. Therefore, we understand why it requires a GLOBAL flood that submerges vegetation, animals, and ten trillion persons suddenly, and then deeply buries them. The world WITHOUT oil, gas, and coal beneath our feet is utterly unimaginable.

2) We wouldn't have the fossil record indicated in the stratified layers of the earth and under the bodies of water. Paleontology has advanced to assist us in creating an overall interpretation of historical data to explain General Revelation, or, how God is revealed in nature. However, the generic explanation EXCLUDES God to assert NON-INTELLIGENCE is revealed in nature.

Paleontology is mainly interpreted to refute any references to God or a worldwide flood. Paleontology also ignores Special Revelation, the explanation of reality as revealed in SCRIPTURE.

The Flood is still traumatic to contemplate, even if God was bringing a blessing along with the horror. The perpetrators of the horror, Abaddon and fallen angels, were not drowned. They didn't die. They were arrested and imprisoned in chains of darkness. The Nephilim, persons created by angel sorcery and human females, although not 100 percent human beings, were drowned. Everyone else, except the eight saved on the Ark, were drowned.

> And, behold, I, even I, do bring a flood of waters upon the earth, to destroy all flesh, wherein is the breath of life, from under heaven; and everything that is in the earth shall die (Genesis 6:17).
>
> They did eat, they drank, they married wives, they were given in marriage, until the day that Noah entered into the ark, and the flood came, and destroyed them all (Luke 17:27).
>
> For if God spared not the angels that sinned, but cast them down to hell, and delivered them into chains of darkness, to be reserved unto judgment (2 Peter 2:4).
>
> And the angels which kept not their first estate, but left their own habitation, he hath reserved in everlasting chains under darkness unto the judgment of the great day (Jude 1:6).

Everyone considered 100 percent human beings who were drowned comprise part of the ten trillion population. They were all Roleplayers. Everyday life devolved to the point of complete corruption. No one identified in scripture separated themselves from the status quo except Noah, although we should include the unnamed, future Missus Noah. Lucifer's challenge that angels were equal to or better than humans has to factor in the integrity of Mister and Missus Noah.

Noah kept himself pure, somehow, and patiently waited to marry and have children. Scripture tells us Noah didn't have his first child until he was 500 years old. We don't know the age of Missus Noah when Noah married her. It could have taken as many as 400 years to find the young, 100 to 400-year-old Miss Right. When the time was set, God coordinated their meeting.

> And Noah was five hundred years old: and Noah begat Shem, Ham, and Japheth (Genesis 5:32)

END OF THE WORLD ROLL CALL

Four groups of actors stand out in the first end-of-the-world scenario:

1. The fallen angels
2. The Nephilim
3. The 100 percent human beings
4. The less-than-100 percent human beings

Let's review the profile of persons who are NOT 100 percent human beings.

1. They are ancestors of the Nephilim family, dating back to the Flood, as a recessive-trait reproduction factor of the family of Noah.

2. Although angels are eternal spirit beings with an authentic identity, and humans are eternal spirit beings with a physical inauthentic identity, anyone born with dominant Nephilim genetic substance has NO spiritual

designation (see Glossary of Colors-Designationism). God creates the spirit, or the soul, which has correspondence with the authentic identity, the Super-Spiritual Identity (SSID), in Paradise, before the world was created.

3. Given that persons less than 100 percent human have no eternal spiritual identity, at death, they cease to exist. Biblical references to the peril of the afterlife apply to fallen angels who impersonate Roleplayers. At death, these agents die physically, but not spiritually.

4. Jesus was promised to be the Redeemer through procreation to atone for the error of sin. He became a 100 percent human being to rescue 100 percent human beings—not angels, not Nephilim, not less-than-100 percent humans, not "aliens", and not animals.

5. The very worst persons and the very best persons roleplay their inauthentic identity based on heredity, environment, and experience. Punishment and reward come as a consequence of day-to-day life before death. Afterlife punishment and reward are qualified in chapters on Hell and Heaven.

6. Victims of Elect and non-Elect Roleplayers receive rewards in Heaven unique to their roleplay identity.

7. Punishment of non-Elect Roleplayers beaten with many or few stripes probably refers to earthly situations. In Hell, the Devil and his angels may receive degrees of punishment.

8. As John Calvin says of the Apostles' Creed (see Chapter 20, "Marvi As Art"), Jesus's descent into Hell was not literal. Jesus on the cross serves as the symbol of Hell. Hell applies as a deterrent throughout the scriptures to dramatize the epitome of error.

9. The stage between Heaven and Hell is present life on Earth. This is Hell for Roleplayers as the Demonstration of Free Will plays out among the insane, the unsane, and other sane Roleplayers day to day (Chapter 17, Insanity Chart).

10. An abbreviation for persons who are less than 100 percent human beings, who are devoid of an eternal spiritual identity, a soul, will be ... what? What name should we use? A great name shorter than the six-word phrase "less than 100 percent human beings" could be useful.

Devoidians? Devoid of a soul—a spirit.

Hephilim? Nephilim and human.

Humalim? Human and Nephilim.

No name? Stay with the six-word phrase?

THE FLOOD 3—POSTSCRIPT

Abaddon and other angels abandon Heaven. Our minds can't grasp this. What a bold, impertinent, presumptive act! They were flawless angels until ... The Act? Planning the act? Starting the act? What act?

1. Colluding with Lucifer to accuse God of favor to humans and disfavor to angels.
2. Accusing God of flawed human and angel design if their liberty is impeded.
3. Seeking to provide an angel redeemer via procreation with human females.

An “immaterial phantom N” chromosome could be an explanation for Abaddon and the angels producing male offspring. The purely artistic impression following from this may be imagined as:

XX = Human female
XY = Human male
NXY = Nephilim male manifested as Nephilim dominant traits
nXX /nXY = Human female and Human male as Nephilim recessive traits.

Thank God that the wizardry fallen angels imposed on human females to produce offspring abruptly ended. Those angels were finally captured and imprisoned. The so-called Nephilim offspring were all drowned in the Flood.

The evil male “giants” referred to in scripture who appear after the Flood could be considered relatives of the Nephilim. If any of the eight persons who survived the Flood were recessive carriers of an immaterial phantom Nephilim essence, that may help us understand inhumane thinking and behavior.

Birth defects and abnormalities may be attributed to the “N” immaterial chromosome. Variation, mutation, evolution, or devolution is further imagery to portray how Nephilim characteristics aren't restricted to large physical stature or evil demeanor. Nephilim characteristics may be defined by numerous other reprehensible qualities all too prevalent throughout history. When we recount any number of atrocities of the past, there are always gut-wrenching examples of inhumane acts. How can people be so cruel to other people?

Maybe because they aren't people—that is, real people. They are LESS than people. They are less than 100 percent human beings. Their role follows Nephilim-dominant immaterial N-phantom chromosomal properties. They won't have a soul or a spirit. This makes them agents for Satan in the quest to blemish, slander, and disrupt those made in the image of God. The ones God sends His Son to save.

Seventy percent of the Christian world probably believes men were so evil and violent that God drowned the majority of them in the Flood. Another 70 percent who hear about angels leaving Heaven to marry human females probably believe it's an awkward and improper biblical translation.
But what if the angel-human female narrative is additional proof of ontological spiritual reality? Satan, Abaddon, Michael, Gabriel, cherubs, and angels are NOT just ghosts. They're real! They have ontological standing. The spirit world exists.

- We fight not against flesh and blood (Ephesians).
- Physical reality is not real. Spiritual reality is real (2 Corinthians).

Atheists, agnostics, and even non-Christians are fond of scoffing at sorcery, miracles, and demons. They openly laugh at scriptures that depict the scene in the Garden of Eden, the Flood of Noah's day, and the virgin birth of Jesus Christ. They shouldn't be ridiculed for their beliefs. Dependability on the natural order of things has much more credibility than the worldview based on the supernatural of the Bible. Until God opens their spiritual eyes, they will be in the dark.

> For we wrestle not against flesh and blood, but against principalities, against powers, against the rulers of the darkness of this world, against spiritual wickedness in high places (Ephesians 6:12).
> While we look not at the things which are seen, but at the things which are not seen: for the things which are seen are temporal; but the things which are not seen are eternal (2 Corinthians 4:18).

Another thing to keep in mind is the line between a 100 percent human being and a less than 100 percent human being is very thin. The WORST 100 percent human being BEFORE God causes their rebirth can be truly evil. Non-Christians don't understand how God changes a person and gives them a new identity. The new Christian transition means sin doesn't cease immediately. The non-Christian assumes typical Christian hypocrisy as the new Christian endeavors to remove sin from their life.

On the other side, a less-than-100 percent human, without a soul or spirit, may very well be a nice person ... until pressed. They also may not even know they are not 100 percent human and couldn't care less.

Similarly, the Elect Roleplayer may have no idea God is going to overrun their demonstration of Free Will. The Apostle Paul is a good example, as he is on his way to imprison Christians when God saves him (Acts).

> And I persecuted this way unto the death, binding and delivering into prisons both men and women. As also the high priest doth bear me witness, and all the estate of the elders: from whom also I received letters unto the brethren, and went to Damascus, to bring them which were there bound unto Jerusalem, for to be punished. And it came to pass, that, as I made my journey, and was come nigh unto Damascus about noon, suddenly there shone from heaven a great light round about me. And I fell unto the ground, and heard a voice saying unto me, Saul, Saul, why persecutest thou me? And I answered, Who art thou, Lord? And he said unto me, I am Jesus of Nazareth, whom thou persecutest
> (Acts 22:4-8).

CHAPTER 32

THE FLOOD—PART 4

Connecting The Dots of Identity has implied the Nephilim as a major influence on why the Earth was corrupted in the days of Noah. The Nephilim may have a continuing influence on why the Earth is corrupted today. Further research has revealed another factor in human corruption. *There was an absolutely staggering number of people alive in the days of Noah.* By the way, did you balk at these four sentences in Chapter 30 – "Flood 2"?

- This event caused huge land mass movement, extremely high winds, and enormous drops in water levels all over the world. Millions, billions, trillions of people all died—at once.

- How could SO MANY people NOT be worth saving in the days of Noah? It's been noted that the population figures of those days could have been ten trillion!

What about these four sentences from Chapter 31 – "Flood 3"?

- The ten trillion population number would then have another piece of evidence for confirmation. The premise of God drowning trillions of non-100 percent humans doesn't seem so ominous.

- Therefore, we understand why it requires a GLOBAL flood that submerges vegetation, animals, and ten trillion persons suddenly, then deeply buries them.

- Everyone considered 100 percent human beings that were drowned comprised part of the ten trillion population.

Did you ask, "What is the Minister of Art talking about? Ten trillion people? This is a major glitch."

What would you guess the human population to be in the days of Noah before the Flood? It probably doesn't matter, or does it? A million people? Ten million? One hundred million people? But when looking at five, ten, fifteen different internet searches on pre-Flood population figures, I was astounded by the preferred presentation. *Calculating the population, before the Flood began was—drum roll please—10,000,000,000,000!* Yikes! Wow! Ten trillion! And ten trillion was the conservative number so as not to embellish the project estimate.

Ten trillion people living at one time on the earth! NO ONE believes this until they realize the time it takes for a population to double, given the starting population, the rate, and a specific time frame. Also, it helps to compare high and low population growth rates in other examples to understand the magnitude of the search results.

Population growth Pre-Flood has to account for the extremely long lifespans of the inhabitants. How many children were born to healthy parents who lived 700, 800, and 900 years? There were no abortions, birth defects, environmental toxins, diseases, or deplorable birth conditions—except, perhaps, in the case of the Nephilim. God's promise of human redemption depended on procreation. There must have been extreme motivation to produce children in those days.

Ten TRILLION POPULATION AT TIME OF FLOOD. (Bible-Science Guy)

How much is a trillion? Comparison of a trillion to seconds: One million seconds is about 11 days. A billion seconds is about 31 years. One trillion seconds is about 32,000 years! A trillion is 1 followed by 12 zeros.

No, no, no. This is impossible. Come on. That population number will be refuted in five minutes. This is what everyone will say ... until they look over the researched material by the mathematician who presents the data. It's interesting to read the comments that agree and disagree with the numbers. It's also interesting to read the replies given by the researcher to those who agree and disagree with his research.

The point is after realizing the possibility of such a large population at the time of the Flood, it's even more reason to assume the diversity of evil with the existence of so many more examples.

Why didn't "good" triumph over all the evil at that time? The people were fresh out of the Garden of Eden. They knew God firsthand. Adam, Eve, Cain, Abel, and all the immediate children of Adam and Eve. There had to be a great number of people who were good.

We could ask a similar question today. It may not be so much that evil triumphs over good as it is "opportunity" that evil will occur.

In the twenty-first century, multiple opportunities to end the human race abound. The opportunities increase as the population grows. Knowledge is cumulative. We build on the advancements others have made in areas of weaponry, science, and technology. Imagine how intelligent and wise you would be if you could add 700 to 800 to 900 more years to your life—a life devoid of medical issues, environmental issues, and rampant crime! And you would be learning from other people who also had an extremely high intellect by way of living hundreds of years longer. This is how pre-Flood Earth may have been.

We could name at least three scenarios that could mean annihilation by accident or by intent. War could end human life. Artificial intelligence could end human life. A global pandemic could end human life.

In Noah's day, pre-Flood, and pre-Nephilim, assuming a multi-trillion population, the ingenuity of those people should have surpassed what we have today. There was one language, one land mass (likely no oceans or seas), and everyone in the same family, though Cain's family line and Seth's family line were slightly apart. They had excellent weather, excellent health, and an excellent future.

Judging from the prowess to build the Tower of Babel and skills developed from Cain's family line, such a large population would solve problems such as food, shelter, and government fairly readily. However, all it takes for the world to come to an end is one rogue egomaniac, a group of elitist power moguls, or an unforeseen event that affects the whole world neighborhood.

Today the earth is about 70 percent water and 30 percent land. Pre-Flood may have been 10 percent water and 90 percent land. The ten trillion people may have needed that much land to live. Then came the time when God declared man's days will be 120 years. Does this mean the lifespan of human beings? Does this mean time until the Flood? The best guess is it means our maximum life expectancy. Life hasn't been anywhere close to the 800-900 years people lived pre-Flood.

Did God wait 120 years to begin the Flood?

Noah was 500 years old when he began to have three children: Shem, Ham, and Japheth. It would take fifteen to twenty years for his sons to reach marriage age and select wives. God told Noah to build the Ark. Noah, Missus Noah, the sons, and the sons' wives begin to build the Ark. No doubt, they hired workers to assist. The Ark is completed sometime between when Noah is 500 to 600 years old. The Flood begins when he is six hundred.

Noah, his family, and hired workers must have become famous in the community, the region, and even the world. The year-after-year process of building the Ark, storing supplies, and gathering animals must have drawn quite a tourist attraction.

Noah and his group answer the questions regarding their tasks. Noah preaches that he is following God's words to prepare for a worldwide event—an aqueous catastrophe. God says mankind is corrupt and has violated His laws of nature. Free Will has pushed man beyond a point of return to godliness.

Finally, as animals of all sorts began to gather, two by two, clean and unclean, male and female, curiosity may have turned to apprehension. But all the highest intelligence among the people gave assurance that no such event as Noah describes would ever transpire. *Why would God bring such a catastrophe? Kill everyone on the planet? Kill ten trillion people at once, with water? A world as big as the earth submerged in water? There isn't that much water—anywhere!* That is preposterous! No way! Besides, God is love. God is patient. And Noah tells us only he and his immediate family are righteous? The gall of that guy. The whole family is bizarre.

> And Noah was five hundred years old: and Noah begat Shem, Ham, and Japheth (Genesis 5:32)
>
> And Noah was six hundred years old when the flood of waters was upon the earth (Genesis 7:6).
>
> Of clean beasts, and of beasts that are not clean, and of fowls, and of everything that creepeth upon the earth, There went in two and two unto Noah into the ark, the male and the female, as God had commanded Noah ... They, and every beast after his kind, and all the cattle after their kind, and every creeping thing that creepeth upon the

> earth after his kind, and every fowl after his kind, every bird of every sort. And they went in unto Noah into the ark, two and two of all flesh, wherein is the breath of life (Genesis 7:8-9, 14-15).

HORROR OF HORRORS

Day Zero. Noah's family is all aboard. Animals are all aboard. All tests run for the Ark are complete. God says that practice is over. *This is not a drill. Today is the day!*

Clouds form in the sky. It gets dark. More clouds. More darkness. Drops of moisture come down from the sky. People run for cover. Rumblings in the air become loud booms of thunder. Noise on the land increases from buildings, trees, and animals. The earth shakes, and water appears from beneath the earth. The noises get louder and louder. Abruptly, huge bolts of blinding, white light appear and disappear, followed by deafening explosions of bloodcurdling thunder. Deep darkness. Brief blinding light flashes. More noise. More water. More earthquakes. More lightning. More thunder.

Terror, pandemonium, and panic hit everyone living. The noises from ten trillion voices try to drown out the cataclysm. Nothing can.

On the Ark, the eight have prepared secure stations for the animals. Now the eight also prepare themselves. We might imagine they made earplugs, blindfolds, and secure straps that bound them to the bedding as all aboard are put to “deep sleep” through the days and nights to come.

Although the Ark is built with great sound and light-dampening features, the sights and sounds of the End of the World must have been a deafening and horrible experience. Noah and his family may have prepared songs and prayers. Perhaps angels joined in to sing away the terrors outside. Even the perfect number of animals making noises could have helped to distract them from The End that was occurring.

The Flood rages. The Mother and Father of all storms—a Class-10 meteorological phenomenon.

Finally, the Flood ends. The Ark comes to rest on Mount Ararat. Noah, his family, and the animals are finally able to leave the Ark. This is about 371 days after the Flood.

What a difference they experience from pre-Flood earth to post-Flood earth.

Free Will as a Demonstration of agents thinking and behaving of their own volition begins now for the third time.

First, in the Garden of Eden.

Second, outside of the Garden of Eden pre-Flood.

Third, outside of the Garden of Eden post-Flood.

It's now up to Noah and his family to get it right—again.

FLOOD 4—POSTSCRIPT

Assuming the Nephilim were the cause of God destroying everyone except eight, humankind had devolved to an intolerable situation.

Assuming the Nephilim is a result of evil spirit activity with humans, and evil spirit activity with humans is explicitly forbidden by God throughout the Bible, demon possession is worse than death. It's worse than death for two reasons:

One, you are cursed – possibly doomed to Hell.

Two, you most likely become psychotic. You are no longer in control; one or more demons are.

Have you ever wondered if demon possession is as common today as it was in New Testament? How prevalent was demon possession in the Old Testament AFTER the Flood? Were demons in greater numbers during the times of Jesus, or did Jesus's presence cause greater awareness of demons?

Connecting The Dots Of Identity paints imagery that affirms:

- Demon possession is present today.
- Demon possession is as common as it was in the New Testament.
- Inhuman evil in the world could be seen as less-than-100 percent human activity. This refers to Nephilim ancestors.

From this, at least two important questions arise:

1. How many of us are related to the Nephilim—those descended from one or more of Noah's family?

2. God DOES save demon-possessed individuals. What if He doesn't save us before we die?

First, MARVI-RPIA indicates all 100 percent humans are already safe in Paradise. As Roleplayers on Earth, we prove the error of Free Will. We are safe. If we are somehow related to the Nephilim, and therefore less than 100 percent human, we still have a chance. Especially if we seem at all concerned about salvation. Even if we are 100 percent AGAINST salvation, it may only reflect our roleplay assignment dictated by heredity, environment, and experience.

Second, if God doesn't save us before we die, at death, or after death, then we were never meant to inherit eternal life. The world is full of people who could not care less. They have no idea unless the Holy Spirit intercedes.

It's not likely people will dispute there are evil people in the world. There are news reports of absolutely inhuman behavior in virtually every country in the world. A large portion of the reports are recent. A larger portion of the inhuman acts are not recent and have never been reported. Just by observation of what we know of human behavior, we know hideous acts of unspeakable horror have been committed as long as people have been on the planet.

This will continue every single day. It will be sensationalized on TV and in the media. That's the nature of business, customer attraction and retention. On the opposite end, it will NOT be sensationalized. It will be covered up, ignored, and lied about. It will be the insidious evil that undermines goodness, seeking to decompose any decency that remains.

What may be helpful is knowing beforehand that the Demonstration of Free Will by Roleplayers is ongoing for another day. Judgment Day is extended. Pray for continuing grace. Pray for the unsane to become sane.

CHAPTER 33

TOWER OF BABEL

As improbable as the story of the Flood is, once the Ark reaches land and the family departs, other notable events occur that are just as improbable.

One of the biggest events affecting everyone's life in the new world began at Babel. Babel was a city under the rule of Nimrod: Nimrod of Cush, Cush of Canaan, Canaan of Ham, Ham of Noah. Nimrod and the people of Babel have an extremely ambitious plan that changes the world yet again.

The Bible does not use the words "Tower of Babel" in the name of Babel. The phrase used is "city and the tower." The story supports the reason for differences in language across the world. For a couple of thousand years, from Adam to Noah and families, there was a common language spoken. Someone, perhaps Nimrod or other group, devised a plan to erect an edifice of enormous height. The building would signify a tangible achievement of human endeavor and progress. God ended the project in that it undermines His plan of human diversity over the whole earth. The Demonstration Of Free Will must be made conclusively and exhaustively.

> And Cush begat Nimrod: he began to be a mighty one in the earth. He was a mighty hunter before the Lord: wherefore it is said, Even as Nimrod the mighty hunter before the Lord. And the beginning of his kingdom was Babel, and Erech, and Accad, and Calneh, in the land of Shinar (Genesis 10:9-10)

> And the whole earth was of one language, and of one speech. And it came to pass, as they journeyed from the

> east, that they found a plain in the land of Shinar; and they dwelt there. And they said one to another, Go to, let us make brick, and burn them thoroughly. And they had brick for stone, and slime had they for morter. And they said, Go to, let us build us a city and a tower, whose top may reach unto heaven; and let us make us a name, lest we be scattered abroad upon the face of the whole earth. And the Lord came down to see the city and the tower, which the children of men builded. And the Lord said, Behold, the people is one, and they have all one language; and this they begin to do: and now nothing will be restrained from them, which they have imagined to do. Go to, let us go down, and there confound their language, that they may not understand one another's speech. So the Lord scattered them abroad from thence upon the face of all the earth: and they left off to build the city. Therefore is the name of it called Babel; because the Lord did there confound the language of all the earth: and from thence did the Lord scatter them abroad upon the face of all the earth (Genesis 11:1-9).

As you think about changes in language, you may wonder how Moses could write about what happened in the Book of Genesis? How did he have access to what transpired in the Garden of Eden, events outside Eden with Cain and his descendants, and with Seth and his descendants? How could he have written the Pentateuch, the first five books of the Bible?

Well, God assisted Moses with what to write. Of course!

And beyond how did Moses achieve such an improbable accomplishment, just read the Book of Genesis. Miracle after miracle after miracle! It all starts with God creating everything from nothing! When you've got God,

Jesus, the Holy Spirit, and a host of angels as your resources, you are truly unlimited.

You may wonder: Why confuse the languages of the people erecting the Tower? God could have brought an end to the endeavor in assorted other ways. Why disrupt the building project by impeding communication? Why not utilize:

- Multi-factor acts of stopping construction such as the building collapsing every three days.
- Evil spirits haunt the building, and the workers get vertigo and acrophobia.
- Demonstration of a sign or wonder from God. Intolerable weather, animals, or angel visitation.

But God had a specific plan that featured language as the prime component.

The scriptural citation that the languages were confused at Babel should include nuances of accent, diction, intonation, pronunciation, and idiom. It may not be that the original language from God to Adam and Eve was now extinct. The original language could have survived but now existed with diverse branches.

And, parenthetically, the use of language in America could also be labeled "confused." It's not that other languages besides English are disruptive. It's that English is frequently redefined, new words are created, and common words are commandeered and reapplied. One generation doesn't understand another generation. One ethnic group's English is misunderstood by another group's English. Adding to the differences is a concerted contempt for misapplication and ignorance of long-established English usage. The situation appears to worsen with each generation.

In the case of what transpired at the Tower, it could lend further support for the roleplay feature needed to portray Free Will in human agents. *The preference for man's Free Will over God's Determined Will must be demonstrated as an error beyond any reasonable doubt.* The proof is achieved by the presentation of immense divergence in free agents. These agents must exercise Free Will under multiple combinations of circumstances. *You can't get that result when there is one great people, in one great location, with one great culture and language.*

In those days, when God disrupted the universal language, there must have been great consternation at the inability to communicate. There must have been further trauma as people were forced to converge based on a common language.

This must be an Act of God. What does it mean? How long will it last? Is this a curse?

This language event was not that far removed from the Flood event. The new challenge now was community participation. Everyone relied on the community for safety, sustenance, and the prevalent mandate of procreation. Now that there are these divergent groups based on language, the first order of business is to provide for the immediate group. Only then are they able to offer help to other groups. People began improvising on communication: sign language, body language, use of objects, illustrations on the ground, illustrations on objects, whatever it took to facilitate intention.

In a sense, I'm doing the same as I speak to you as an artist. I'm giving an abstract illustration of reality using unfamiliar phrases and concepts. As I provide further details of the biblical story, I portray a modern, abstract impression. I do so in the spirit of the Christian Reformed theological doctrine. Your salvation was guaranteed before you were born. The identity you are born with is part of the Demonstration of Free Will through living Roleplayers who began with Adam and Eve (and the Serpent, who also has Free Will but no soul). This is a model of Christian Reformed Impressionism.

Jesus's number one message declared you are not your body, but rather you are a spirit in a physical dimension. Jesus relived the role Adam was given to perfect it. Once perfected, Jesus fulfills the promise to redeem humanity. We are to follow the example Jesus preached. We may be given the Holy Spirit that assists us through our roleplaying assignment. Our physical identity assignment was forced upon us by birth, but we're to overcome that as much as possible by recognizing it is not our true identity. Our true identity is spiritual, safe in Heaven.

And if you are not one of the Elect? Do you have no Super Spiritual Identity (SSID) counterpart in Heaven? How is that imagery portrayed in MARVI-RPIA?

You have no soul, no eternal spirit. You are not 100 percent human. Non-Elect Roleplayers may not know their authentic Elect identity until late in life or the last moments of life, as demonstrated by the thief on the cross. They may never realize it. There is no reason to give up hope in a fatalist way of thinking. If you are not Elect, at death your Free Will roleplay mission ends. You die. You cease to exist. There is no afterlife.

As a Roleplayer, the Identity Array you possess means any afterlife identity not fit for continuing life in Heaven will be explicitly discarded as waste. Waste is a by-product of living. Animals, plants, trees, food, water, and organic matter provide sustenance to the living person. Life produces waste. Similarly, non-Elect Roleplayers, once living, may function as temporary, transient, assistants to the Elect Roleplayers, perhaps even as intimately as a lover or spouse. But once life ends for them, they will simply no longer exist.

Does it sound crude to think of a human as waste? The analogy is to dung, vessels fitted for destruction (Romans 9:22). The vessels designated are suited for a future non-life in the afterlife. Oblivion. Forgotten. Extinguished.

And if not 100 percent human? What about 99 percent, 80 percent, 70 percent, even 55 percent? This is still MOSTLY human. Isn't that good enough for God to save? Where is His mercy?

To us, yes. Less than 100 percent human is acceptable. To God, not likely. Why? Jesus was a 100 percent HUMAN BEING. His redemption was for 100 percent human beings. Not angels, not angel-human hybrids. Not aliens from space. Not animals.

Adam and Eve were 100 percent human beings. Jesus became 100 percent human to correct THEIR sin that doomed US all—the "us" that qualifies as 100 percent human.

Don't forget: MARVI-RPIA has it that your true identity is ALREADY in Paradise.

Continuing with the story of Babel …

Once it is deserted and the Tower left incomplete, people disperse. Later, they converge in groups of similar languages. A new assortment of Roleplayer attributes applies to various new communities. The second layer of factors is about to be added to the human race. Besides language, up next is geography, or location, as a maneuver to affect human diversity. The Earth will be divided.

CHAPTER 34

PELEG

> And unto Eber were born two sons: the name of one was Peleg; for in his days was the earth divided; and his brother's name was Joktan (Genesis 10:25).

Why don't we hear more about Peleg? Considering the earth was divided in his days, it would seem Peleg would be famous. Of course, the phrase "earth divided" can have more than one meaning. Assuming the context refers to PEOPLE of the earth divided, that supports the theme of Babel, where the people are no longer ONE group, but groups divided by language.

What if the division of the earth is PHYSICAL, as in landmass division? How many continents were there before the Flood? How many continents after the Flood? We know any great earthquake that causes the separation of large landmasses must be a catastrophe of great proportions. One suggestion, advanced by John Morris of the Institute of Creation Research, cites an Ice Age solution:

I am convinced that Genesis 10:25 should not be understood to imply that "In the days of Peleg the Atlantic Ocean opened up." This would have caused devastation comparable to Noah's Flood, and the Bible has no mention of it. If the continents separated, they did so during Noah's Flood.

The traditional interpretation relates Peleg's day to the division of language/family groups at the Tower of Babel. Comparing the lineage of Shem, which includes Peleg, to the lineage of Ham, which includes Nimrod, leader of the rebellion at Babel, we find it likely that Peleg was born soon after the dispersion (assuming the genealogies are complete). Thus, it would have been reasonable for his father Eber to name a son in commemoration of this miraculous event.

One "separator" did occur sometime after the dispersion. The Ice Age, which followed the Flood, would have caused sea level to be an estimated 600 feet lower than today, since such a great volume of water was trapped as ice on the continents. Such a lowering of today's seas would reconnect the continents once again. The connected continents would have aided in both animal and human migration following both the Flood and the dispersion, as commanded by God (Genesis 8:17,11,4,8,9). Then the ending of the Ice Age and the melting of the ice sheets would cause sea level to rise, covering the land bridges and "dividing" the continents after migration had occurred. Morris, John D. 1993. *What Happened in the "Days of Peleg"?*

An image of people living across the world speaking different languages now emerges. How do the people look and behave? How do we get the disparity between skin color, facial features, hair texture, physique, and abilities? What caused ethnic differentiation?

Science has no uniform answer as to when, where, why, or how the classifications of race originated. Religion assumes everyone began with the male and female in the Garden of Eden. *Connecting The Dots Of Identity* imagery supports racial differentiation that began in Eden. How would that be so?

Given that the lands of Canaan, Cush, and Nimrod were North African or Middle Eastern, dark skin was not uncommon in that region. Families of the sons of Noah settled in various separate regions. Light skin color and other ethnic markers serve as a pattern to point of origin. Going further into the ancestors of the family of Noah reveals the three wives of the sons of Noah. Were the wives dark-skinned or light-skinned? Did they exhibit physiological features other than that of Noah's sons? What about Mister and Missus Noah? What about Adam and Eve? What types of differentiation did God implant in Adam and Eve so that all races evolved from them?

God could certainly have placed dominant and recessive racial traits in Adam and Eve. Perhaps Cain and Abel resembled their parents, perhaps not as much. Did the Nephilim affect dominant and recessive racial traits? Did the post-Garden of Eden environment affect the embryos in Eve's womb? We know absolutely that environmental factors contribute to birth defects. Birth defects are rare and don't proliferate. However, the devolution of Adam and Eve by way of sin certainly instigated diminishing qualities of their identity—mental ID, spiritual ID, and physical ID.

In the post-Flood world, the air, land, waters, plants, animals, and fish were all now changed. Food and drink are not as they were. The weather was different. Families and newborn children are now a product of the new environment. This new environment is partially submerged under tons of organic and inorganic matter. *But people must live from the products produced by the transformed environment.*

Birth defects today are just a tragic fact of life. Knowledge is limited regarding how to prevent or appropriately classify them. *They are not all physical or structural. They can be genetic, chromosomal, or biochemical.* If a mother and father of a newborn child experience abnormalities in the child, treatment is available to them. Treatment may be ineffective. The parents may not know of the defect until the child is much older, *or they may never know.* Some defects are moderate, others are deadly—slow death, sudden death, mysterious death, and suicide.

What may be considered a birth defect may not be considered a defect to the person in question. The defect may simply be a deviation from a normal range of acceptable conditions. When we look at the wide range of variables affecting the fetus in the womb, the challenge is to determine what feature or combination of features plays the determining role in physical/mental attributes. Factor in the medical history and habits of the mother and her ancestors, before and during pregnancy. Factor in the medical history of the father and his ancestors in roleplay expressions. How do types of radiation, pollutants, toxins, and undiscovered elements affect mental and physical development?

The takeaway is that from biblical history, the genetic code, the blueprint God had for Adam and Eve, was compromised by sin. *One of the popular lines used by pastors is "God made them (Adam and Eve) male and female."* This is taken to mean there cannot be gender changes or true gay people. I will attach a second line. *Sin made Adam and Eve's progeny a corrupted blueprint of male and female, not God.* People often say, "God made me gay." No. God made the blueprint. Sin modified the blueprint. You may be gay, but not because of God. *Adam and Eve made you gay via cursed heredity, cursed environment, and cursed experiences.*

Is same-gender attraction a birth defect? Yes. Absolutely. Is it abnormal? No. Not at all.

Birth defects are simply an indication of heredity, environment, and experience of Roleplayers in the Demonstration of Free Will.

Is sin a birth defect? Yes. Absolutely. Is sin abnormal? No. Not at all.

According to scientific consensus worldwide, same-gender attraction is normal. This means it is not so unusual to be considered outside the norm of society. The act itself is not in judgment. The basis of acceptance became the frequency and popularity of the act. Really?

Murder is popular. Theft is popular. Rape is popular. Pedophilia is popular. Are they accepted?

Murder is frequent. Theft is frequent. Rape is frequent. Pedophilia is frequent. Are they accepted?

Think about it. Don't answer so quickly.

Let's get back to biblical history.

From the heavenly hosts to Adam and Eve, Nephilim, the Flood, Noah's descendants, Babel, and Peleg, there has been a roller-coaster ride of developments. A new group now comes to focus as the Lord singles out a people to produce the Messiah. The Error in the Garden of Eden will be resolved in a magnanimous, beautiful, gracious way—Jesus the Christ.

CHAPTER 35

GOD'S CHOSEN PEOPLE

God's chosen people are the Elect – the ones chosen from before the foundations of the world (SSIDs). Let's call this Group 1. Group 2 of God's chosen people are the ones who receive the Holy Spirit (HSIDs). This comes near conception, at birth, or after being born. The Holy Spirit may have secured you without any apparent manifestation. Some people are confident about which day God intervened to save them, and others don't know the year God intervened in their life. The point is that He does it. The timing runs the gamut, from John the Baptist in the womb of his mother Elizabeth to the thief on the cross with Jesus in the last moments of life.

> And it came to pass, that, when Elisabeth heard the salutation of Mary, the babe leaped in her womb; and Elisabeth was filled with the Holy Ghost: And she spake out with a loud voice, and said, Blessed art thou among women, and blessed is the fruit of thy womb. And whence is this to me, that the mother of my Lord should --come to me? For, lo, as soon as the voice of thy salutation sounded in mine ears, the babe leaped in my womb for joy (Luke 1:41-44).

> And one of the malefactors which were hanged railed on him, saying, If thou be Christ, save thyself and us. But the other answering rebuked him, saying, Dost not thou fear God, seeing thou art in the same condemnation? And we indeed justly; for we receive the due reward of our deeds: but this man hath done nothing amiss. And he said unto

> Jesus, Lord, remember me when thou comest into thy kingdom. And Jesus said unto him, Verily I say unto thee, Today shalt thou be with me in paradise (Luke 23:39-43).

There is a third group of God's chosen people: the people of Israel. As the Book of Genesis continues with documenting the descendants of Noah through Shem, Peleg, and others, the names conclude with Abraham. God speaks directly with Abraham as He did with Noah. God makes a covenant with Abraham that includes Abraham's descendants, and from them to the rest of the world.

Abraham's blessed son is Isaac, and Isaac's blessed son is Jacob. From Jacob comes the name Israel. One of Jacob's blessed sons is Judah. From the name Judah, the term "Jews" is derived.

In the New Testament Books of Matthew and Luke, the ancestors of Jesus Christ are listed. In Matthew, the line is traced from Abraham, going up through the Old Testament, and concludes in the New Testament at Jesus's stepfather, Joseph, the husband of the Virgin Mary.

> The book of the generation of Jesus Christ, the son of David, the son of Abraham. Abraham begat Isaac; and Isaac begat Jacob; and Jacob begat Judas and his brethren; And Judas begat Phares and Zara of Thamar; and Phares begat Esrom; and Esrom begat Aram; And Aram begat Aminadab; and Aminadab begat Naasson; and Naasson begat Salmon; And Salmon begat Booz of Rachab; and Booz begat Obed of Ruth; and Obed begat Jesse; And Jesse begat David the king; and David the king begat Solomon of her that had been the wife of Urias; And Solomon begat Roboam; and Roboam begat Abia; and Abia begat Asa; And Asa begat Josaphat; and Josaphat begat Joram; and Joram begat Ozias; And Ozias begat

> Joatham; and Joatham begat Achaz; and Achaz begat Ezekias; And Ezekias begat Manasses; and Manasses begat Amon; and Amon begat Josias; And Josias begat Jechonias and his brethren, about the time they were carried away to Babylon: And after they were brought to Babylon, Jechonias begat Salathiel; and Salathiel begat Zorobabel; And Zorobabel begat Abiud; and Abiud begat Eliakim; and Eliakim begat Azor; And Azor begat Sadoc; and Sadoc begat Achim; and Achim begat Eliud; And Eliud begat Eleazar; and Eleazar begat Matthan; and Matthan begat Jacob; And Jacob begat Joseph the husband of Mary, of whom was born Jesus, who is called Christ. So all the generations from Abraham to David are fourteen generations; and from David until the carrying away into Babylon are fourteen generations; and from the carrying away into Babylon unto Christ are fourteen generations (Matthew 1:1-17).

In Luke, the line of Jesus begins with Joseph (Jesus's stepfather) and identifies persons going back from the New Testament through the Old Testament, concluding with Adam as the son of God.

> And Jesus himself began to be about thirty years of age, being (as was supposed) the son of Joseph, which was the son of Heli, Which was the son of Matthat, which was the son of Levi, which was the son of Melchi, which was the son of Janna, which was the son of Joseph, Which was the son of Mattathias, which was the son of Amos, which was the son of Naum, which was the son of Esli, which was the son of Nagge, Which was the son of Maath, which was the son of Mattathias, which was the son of Semei, which was the son of Joseph, which was the son of Juda, Which was the son of Joanna, which was the son of Rhesa, which

was the son of Zorobabel, which was the son of Salathiel, which was the son of Neri, Which was the son of Melchi, which was the son of Addi, which was the son of Cosam, which was the son of Elmodam, which was the son of Er, Which was the son of Jose, which was the son of Eliezer, which was the son of Jorim, which was the son of Matthat, which was the son of Levi, Which was the son of Simeon, which was the son of Juda, which was the son of Joseph, which was the son of Jonan, which was the son of Eliakim, Which was the son of Melea, which was the son of Menan, which was the son of Mattatha, which was the son of Nathan, which was the son of David, Which was the son of Jesse, which was the son of Obed, which was the son of Booz, which was the son of Salmon, which was the son of Naasson, Which was the son of Aminadab, which was the son of Aram, which was the son of Esrom, which was the son of Phares, which was the son of Juda, Which was the son of Jacob, which was the son of Isaac, which was the son of Abraham, which was the son of Thara, which was the son of Nachor, Which was the son of Saruch, which was the son of Ragau, which was the son of Phalec, which was the son of Heber, which was the son of Sala, Which was the son of Cainan, which was the son of Arphaxad, which was the son of Sem, which was the son of Noe, which was the son of Lamech, Which was the son of Mathusala, which was the son of Enoch, which was the son of Jared, which was the son of Maleleel, which was the son of Cainan, Which was the son of Enos, which was the son of Seth, which was the son of Adam, which was the son of God (Luke 3:23-38).

In order to arrive at the promised Messiah, Jesus, care had to be taken to ensure the BLOODLINE didn't become corrupted and also matched PROPHECY throughout the Old Testament. Life in those days was no bed of roses. People often reject the whole basis of religion solely on the depiction of Old Testament life.

At that time, there were no police departments, fire departments, hospitals, pharmacies, newspapers, electricity, running water, refrigerators, clothing stores, dentists, surgeons, public transportation, or broad communication. The Bible even states that people just behaved in a way they felt was satisfactory in their own eyes.

> In those days there was no king in Israel: every man did that which was right in his own eyes (Judges 21:25).

Doing the things that seem right in your eyes may not be right in someone else's eyes. There was no universal standard of rightness that could be applied, given the logistics of the undertaking at that time. There were lawyers, courts, and judges, but they were for a generalized locale and not applicable to persons outside of a community who didn't respect local law.

People did what was right in their own eyes until judges were installed that ruled the "civilized" people of God. After this, the kings ruled the people of God. We follow along in the Old Testament Books of Judges, I Kings and II Kings, and other books of that period. There were frequent wars. The people of God were often despised by people of the lands who were not of God. Some groups of people had kings, some had various leaders, and some lived and died by power, shrewdness, and guile. The strong survived; the weak were taken advantage of. The weak died. The weak were killed.

Particularly galling to atheists and agnostics is how God Himself participated in killing those of His own chosen people. God also killed people who did not believe in Him. It appears that not only is God unfair in His concern for every person, but He also brutalizes men, women, children, animals, and even the environment, without pity.

Further, the laws and commands that God institutes are obviously crude. Capital punishment for the most minor infractions is standard fare. Women, children, ethnic groups, the poor, and the uneducated seem to have no rights or standing. Not until the New Testament, when Jesus arrives on the scene, is there a semblance of decency and love. *Yet even Jesus Himself condones and affirms the credibility of the Old Testament.* The message of the "Good News" given over the centuries may be adequate for Christians but seems inadequate to the general public. *Connecting The Dots Of Identity* could help change that.

The change started with a realization of what Jesus's number one message may have been: you are not your body. From this, the implication comes that you are a spiritual creature in a physical dimension. Jesus taught that He came to undo what Adam and Eve caused to happen to humanity, namely sin and death. Jesus lived a sinless life, died, and conquered death by rising again.

From this, we who are born into the circumstances of life must overcome the apparent identity we have to recognize we have a spiritual inheritance from God who has adopted us. We are temporarily imprisoned in physical reality. Meanwhile, we strive to overcome the plight that is not of our choice or knowledge. You are a Roleplayer in a temporal domain. *Your true identity is already guaranteed in Heaven before you were born.* "Trust Me," says Jesus. He is perfectly trustworthy.

Certainly, that should be good news. Is Jesus trustworthy enough? Is the Bible trustworthy enough? Whom can you trust? Scientists? Intellectuals? Friends? The Church? Do you trust the culture in which you were raised? Maybe you don't trust anyone. You believe your innermost gut feeling.

Whether you trust the religious view or the secular view, MARVI-RPIA aspires to reimagine your position. You may still hold your position while wondering if MARVI-RPIA has any real value. If it is only art, is that art helpful? If it is more than art, is it meaningful as a worldview? A good test may be how well MARVI-RPIA answers questions of substance. The best answers to the most influential questions should be featured. They will be featured.

GOD'S CHOSEN PEOPLE—POSTSCRIPT

Read through the Old Testament Book of Numbers, Chapter 18. As you read, it becomes obvious this passage is specifically for Jews and not Gentiles. God lays out His plan for the sons of Israel, for the tribe of Levi among the sons of Israel, and for the priesthood. It's pretty straightforward. However, with repeated reading, a spirit of the words atop the letter might produce something like this:

Verses 20, 29, 31, and 32 speak of a specific group within the group of God's people who will NOT have a portion or inheritance. This is the tribe of Levi. Everyone wants a portion and inheritance, provisions that ensure security for the future. These provisions are typically a spouse, children, and valuable possessions such as land, animals, food, and wealth. The scriptures in the chapter declare God, Himself, will be their portion and their inheritance. In doing so, God commands the people to give their best as gifts to the Levites and priests for their service to the people and for performing their assignment from God.

So long as the priests, the ones who speak for God, sacrifice and offer their best in honor of God, no sin is counted against them. No sin means their heart is pure.

But I don't want to be a priest within a group like the Levites. I don't want to be in a group like the Levites. I want to be one of the people who makes their own portion and inheritance. I want to have a spouse, children, land, and wealth. I want things in my own hands. If I depend on God, my prayers may not be answered, especially if it means I must depend on the people of God to support me. That sentiment is well understood.

But these verses look at the *letter* of the program, not the *spirit* of the program God instituted for Israel. In the Book of Genesis, the spirit of the program Adam and Eve may have been given was the authority over God's Garden. Adam and Eve were the epitome of beauty in the Garden. They were charged with representing the life and beauty of the Garden. They were not only working FOR the Garden, but they WERE the Garden.

Our responsibility is possibly like their responsibility. If you are a male, be a Gardener. If you are a female, be a Gardener. Maintain the beauty and life source of your environment, the animals, the plants, the waters, and the land.

And after the Fall? Now that the mandate has shifted from providing the Redeemer through procreation, the responsibility shifts back to caring for the environment. *The environment now is the environment of PEOPLE.* To be a Gardener of the People requires tending a garden that is overrun with fellow gardeners who are corrupt, disinterested, and oblivious to the plight of the environment. *They don't see themselves as part of the environment.* They are individuals, independent sovereignties of their own little worlds.

Even so, with objective moral leadership and a great program, the Garden's chances of evolving versus devolving increase.

Be a Gardener of the People.

CHAPTER 36

IDENTITY ARRAY—CONTINUED

The essence of *Connecting The Dots Of Identity* is to illustrate the discrete identity of the Elect. From this identity flows the imagery of an eight-part identity array of who we are. At this point, the very height of who you are is a spiritual essence in Paradise with the Lord. We are the Elect, the persons identified in scripture as granted salvation before the foundation of the world (Ephesians). This is a vision of ontological status—being—before birth on Earth.

> According as he hath chosen us in him before the foundation of the world, that we should be holy and without blame before him in love: Having predestinated us unto the adoption of children by Jesus Christ to himself, according to the good pleasure of his will (Ephesians 1:4-5).

Here we see individual acknowledgment of personhood by God. He knows us. He has a name for us. That name, noted in scripture, is written in the (Lamb's) Book of Life. God has our unique God-given name reserved there in Heaven. This is different from God knowing who we would become after being born because of His omniscience. God does know that person too. That is a separate creation. That earthly creation is based on a blueprint for human beings. That occurred when God created Adam and Eve. That blueprint was altered by sin.

> And there shall in no wise enter into it any thing that defileth, neither whatsoever worketh abomination, or

> maketh a lie: but they which are written in the Lamb's book of life (Revelation 21:27).

Since there is no specified name for the Elect persons God has saved before the world was created, *Connecting The Dots Of Identity* names them Pre-Life Elect or Super-Spiritual Identities (SSIDs). They are with the Lord, outside of time, in Paradise. Conscious? Alive? The relevant imagery is that SSID beings are recognized as *non-born individual persons residing in Paradise, in an unknown state with the Lord.*

The distinction of the SSID outside time from the Free-Will Roleplayers inside time supports a reason for two human identities: an *authentic* identity and an *inauthentic* identity. Additionally, God established spiritual life, the angels, and heavenly hosts.

Did God actually create SSIDs? We know the Father, Son, and Holy Spirit are not created. They are self-existent. Angels were created. The world was created. But are the Pre-Life Elect, those saved from the foundation of the world, in existence right now? Do SSIDs possess the same spiritual existence as angels and other heavenly hosts? Do they possess a similar spiritual essence as deceased elect humans who are now in the presence of the Lord? Do they possess a similar spiritual essence as Virgin Mary and John the Baptist? Adam and Eve? Melchizedek?

Does God have a sense of obligation to create SSIDs before they assume ontological status?

Continuing the MARVI-RPIA impression, the world is created to demonstrate the Free Will of a flawless person made in the image of God. The angels also have Free Will, but they are not made in the image of God, and they do not have a test (as in the Tree of Knowledge of Good and Evil).

The flawless creatures made in God's image acted of their Free Will. They choose to disobey God's will to pursue their own will. The penalty was death, but death was worth the risk to act freely. God imposed the penalty but provided mercy. A promise was given to rectify the death penalty by procreation. A Redeemer will emerge in the future.

The flawless creatures were created spiritually, mentally, and physically. They differ from the heavenly hosts, who were created spiritual and mental—not physical creations. The flawless creatures, Adam and Eve, are now no longer flawless. They are dying. Their only solution to correct their error is to procreate. Their offspring will produce the Antidote to their disastrous failure.

The spiritual, mental, and physical identity of Adam and Eve is expressed as SID, MID, and PID. *So now, along with SSID, we have four of the eight identity array names.* When Adam and Eve experience life outside the Garden, another facet of identity becomes evident: dreams. They both have visions while sleeping. They dream of themselves who are not themselves but have their personal point of view. This dream identity is abbreviated as DID. *There are now five of the eight identity array names.*

Once outside the Garden, Adam and Eve are taught procreation. God instructs them on intercourse, pregnancy, delivery, nurturing, and child-rearing. *The first child, Cain, initiates the sixth named identity, which is the childhood identity—CID.* Interestingly, Adam and Eve also possessed a childlike identity of sorts. Adam and Eve have an obscure recollection of their pristine identity in the Garden. In their present flawed condition, recall of the past is limited and seems to decrease over time. Who they were is no longer 100 percent accessible. In the Garden, partaking of the Tree of Life from time to time, meant they didn't age. Every day was yesterday, today, and tomorrow. Now, they age, and their children age. Their childlike innocence in the Garden of Eden ended.

The second child, Abel, arrives. One day, Cain kills Abel (Genesis 4:8). Adam, Eve, and Cain experience the death of Abel. Finally, the three know what sudden death is. They bury Abel. Cain is banished to another land. Brothers and sisters leave home to assist Cain. It's important that the Bible indicates Abel was in favor of God. *This introduces the seventh identity marker: Holy Spirit Identity (HSID).* We can see a contrast in the character of Cain and Abel.

When a person is transformed from being a Free Will Roleplayer, initiated by the error of Adam and Eve, to an Elect Roleplayer, this is evidence of Holy Spirit intercession. They say that falling in love is meeting a special someone who is so unique, so wonderful, and so interesting that you are irresistibly drawn to them. Your wish is to be inseparable. You want to know more about them. You are constantly surprised and delighted by their presence. This is how God introduces Himself to you. It may be gradual, in flashes, or a memorable moment.

It's reasonable to fear a spiritual entity that intervenes in your personal space. But as described above, you are irresistibly drawn. There is no fear. God doesn't overrun you, intrude, or interfere. This intervention is an introduction to the One that loves you, the One that absolutely knows and absolutely loves you.

Think of a blind date. Your relatives and friends are telling you they have someone they want you to meet. They say this person is truly beautiful, truly romantic, truly fun, truly smart, truly confident, and truly ready to begin a relationship. They know what you like and GUARANTEE you will not be disappointed.

As a single person, you feel apprehension. (1) The person sounds too good to be true, (2) you wonder if you are worthy of such a person, and (3) what if this person rejects you?

With HSID, the Person IS too good and IS true, you ARE worthy of such a Person because THEY choose YOU and will NOT reject you. In fact, the blind date is ALREADY a success. The timing may not be apparent.

The last-named form of identity a Roleplayer may possess is the evil spirit identity (ESID). The situation is a Roleplayer who is not an Elect person and becomes compromised by evil. No Elect Roleplayer (SSID) can be possessed or compromised by ESID. You have 100 percent protection. You may be harassed, troubled, or bothered from time to time by evil forces, but never in jeopardy of damnation.

By the way, there have been, and may continue to be, those who actually are demon-possessed. However, if that person is an Elect Roleplayer, HSID exorcizes ESID. In scripture, no Christian is, or remains, demon possessed.

> Ye are of God, little children, and have overcome them: because greater is he that is in you, than he that is in the world (1 John 4:4).

There are concerns regarding King Saul in the Old Testament.

> But the Spirit of the Lord departed from Saul, and an evil spirit from the Lord troubled him. And Saul's servants said unto him, Behold now, an evil spirit from God troubleth thee (1 Samuel 16:14-15).

> And Saul was afraid of David, because the Lord was with him, and was departed from Saul (1 Samuel 18:12).

In the New Testament, the old woman whose stature is bent over from affliction is due to an evil spirit. Is the phrase "daughter of Abraham" a child of God or simply a title of a group?

> And ought not this woman, being a daughter of Abraham, whom Satan hath bound, lo, these eighteen years, be loosed from this bond on the sabbath day? (Luke 13:16).

We come to understand the Elect and non-Elect may suffer demon oppression from time to time. If the Elect or non-Elect does become demon possessed, the Holy Spirit depossesses at His will.

> And certain women, which had been healed of evil spirits and infirmities, Mary called Magdalene, out of whom went seven devils (Luke 8:2).

> Now when Jesus was risen early the first day of the week, he appeared first to Mary Magdalene, out of whom he had cast seven devils (Mark 16:9).

BAD AS IT LOOKS?

As bad as things can look, as in demon possession, there seems a chance God may still intercede on your behalf. Once again, the thief on the cross, a condition that may not be as dire as demon possession, but you are in the last seconds of life. Does God rescue you?

Think of Judas Iscariot. How much worse can life get? He betrayed Jesus Christ. He was indwelt by Satan. Is there any chance Judas also asked Jesus to remember him? How much time passes as he hangs by the neck, the rope breaks, he drops and is disemboweled?

Someone must be the person to play the role in the life of Jesus that contributed to His well-publicized death. Judas, as well as various other Roleplayers, bore crucial "assignments" centered around Jesus's life and death. This event could not be left to chance or a haphazard series of everyday affairs.

The death of Jesus could not be a natural death of old age or dying in His sleep. It could not be circumstantial, accidental, or a case of manslaughter. His trial and sentence should carry the drama of blasphemy, treason, or sorcery. *The details must stand the test of time.* His death would be slow, purposeful, assured, tragic, public, and memorable. *Crucifixion fits the part!*

He was a famous person. Yes—confirmed.

He was the person claiming to be God. Yes—confirmed.

He was the same person confirmed deceased. Yes—confirmed.

Roman law and religious law document His demise. Yes—confirmed.

Several people had major roles to play in making sure Jesus died at a certain time. The someone who had the major role of the traitor was Judas Iscariot. Yes, Jesus said it would have been good for that man if he had not been born (Matthew 26). We could say the same for Roleplayers such as Pharaoh, Jezebel, and Pilate. It's good if you are not born to fulfill a bad role. But everyone has an individual role to play. Otherwise, they wouldn't be conceived.

Even if a mother loses a child without ever knowing she was pregnant? Even in unsuccessful in vitro fertilization situations? Does the unrealized person have a role to play? What role would that be?

The role in such cases is mainly through the persons who produce the conception rather than by the conceived person.

> The Son of man goeth as it is written of him: but woe unto that man by whom the Son of man is betrayed! it had been

> good for that man if he had not been born (Matthew 26:24).

Do I think Judas has an SSID counterpart in Heaven? Do I think Judas was a non-Elect Roleplayer? Was he a person destined for oblivion being less than 100 percent human? In the Book of John, Jesus is speaking of not losing any of the Elect except the son of perdition. Is that Judas, under damnation before he died?

> While I was with them in the world, I kept them in thy name: those that thou gavest me I have kept, and none of them is lost, but the son of perdition; that the scripture might be fulfilled (John 17:12).

I think of the second thief on the cross. He hears the first thief asks to be remembered. Jesus assures him he will be with Him in Paradise. Does the second thief remain silent? Is he already dead? Does he observe what happens when Jesus died, Jesus's last words, darkness, earthquake, etcetera? Does the first thief entreat the second thief? Is there strength to talk during the hours all three are dying?

Being a Free Will Roleplayer means the identity you possess is not really you. Jesus's number one message may have been you are not your body. You are a spiritual creature in a physical dimension. This is the abstract impression I have that I try to illustrate. You ask yourself why you do what you do. Why do you think what you think? That was me in the dream, at least it was my point of view, but that person is not me. I don't want to look the way I look. I don't want the brain I have inherited. I really don't want to be me because I had no say-so in creating this version of me.

We know who we are comes from our parents, grandparents, great-grandparents, and others as heredity. The environment shapes our thinking and behavior. Experiences also dictate how we have developed. In a certain sense, we're not 100 percent responsible for who we are because of so many factors that aren't in our control, never have been in our control, and never will be in our control.

A two-year-old girl in a remote village isn't mature enough to understand General Revelation—the truth of God as revealed in natural phenomena. No Special Revelation, the "good news" of Jesus Christ in scripture, ever arrives. She dies young of malnutrition and disease.

Is she a non-Elect Role Player, destined to be nonliving waste matter in Hell?

Is she less than 100 percent human and simply ceases to exist at death, like an animal?

Is she Elect before the foundation of the world, before she was born, with an SSID counterpart in Paradise?

And another person is sixty-six years old, overweight, and gay. He has molested and abused six people. He is passing away in the hospital from alcoholism and drug addiction. He's mad at the world because he's deathly ill and his family mistreats him. Life has always seemed so unfair to LGBTQ people.

Is this guy a non-Elect Role Player?

Will he have any change in identity before death?

If he is Elect, identity change should occur. He will not think and behave as before. It will take time, but he has to change. If he does not change or dies before change occurs, he should still have an SSID counterpart in Paradise. He dies. His Free Will roleplay identity has played out. Yes, it shows error. We all show errors. Unless and until the Holy Spirit intervenes, no roleplayer has a significant change in objective morality. We don't do this by our own will. God does it.

It is so wonderful that even an embryo in the womb can achieve Elect status. Remember John the Baptist in his mother Elizabeth's womb? A person in the last seconds of death can achieve Elect status, just like the thief on the cross. And the opposite may also apply. An embryo may not be Elect. It may not be 100 percent human. *It has a unique role, but chronological age is no factor in how God views identity.*

LOOKING INTO THE FUTURE

A major question you may have is: *On what basis does the Holy Spirit choose to grant salvation to Roleplayers? Is it a relationship to the number of SSIDs in Paradise—one-to-one?*

A second question in the back of your mind may be: *If life is a roleplay Free Will demonstration, when will the demonstration end?*

Good questions. Fair questions. No answers ... yet. Maybe when more material is fleshed out in the second book, *Connecting The Dots Of Identity-2*. The chapters coming up next on Hell and Heaven may provide further insight.

Meanwhile, the advantage of the MARVI-Roleplay Identity Array is to describe components of who you are to prevent disassociation. Disassociation comes from layers of subordinate identities. These eight identity array classes are simple. Complexities of identity models confound the definition of who you are. You are not your occupation, your spouse, your child, your hobby, your fantasy, or your idol. You are a discrete being. Your role is not who you are. It's a role.

Roleplay is the Free Will error instigated by Adam and Eve that you inherited from every person in your ancestral line. You had no say-so in being conceived. You are you without your knowledge or permission. You go through the motions you are taught until you learn for yourself how-to-live skills. Your life proceeds through circumstances of heredity, environment, and experiences. If you are one of the Elect, the Holy Spirit intervenes between the time of conception and death. If not, your roleplay mission of demonstrating Free Will is in process until death. Adam and Eve set it in motion. You continue it.

Why should you suffer because of Adam and Eve? This debacle is not your fault. But it is your fault. You would have done the same thing they did, given the same set of circumstances, with the same superb intellect. Do you really think you are more intelligent than Adam and Eve were in the Garden of Eden? You don't have any way of understanding what was on the minds of flawless creatures in a flawless environment. You are a flawed creature in a flawed environment.

The consoling point MARVI-RPIA attempts to provide is that there is more than one "you." Identifying which you is the true you (SSID), and offering the Roleplayer you as a temporary "you" that demonstrates the Free Will error of Adam and Eve—which is rectified by Jesus Christ who has guaranteed your salvation before you were born, proving it by becoming a second Adam, living a sinless life publicly, dying publicly, and overcoming death publicly so we have a trustworthy historical record of what life is all about—is the you that is being painted.

We can know who we are. We can know why we're here. *When bad things happen, we know it's not happening to us. Bad things happen to our roleplay identity. That identity has nothing to do with us. We are not our body, our brain, our childhood, or our dreams. Those things were crammed down our throats years ago without our permission or our knowledge.* Half of the things in our distant past we don't even recall accurately. Our mission is to recognize we're not trapped by circumstances of the past, present, or future. We have hope. We have comfort. We have a future.

Jesus Christ proclaimed in his acts of healing that following His principles gives eternal life. When he healed blindness, deafness, lameness, and deadness back to life, He illustrated spiritual ideals. *When the Holy Spirit intervenes in a person's life, they now see, hear, walk, and live with new understanding. Words have new meanings. Life is transformed. You are a different person.*

So what you were raped, molested, assaulted, robbed, cheated on, and became ill. Or maybe you were the one who raped, molested, assaulted, robbed, cheated, and caused illness. *You must not accept those events as part of who you are. You must not relive those events as a part of who you are. You are not trapped in your body. You are not trapped in your mind. You are temporarily in possession of them, but you are essentially a spiritual creature. You cannot be trapped.* It seems traumatic, confining, and excruciating; but it's temporary. It will end. Life is a feature of what Adam and Eve passed down to every person. It's a Demonstration of Free Will.

The exercise of Free Will, at the risk of death by partaking of the Tree of the Knowledge of Good and Evil, didn't cause death right away. Or maybe it did. Maybe Eve dropped dead fairly quickly. God started over. Eve goes to Adam, and he eats. They both drop dead moments later. God starts over. It could be as God goes through scenarios, losing their life doesn't teach them anything new. They eat of the tree, no matter the scenario. So, God changes death to become a prolonged, ongoing, extension of dying, with all its better or worse, sickness or health, richer or poorer woes.

All the progeny from Adam and Eve inherit and then pass down to their children the error of Free Will. There is no way to recreate what Adam and

Eve felt about their decision to pursue knowledge of good and evil. The transition from being a flawless creature in a flawless environment to a flawed creature in a flawed environment must have been the trauma of all traumas.

As one of the first reminders of their error, they are exposed to death in animals, trees, plants, birds, and fish—all the things they cared for in the Garden. Then they experience the death of Abel. That is bad enough, but it is at the hands of their firstborn child, Cain. Their own child, their flesh and blood, took his brother's life. He committed an act only God has the right to commit. What should we do with Cain? He can no longer be trusted.

Perhaps they attempted to revive Abel. They could not. Maybe preserve Abel's body. They could not. Abel had to be removed from sight. Just imagine their distress. Decomposition of a loved one's body. Is decomposition what they will also experience?

Now, the best course of action is to ensure recovery of what has been lost by continuing childbirth so that the Redeemer may appear as promised by God. Death is horrible. It must be conquered. Life must be redeemed.

And now, the Redeemer has appeared. Death is conquered. It's thousands of years later and an innumerable number of deaths later. However, it's all for the best. Isn't it?

Then why does the Demonstration of Free Will continue? Does the whole world have to hear about Jesus Christ through the Special Revelation of scripture? Doesn't the whole world need to receive the General Revelation of God through Nature? Salvation is granted based on grace, not granted on works of knowledge or behavior. How many lives does it take to prove God's Determined Will for humans is superior to a human's Free Will for itself? It's not known what number of lives it takes to prove the point, but adding your life to the proof may hasten the end of the Demonstration.

The end of the Demonstration indicates Judgment Day for all Roleplayers. The inauthentic identities of Roleplayers are judged based on roleplay circumstances. Roleplay is judgment. Life is judgment. There is no “day” of Judgment. Judgment is outside time. No more days.

Those graced with salvation before the foundation of the world are NOT judged.

Those less than 100 percent human cease to exist. Judgment for them is oblivion.

This leaves the Devil and his angels. Hell is created for them. That’s their judgment.

CHAPTER 37

HELL—PART 1

Two of the most dynamic elements of MARVI-RPIA are the images of Hell and the images of Heaven. In the transition from childhood, through adolescence, and into adulthood, the afterlife is a haunting mystery. Death is inevitable. What happens to me after I'm dead? Something or nothing?

If NOTHING happens, this is almost the best-case scenario. Almost the best case, because Heaven is obviously the best case, but this is only if SOMETHING happens after death.

If something DOES happen after death, will that be Heaven or Hell? Heaven is the sure choice, but how do you get there? The belief is you get there by being good and not being bad. This is accomplished by following the guidelines set forth in "religion."

What about Hell? Too horrible to think about. It can't possibly be true. DON'T think about it. If you must consider it, treat it as humor, fable, or satire.

In the meantime, you're in a quandary as you sort through how you want to live your life. Your identity develops through trial and error, circumstances and desire, talent and necessity. *All the while, in the back of your mind, there's this little bit of dread. You have no idea when you are going to die.* It could be five minutes from now. It could be in five months, five years, or in fifty years. Would you go to Hell? Do you have to believe in Hell to go there? What if there is no Heaven or Hell, and you throw your life away in the interest of achieving Heaven—or simply doing what's necessary to avoid Hell?

Which worldview is best?

The atheist-secular worldview? They propose Heaven and Hell do not exist. There is no acceptable definition of God – especially the God of the Bible.

The agnostic view? Though agnostics don't commit to atheism, they live as atheists. Being spiritually blind, there's no belief in God or an afterlife until God opens their spiritual eyes.

The theistic worldview? Heaven and Hell are real destinations.

Connecting The Dots Of Identity illustrates another worldview: You are ALREADY in Heaven—the authentic you which is SSID. The inauthentic you are the Free Will Roleplayer here in the present.

No one goes to Hell except those who have no SSID counterpart in Heaven—the non-Elect Roleplayer.

Those who have no SSID counterpart in Heaven aren't 100 percent human beings. As Roleplayers, they are conceived, demonstrate Free Will based on heredity, environment, and experience, and die. Their roleplay ends. They cease to exist. There is no afterlife.

Persons who die as non-Elect Roleplayers, not receiving HSID, have no soul—no spirit. Were they to continue into the afterlife, it would mean joining Satan and his angels in Hell. Hell is created for the Devil and his angels.

Now a reminder from Chapter 18. The *figurative* image of Hell as only for the Devil and his angels can be seen at the time of the Flood. Who's in Hell—the Abyss—A, B, or C?
A) Abaddon and other Third-Class Angels.
B) The Nephilim.

C) Human beings.

A! *Only the evil angels were put into Hell.*

Why not the Nephilim—half human, half angel? Why not human beings—all except eight?

> For if God spared not the angels that sinned, but cast them down to hell, and delivered them into chains of darkness, to be reserved unto judgment (2 Peter 2:4).
>
> And the angels which kept not their first estate, but left their own habitation, he hath reserved in everlasting chains under darkness unto the judgment of the great day (Jude 1:6).
>
> And they had a king over them, which is the angel of the bottomless pit, whose name in the Hebrew tongue is Abaddon, but in the Greek tongue hath his name Apollyon (Revelation 9:11).
>
> Then shall he say also unto them on the left hand, Depart from me, ye cursed, into everlasting fire, prepared for the devil and his angels (Matthew 25:41).
>
> And fear not them which kill the body, but are not able to kill the soul: but rather fear him which is able to destroy both soul and body in hell (Matthew 10:28).

Of course, there are implications MARVI-RPIA raises. *Are the worst people in history escaping Hell and now abiding in Heaven? Since I'm 100 percent human, I can do whatever I want and still go to Heaven?*

Doesn't Hell lose its deterrent status if only non-Elect Roleplayers go there, who are actually not 100 percent humans?

Do non-Elect Roleplayers have a sense they are not Elect, especially considering someone like the thief on the cross with Jesus? He must have assumed he was not a follower of God until the last few seconds of his life. But ... he joined Jesus in Paradise.

The worst people in history are just Roleplayers. They either transition to their authentic identity in Paradise or cease to exist.

- You won't want to do whatever you desire when you are born again by the Holy Spirit. You are a NEW creature. You won't change overnight, but you should grow in spiritual maturity.

- Non-Elect persons do not know they are not Elect. They have no way of knowing without divine intervention. They're still spiritually blind. Some of them may ASSUME they will be in Heaven. They're led astray by family, culture, and religion. Once again, assurance can only be valid, no matter the feeling, when bestowed by the Holy Spirit. As scripture warns:

  > For such are false apostles, deceitful workers, transforming themselves into the apostles of Christ. And no marvel; for Satan himself is transformed into an angel of light (2 Corinthians 11:13-14).
  >
  > For there shall arise false Christs, and false prophets, and shall shew great signs and wonders; insomuch that, if it were possible, they shall deceive the very elect (Matthew 24:24).

Theologians teach that Jesus preached more about Hell than Heaven. That may be so. It stands to reason that, when you're a child, your parents use the most negative term, “no,” more often than the most positive term, “yes,” to shape your development of what is right. Similarly, a strong threat of destruction is a credible deterrent to wrongdoing. What more negative term exists than Hell?

Also, Jesus taught in parables.

> All these things spake Jesus unto the multitude in parables; and without a parable spake he not unto them (Matthew 13:34).

Does the concept of Hell go beyond what is credible as a deterrent for misconduct? *Ninety-nine people out of one hundred would probably say "Hell, YES!"* Hell is way, way, WAY more of a punishment than the crime warrants. Torture forever? How is that equitable? What crime could be so heinous to deserve eternity in Hell?

There is some contention about the difference between Hell being PUNISHMENT forever versus PUNISHING forever. Punishment is the penalty that APPLIES forever versus punishing is the penalty that is ONGOING forever. A distinction may have standing if God ultimately destroys souls in Hell. He’s able. Is He willing?

> And fear not them which kill the body, but are not able to kill the soul: but rather fear him which is able to destroy both soul and body in hell (Matthew 10:28).

The one person in a hundred who agrees the concept of Hell is a just punishment is usually a theologian. They say the crime of sin is against His Holy Majesty God. The penalty of misconduct escalates as it applies to the importance of the person the act is against. The classic example goes something like this: You slap your sibling. Crime level 100. You slap your mother. Crime level 1,000. You slap a police officer. Crime level 10,000. You slap the state governor. Crime level 100,000. You slap the president of the country. Crime level 1,000,000. You slap God. Crime level is innumerable.

If God is a God of love, how can He send people to Hell forever?

Life is not an equal opportunity venture. People are born, live, and die under all manner of circumstances. No one has the capability to structure their life and the lives in their circle of influence to choose God. No one can come to the Lord except the Lord draw him.

> No man can come to me, except the Father which hath sent me draw him: and I will raise him up at the last day (John 6:44).

Following conventional Bible teaching on Hell is to affirm everyone will be brought to trial on Judgment Day. The good people will go to Heaven, the bad people to Hell. Here are several verses that speak to the plight facing non-Christians in the afterlife.

> The Son of man shall send forth his angels, and they shall gather out of his kingdom all things that offend, and them which do iniquity; And shall cast them into a furnace of fire: there shall be wailing and gnashing of teeth (Matthew 13:41-42).

> And I saw the dead, small and great, stand before God; and the books were opened: and another book was opened, which is the book of life: and the dead were judged out of those things which were written in the books, according to their works. And the sea gave up the dead which were in it; and death and hell delivered up the dead which were in them: and they were judged every man according to their works. And death and hell were cast into the lake of fire. This is the second death. And

> whosoever was not found written in the book of life was cast into the lake of fire (Revelation 20:12-15).
>
> He that overcometh shall inherit all things; and I will be his God, and he shall be my son. But the fearful, and unbelieving, and the abominable, and murderers, and whoremongers, and sorcerers, and idolaters, and all liars, shall have their part in the lake which burneth with fire and brimstone: which is the second death (Revelation 21:7-8).

MARVI-RPIA images support those conventional views but through rose-colored glasses. Role Play Identity Array imagery portrays those Hell-bound identities as not totally human. Of course, this does not mean they are not human. I'm an artist. I'm rendering an abstract impression using words as a way to grasp Reformed theology.

The Bible also makes use of imagery to convey meaning. Hell is depicted as a place and time to burn waste (New Testament Book of Matthew) and a continuously burning garbage dump outside the city for animals and criminals (Old Testament Book of Isaiah).

> Whose fan is in his hand, and he will thoroughly purge his floor, and gather his wheat into the garner; but he will burn up the chaff with unquenchable fire (Matthew 3:12).
>
> For Tophet is ordained of old; yea, for the king it is prepared; he hath made it deep and large: the pile thereof is fire and much wood; the breath of the Lord, like a stream of brimstone, doth kindle it (Isaiah 30:33).
>
> And they shall go forth, and look upon the carcasses of the men that have transgressed against me: for their worm

> shall not die, neither shall their fire be quenched; and they shall be an abhorring unto all flesh (Isaiah 66:24).

Hell is being described as a place of disposal for wasted lives—or identities. The MARVI-RPIA names of the identities are nonliving waste matter and non-Elect Roleplayers. Hell is referred to as a place made for the Devil and his angels.

> Then shall he say also unto them on the left hand, Depart from me, ye cursed, into everlasting fire, prepared for the devil and his angels (Matthew 25:41).

Does this mean no 100 percent human identities will be in Hell? Less than 100 percent human is a term that suggests two concepts:

a) *The one-drop rule of Nephilim blood (phantom genetic substance) that produces a hybrid angel-human identity.*

b) *An angel impersonating a human being.*

By now, you may say it's not hard to paint almost any picture by isolating specific scriptures and stringing them together. The picture that develops from this doesn't mean it's substantive or significant. Yes, that accusation could apply to MARVI-RPIA. But MARVI-RPIA isn't religion. It's a mural on the surface of a church. A religious IMPRESSION. An artistic IMPRESSION. There's no responsibility to be substantive or significant. It's art appreciation, or not.

Continuing with popular teaching on Hell, the lesson frequently refers to the rich man and Lazarus found in the New Testament Book of Luke. Just as in other books, Matthew and Revelation, for instance, the use of analogy and metaphor occurs. In Hell, there can be no tears or gnashing of teeth. There are no eyes or teeth. Asking for water on the tongue doesn't follow, as there can be no physical attributes in Hell (eyes, teeth, tongue, etcetera). And how long could water last in Hell?

Weeping and gnashing of teeth suggest anguish. Hell is meant to epitomize anguish.

> There was a certain rich man, which was clothed in purple and fine linen, and fared sumptuously every day: And there was a certain beggar named Lazarus, which was laid at his gate, full of sores, And desiring to be fed with the crumbs which fell from the rich man's table: moreover the dogs came and licked his sores. And it came to pass, that the beggar died, and was carried by the angels into Abraham's bosom: the rich man also died, and was buried; And in hell he lift up his eyes, being in torments, and seeth Abraham afar off, and Lazarus in his bosom. And he cried and said, Father Abraham, have mercy on me, and send Lazarus, that he may dip the tip of his finger in water, and cool my tongue; for I am tormented in this flame. But Abraham said, Son, remember that thou in thy lifetime receivest thy good things, and likewise Lazarus evil things: but now he is comforted, and thou art tormented. And beside all this, between us and you there is a great gulf fixed: so that they which would pass from hence to you cannot; neither can they pass to us, that would come from thence. Then he said, I pray thee therefore, father, that thou wouldest send him to my father's house: For I have five brethren; that he may testify unto them, lest they also come into this place of torment. Abraham saith unto him, They have Moses and the prophets; let them hear them. And he said, Nay, father Abraham: but if one went unto them from the dead, they will repent. And he said unto him, If they hear not Moses and the prophets, neither

> will they be persuaded, though one rose from the dead (Luke 16:19-31).
>
> And shall cast them into a furnace of fire: there shall be wailing and gnashing of teeth (Matthew 13:42).

Considering the Bible testifies to the many lives that were cursed—and that, seemingly, being in direct confrontation to the Lord, were destined to Hell—is that actually the case? It may not be. If any person is cursed and dies or is killed by the Lord Himself, the damnation is death. In countless examples, persons commit deadly sins without knowledge of the consequences. Ignorance is no excuse for being unaware of the law, but it certainly happens. Hell, eternal torment, is the consequence? You're dead. You don't learn anything from the offense you committed. You're the example to others, not yourself.

Adam and Eve could have been executed on the spot. They weren't. They were given the opportunity to experience their error every day for about a thousand years. From them, and their ancestors, their lives became examples for us to learn from. Being an example often meant the first person(s) to be killed by doing something stupid, against the law, or being in the wrong place at the right time. They got caught. Don't they deserve mercy for being the example? MARVI-RPIA says yes, but much more than that.

Again, the question may be raised: Why would Jesus preach so much about Hell if everyone is already in Heaven? If there is NOTHING I can do about avoiding Hell and going to Heaven, according to election/predestination, why preach the Gospel? And specifically, if Hell is for the Devil and the evil spirits, why would humans be in jeopardy?

The Free Will Roleplay Demonstration is SO important that God Himself interacts with humans (Adam/Eve/Noah/Abraham/Moses/David, et al).

He does so through General Revelation and Special Revelation. *Life may be the most superb gift God gives His creatures: humans and angels. Their freedom to be autonomous from God is of the highest order for a flawless living creature. The abuse of such a beautiful gift must be allowed if they are indeed free.* In an absolutely magnanimous gesture, God protected humans from eternal damnation. They are identified as being saved before the foundation of the world—the so-called SSIDs.

Not so the angels. Not so those who are not 100 percent human. This lack of protection means no specific provision for persons not identified before the world was created.

So, 100 percent human beings are not in jeopardy?

They're not in jeopardy. But ... *are you a 100 percent human being?*

CHAPTER 38

HELL—PART 2

As you read the scriptures, concepts of Hell make extensive use of analogy, metaphor, and symbols. They are used to build obstacles, preventative measures, and defenses against our natural sinful tendencies. *But if Hell is created for the Devil and demons, is this the reason Hell is such an empty threat to 50 percent of the world?* If Hell is the most effective deterrent against sinful behavior, does this lead to loving God with all your heart, mind, and soul? Does fear of God sending you to Hell inspire you to love Him?

Perhaps Hell is a designated, necessary, exaggerated counterbalance to Heaven. Behave badly, get severely punished. Behave well, get wonderfully rewarded.

Apparently, the opportunity to enter Heaven is insufficient to diminish the degeneracy inherent in all of us. As grandiose as Heaven sounds, people are never sufficiently motivated to NOT behave badly. *If people had the ability to choose Heaven and reject Hell, they certainly would. Why wouldn't they? It seems obvious. But it isn't obvious.* This underscores the principle that unless the Holy Spirit arrives to open our eyes and recreate our identity as new creatures, we will NEVER choose God's will for our life. We choose our own will. It's from Adam and Eve.

Let's assume you COULD choose freely. This is the consensus in most of the world. We think we have Free Will to be agnostic, theistic, or atheistic. So, why not choose to be good and go to Heaven?

Reason 1 – No life-altering examples of Heaven exist. *Heaven has to be a LOT more compelling.*

Reason 2 – No life-altering examples of God exist. *God has to be a LOT more compelling.*

Okay. But in the case of Satan, who has life-altering examples that God exists, why wouldn't he throw himself on God's mercy and avoid Hell? He must know he can't defeat God. If Hell is created for him and his team, why continue the evil misbehavior? Why continue to live?

Reason 1 – *He can't change his mind.* A flawless creature's decision to oppose God is final.

Reason 2 – *He can't prevent living.* He's an eternal spiritual creature. Suicide isn't an option.

Reason 3 – Being flawless creatures, Satan, Abaddon, and others had first-person, direct contact with God. *Exercising their Free Will to oppose God effectively DISFIGURES their flawless image.* Their intellect becomes flawed. This may have been comparable to spiritual suicide. They renounce their God-determined life for an angel-determined life.

The Serpent, Adam, and Eve also opposed God's will. Adam and Eve knew the penalty was death. They exercised their opposition knowing death would follow. That would be suicide.

The Serpent was a flawless creature but possessed no eternal spiritual identity. Should he die, he would cease to exist. No afterlife.
But the Serpent wasn't threatened with death. What did he understand about death? He told Eve she would NOT die. Did he think he would not die?

Adam and Eve knew they would die if they disobeyed God. Then what? There was no Hell to speak of at that point in creation. Was there Heaven to speak of? Would they go out of the physical realm into the spiritual realm? Is the spiritual realm composed of tiers of Heaven? Tier one, tier two, tier three? Is tier three the most Heavenly, and tier one the least Heavenly, but still an abode of spiritual creatures?

What did Satan, Abaddon, and others think would happen to them if they opposed God's will for their life? What penalty for opposition existed? What was God's will for their life before humans were created and after? Were they always deemed ministering spirits? How much freedom does a ministering spirit have? Serving God is one thing. Serving humans must be a whole other story. How did the angel's assumptions, conclusions, and reactions change as human beings became the center of the universe?

Was death a penalty for opposing God's will? Certainly, a flawlessly created being such as an angel, the Serpent, Adam, and Eve could comprehend the cessation of life. What's next? *Would God recreate them? Would recreation change their identity?* The angels were already in Heaven, or Paradise, or a version of Heaven. Would they go into another Heaven if God removed their eternal life? Would they go into oblivion? *Would Adam and Even simply return to the presence of the Lord again, anew, if they ate of the forbidden Tree?* It's not likely Hell was a concept to any of them.

What manner of penalty was death? Soul sleep or a state of total inactivity and unawareness? Do flawless creatures discern the concept of sleep? Do they ever experience fatigue or loss of energy?

Would God have revealed an afterlife to the angels? Would He have revealed an afterlife to Adam and Eve? The Super-Spiritual Identities

(SSIDs) are essentially "before life" identities. There is no before-life counterpart to an angel. God may not have disclosed there was an SSID, a before-life before-time counterpart to Adam and Eve, before they ate of the Tree of the Knowledge of Good and Evil.

The premise of Lucifer's Postulate challenged God's Determined Will for the lives of angels. God's proposed Demonstration of Free Will would prove the liability of Free Will, but would the liability include severe penalties? Would such a penalty describe death? *Would such a penalty go beyond death to introduce the concept of Hell?*

Lucifer was certainly aware of the group of angels who did not approve of his challenge. They accepted God's will for their lives, no matter what. It may not have mattered to Lucifer and his group if God secured another group of heavenly hosts—the non-living Super-Spiritual Identities. What mattered to Lucifer was unrestricted Free Will. If there was anyone who could make that case, He was the person. He was going to push as hard and far as he could to secure ABSOLUTE FREEDOM for every living creature. If God was God, He should be able to make that happen.

Otherwise, was life REALLY worth living? We're obviously locked down by restrictions on our liberties. Have we been created the RIGHT way? If so, why are we displeased? *We may not be flawless after all. There may be a substantive design flaw by our Designer.*

By the way, WHEN was Hell created? Before the foundation of the world? For whom was it created? No one was alive then. Or were they? Probably not the SSID, the ones saved before God created the world. They weren't created to live before time began. Their identity is known but has no ontological status, except as MARVI-RPIA. *Were the angels living when Hell was created? Were Adam and Eve alive when Hell was created?* Do we KNOW that Hell exists?

WHERE is Hell? Is Hell a literal destination or a state of non-being in a non-location where there is no time, no up or down, no in or out, only darkness and disorientation? An eternal spirit creature may experience death, but does that mean they cease to exist? An eternal spirit is eternal. *Is spiritual death a critical loss of self-awareness, the lowest level of cognitive identity?*

The Book of Revelation conveys lurid imagery of Hell. Vivid, graphic, and violent, it ends the Greatest Story Ever Told in horror, dread, and revulsion. It is a phenomenal contrast to the splendor and wonder of Heaven. Is Hell similar to the bottomless pit of Revelation where the evil angels are imprisoned—the Abyss? It's similar in at least two ways.

One is a realization that God exists. He is not for you but against you. *He has sentenced you to an inactive non-life separated from His presence.* What could be worse?

Two is the loss of a most prized possession: freedom. The loss of freedom that defines imprisonment connotes the most oppressive of individual restrictions. This, coupled with darkness, discomfort, and disorientation, substantiates the gravity of the penalty. In this case, *the comparison between capital punishment and life imprisonment brings an added perception, which is that DEATH is impossible.* There is NO escape route. Is the Abyss identified in the Book of Revelation a location in the spiritual world? Is the Abyss metaphorical? Are the angels in the Abyss responding to "psychological" control that creates the environment of incarceration?

And, again, we are often told that Jesus spoke more about Hell than Heaven. We also know that Jesus spoke in parables. In fact, you may recall that scripture states "without a parable He did not speak to them" (Mark 4). Also, Reformed theology teaches no one can come to the Father unless the Father draws him. Opponents of religion shake their heads in disgust. It doesn't make sense. *God is not allowing the freedom to be a good person. And God also allows people to go to Hell because they are not a good person.*

If the Father doesn't draw you, you go to Hell. If you don't figure out Jesus's parables, you go to Hell. The retort from the spiritually blind? Keep your utterly stupid religious barbaric ideas to yourself. It's an insult to our intelligence.

Connecting The Dots Of Identity sympathizes with nonreligious worldviews. How can this God of the Bible in any way be attractive to the average person?

> No man can come to me, except the Father which hath sent me draw him: and I will raise him up at the last day (John 6:44).
>
> And the disciples came, and said unto him, Why speakest thou unto them in parables? He answered and said unto them, Because it is given unto you to know the mysteries of the kingdom of heaven, but to them it is not given. For whosoever hath, to him shall be given, and he shall have more abundance: but whosoever hath not, from him shall be taken away even that he hath. Therefore speak I to them in parables: because they seeing see not; and hearing they hear not, neither do they understand. And in them is fulfilled the prophecy of Esaias, which saith, By hearing ye shall hear, and shall not understand; and seeing ye shall see, and shall not perceive: For this people's heart is waxed gross, and their ears are dull of hearing, and their eyes they have closed; lest at any time they should see

with their eyes and hear with their ears, and should understand with their heart, and should be converted, and I should heal them. But blessed are your eyes, for they see: and your ears, for they hear. For verily I say unto you, That many prophets and righteous men have desired to see those things which ye see, and have not seen them; and to hear those things which ye hear, and have not heard them (Matthew 13:10-17).

This know also, that in the last days perilous times shall come. For men shall be lovers of their own selves, covetous, boasters, proud, blasphemers, disobedient to parents, unthankful, unholy, Without natural affection, trucebreakers, false accusers, incontinent, fierce, despisers of those that are good, Traitors, heady, highminded, lovers of pleasures more than lovers of God; Having a form of godliness, but denying the power thereof: from such turn away. For of this sort are they which creep into houses, and lead captive silly women laden with sins, led away with divers lusts, Ever learning, and never able to come to the knowledge of the truth (2 Timothy 3:1-7).

And they had a king over them, which is the angel of the bottomless pit, whose name in the Hebrew tongue is Abaddon, but in the Greek tongue hath his name (Revelation 9:11).

And I saw an angel come down from heaven, having the key of the bottomless pit and a great chain in his hand. And he laid hold on the dragon, that old serpent, which is the Devil, and Satan, and bound him a thousand years,

> And cast him into the bottomless pit, and shut him up, and set a seal upon him, that he should deceive the nations no more, till the thousand years should be fulfilled: and after that he must be loosed a little season (Revelation 10:1-3).

> And with many such parables spake he the word unto them, as they were able to hear it. But without a parable spake he not unto them: and when they were alone, he expounded all things to his disciples (Mark 4:33-34).

HELL 2—POSTSCRIPT

There are three prominent possibilities of the afterlife: Heaven, Hell, or Nothing.

Possibility One: Good people, the Elect Roleplayers, will transition to HEAVEN as SSID persons.

Possibility Two: Bad people will be in HELL with the Devil and his angels.

Possibility Three: Disbelief in an afterlife means NOTHING happens. It's oblivion. The End.

Connecting The Dots Of Identity extends afterlife imagery to include three more possibilities: the Super-Spiritual Identities, First-Class Angels, and Non-Elect Roleplayers. However, the Pre-Life disposition of Super-Spiritual Identities (SSIDs) doesn't qualify for the afterlife. They were never alive. Likewise, First-Class Angels who never rebelled against God aren't subject to an afterlife. They're always living.

This leaves Non-Elect Roleplayers.

So, as MARVI-RPIA envisions The End, there are Elect Roleplayers and Non-Elect Roleplayers. Non-Elect Roleplayers are either 100 percent human or are less than 100 percent human.
One hundred percent human Roleplayers who don't receive the Holy Spirit before death live out their role and transition to Heaven to join authentic identity as SSID. Their ROLE was that of a Non-Elect Roleplayer.

Less than 100 percent human Non-Elect Roleplayers cease to exist at death.

In the sense that bad people, Non-Elect Roleplayers, are damned and go into eternal punishment, we might envision at least three things:

One: The punishment of forever being excluded from Heaven is devastating eternal punishment. Even though our best concepts of Heaven are good to great in imagination, nonetheless, *the gut-wrenching loss of what Heaven actually is has to be immeasurable.*

Two: To cease to exist could be considered sufficient PUNISHMENT rather than some other continual PUNISHING, as in the concept of Hell. This comparison of a person to other life forms, like animals that cease to exist at death, seems to further punishment. They can neither rejoice at avoiding Hell nor mourn the exclusion of Heaven. They have no soul, no spirit. They may as well be beasts. Not bad enough? Can anyone truly cease to exist? Is energy capable of being destroyed, relative to the First Law of Thermodynamics? What actually happens?

Three: The definition of nonexistence after death might include the type of identity we have while dreaming. Our dream identity does not exist. Nothing in our dreams exists. They are just images. But is it true that dead people do not perceive images or anything else? The dead know nothing. When there is no consciousness, there is no knowledge.

But when a death occurs, are there lingering images that do not instantly disappear? How long do they linger? Does time exist at that point? How long does one second last where no timekeepers exist—no light, no sun, no moon, no stars, no planets?
In our dreams, as our eyes are closed in darkness, no timekeepers exist. Our mind creates everything. If there are nightmares, they are from our imagination. We create them consciously and subconsciously. Will those who are less than 100 percent human "experience" the prophetic warnings of Hell? Perhaps as religious nightmare imagery? Does Judgment Day render this form of judgment on those who cease to exist?

Orthodoxy teaches the "good dead" go immediately to Heaven. The "bad dead" either go to a place of silence awaiting Judgement Day or regain consciousness in Hell. MARVI-RPIA paints the "Last Day" something like this:

Those who are not 100 percent human beings cease to exist at death. There will be no afterlife in Heaven or in Hell. However, on Judgement Day, we are all PRE-JUDGED by how we lived or were conceived. The so-called Last Day could be more like a separation stage for those going to Heaven, those to Hell, and those who will cease to exist. *Life itself becomes the proof of judgment regarding the Demonstration of Free Will. When life ends, so does the Demonstration. Judgment is built in.* Why have a formal arraignment? The verdict is the Demonstration. There is no "day" of judgment where time does not exist.

The Bible gives us clues and examples of the afterlife so that we have some ideas. What literally happens outside time and in the spiritual realm may not be so straightforward. This we should assume.

Some of you might think, let's see if I have this straight ...

If I'm 100 percent human, no matter how my life goes, I'm in Heaven.

If I'm not 100 percent human, no matter how my life goes, I go into Oblivion.

Otherwise, I'm like one of the Devil's angels whom Hell is created for.

But there is no way to prove I'm 100 percent human. Or is there?
And why should I care? It's either Heaven or Oblivion, and I have no say-so in the matter. I can't get myself saved. I can't get myself lost. Only God does the action.

It matters in the sense that life has the essential ongoing drive to know what life is. More knowledge means more control over life, which means more life or more quality of life. Less knowledge means less control, which leads to loss of life.

Lucifer desired full control. Adam and Eve desired full control. Angels and humans gave their lives to procure control.
Knowledge is power. Knowing more than others gives advantages to the intelligent ones. Knowledge helps defend against the advantages of the intelligentsia.

CD1/CD2 isn't knowledge, it's LEVERAGE; leverage against assertions atheists or theists offer as truth. If you have leverage that is reasonable and useful in defense against the best cases for the truth atheists and theists claim, does it matter what you call it? Does it matter if it's not real?

CHAPTER 39

HELL—PART 3

Everybody goes to Heaven because they're already there. Nobody goes to Hell who is 100 percent human. Now, let's review how MARVI-RPIA envisions this impression.

Who goes to Hell?

1) The Devil and his angels. These are Second-Class Angels, Satan and group, and Third-Class Angels, Apollyon and group.

2) Less than 100 percent human beings. These may be those hybrid humans who are compromised by evil spirits. They are non-Elect Roleplayers participating in the Demonstration of Free Will who do not receive salvation (HSID). They do not have a corresponding Pre-Life Elect identity residing in Paradise.

Why don't ALL Elect Roleplayers receive salvation before death?

1) *They DO receive it before death. It's election-predestination! Otherwise, some receive HSID before death. The ones that don't are still Elect.* Free Will roleplay is to prove that unless God intervenes no one chooses salvation, even to the last moments of life.

2) Salvation is improbable to anyone compromised by evil spirits. Jesus appeared as 100 percent human to redeem 100 percent humans—not angels, not hybrid angel-humans, not aliens, not animals.

How do Roleplayers become compromised by evil spirits?

1) Heredity – an ancestor was compromised (Nephilim)

2) Environment and experiences

It seems the idea of being born demon possessed is totally unfair. It isn't the same as being born a sinner, then receiving the Holy Spirit. A person born demon possessed, not 100 percent human, means they have no chance at salvation.

If a person is born demon possessed or is less than 100 percent human, they won't be subject to an afterlife. No Heaven. No Hell. They cease to exist. Their roleplay ends.

Hundred-percent humans who become demon possessed, or oppressed, are another story. Consider King Saul in the Old Testament Book of 1 Samuel. Saul was oppressed by a spirit from the Lord. Later, Saul consulted with the Witch of Endor, which is strictly forbidden by God, to bring Samuel from the dead. Also consider the woman in Luke 10, who was physically impaired by an evil spirit. Saul and the woman received healing from their oppression. Evil spirits were cast out by Jesus, and followers of Jesus could perform exorcisms. Mary Magdalene had seven devils cast out (Luke 8:2). So, demon oppression/possession isn't a condemnation to Hell. Demon possession or oppression isn't necessarily permanent.

> Then said Saul unto his servants, Seek me a woman that hath a familiar spirit, that I may go to her, and enquire of her. And his servants said to him, Behold, there is a woman that hath a familiar spirit at Endor (1 Samuel 28:7).

> And certain women, which had been healed of evil spirits and infirmities, Mary called Magdalene, out of whom went seven devils (Luke 8:2).

> And ought not this woman, being a daughter of Abraham, whom Satan hath bound, lo, these eighteen years, be loosed from this bond on the sabbath day? (Luke 13:16)

The other side of the coin is that being born demon possessed goes all the way back to the Nephilim. The following groups "removed" in the Flood include:

- **Group 1:** 100 percent humans. These were babies in the womb, babies born, toddlers, children, adolescents, and adults.
- **Group 2:** Persons produced by angels and human females (Nephilim).
- **Group 3:** Persons produced by Nephilim and human females (Nephilam).
- **Group 4:** Persons produced by Nephilam and human females (Nephilom).
- **Group 5:** Persons produced by Nephilom and human females (Nephilegion).

Of course, groups three, four, and five are made-up names to portray generations of family types existing before the Flood. These families indicate the progression of offspring initially produced by Nephilim and human females. The offspring was "engineered" to produce the male gender.

If angels and humans produced offspring 500 years from the time Enoch was "no more" at age 365 to Methuselah's last years of life at age 969, imagine their effect on the population for that period of time.

Finally, it all comes to The End.

All these groups of people died in the Flood. The angels who initiated contact with human females—Abaddon and group—did not die in the Flood. They were captured and relegated to chains of darkness. Noah,

Noah's sons, and Noah's son's wives did not die in the Flood. As hopeless as life seemed, God had mercy on those eight people. They were sinners like all the others who were killed. God saved a few.

Of the eight sinners that were saved, the possibility exists that so-called Nephilim genetic material or immaterial would be present in subsequent generations. This would account for the appearance of "giants" in scripture after the Flood. This also accounts for other people who exhibit less-than-human attributes in their thinking and behaving. If they don't seem human, maybe they aren't 100 percent human.

Using the phrase "one-drop rule" to suggest evil spirit immaterial-genetic-substance as a "drop of blood" that corrupts human blood is artistic impressionism. Though we accept the XX and XY chromosomal definitions for gender, other factors influence identity. If human females are XX and procreate with an angel AA, the progeny could be:

–AA/XX = Axy hybrid person (male Nephilim giant). Dominant angel. Recessive human.

–AA/XX = aXY or aXX hybrid person (human male or human female). Dominant human. Recessive angel.

Do angels have tangible chromosomal markers? Are all angels male? The "giants" who are referenced in the Bible were always male, and always evil.

Were there female giants?

If angel-human female offspring produced female Nephilim, were they considered "normal" human beings with recessive Nephilim chromosomal immaterial? Did human females know their babies were going to be giants? Parents never know with 100 percent accuracy how their children will turn out. The children themselves are always discovering components of their own identities.

Is it ever apparent that a person is not 100 percent human? No. Not without the assistance of the Lord. God witnesses with our spirit that we are children of God. Otherwise, how can we ever know? The Devil is the master deceiver. Humans aren't capable of discerning Satan's deception without God's help. Additionally, we deceive other people and are deceived by our own nature.

> The Spirit itself beareth witness with our spirit, that we are the children of God (Romans 8:16).
>
> And the great dragon was cast out, that old serpent, called the Devil, and Satan, which deceiveth the whole world: he was cast out into the earth, and his angels were cast out with him (Revelation 12:9).
>
> There were giants in the earth in those days; and also after that, when the sons of God came in unto the daughters of men, and they bare children to them, the same became mighty men which were of old, men of renown (Genesis 6:4).
>
> And there we saw the giants, the sons of Anak, which come of the giants: and we were in our own sight as grasshoppers, and so we were in their sight (Numbers 13:33).

The MARVI-RPIA imagery of nobody going to Hell who is 100 percent human isn't beautiful for everyone. There are people who don't feel human, don't want to be human, and just do not care. There are people who lack confidence that they are 100 percent human. If asked, they will readily affirm being human. But as Free Will Roleplayers demonstrate the effects of heredity, environment, and experiences, how would they know who they really are? No one can know until God reveals it to them. God may not reveal it. Full-on humanness may apply even without knowledge of it. In the case of abortion or early death, that person may have never thought about humanness.

The consolation is that God is running the show. We know there are three groups of people we are concerned about when we look at the Flood and when we look at non-Elect Roleplayers. The three groups are:

1) those in the womb of the mother;

2) children; or

3) mentally deficient adults.

Our concern regards the apparent innocence of individuals. Our sense of innocence is subjective. We have no access to the true identity of a person. God does. He doesn't see an embryo, a baby, or a child. He sees them as whole identities. Chronological age is never a factor in how innocent and pure a person is. We are all sinners at conception.

The overarching principle to keep in mind is that Jesus Christ is the Savior for human beings, not angels. Jesus is 100 percent human. Jesus is 100 percent God. Jesus accomplished what Adam did not accomplish: perfection. God's flawless human creations committed a gross error, but God Himself became a flawless human to recover the devastating loss.

A remaining question to be answered regards the 100 percent human beings that Jesus redeems. How much humanity is required to be redeemed by Jesus's saving grace? Does 1 percent human qualify? Is 10 percent human enough to merit salvation? Must a person be 100 percent human in every single case? Why can't 99.9 percent of human identity qualify for redemption?

Adam and Eve were 100 percent human, but their error was the worst error in human history! Abaddon (Hebrew name) or Apollyon (Greek name) and the angels who sought a redeemer for angels through procreation with human females surely committed a lesser sin than Adam and Eve. Angels simply wanted what humans were promised—a savior.

And Lucifer, before he becomes Satan, the accuser, was even less worthy of damnation when asking for angel omnipotence to behave as desired (Glossary/Chapter 19 – "Lucifer's Postulate"). A flawless living creature expects absolute freedom. That seems a reasonable inquiry.

Whether God saves all 100 percent humans or not rests with Him. Whether or not persons can be saved who are not 100 percent human rests with Him. God's salvation plan for Roleplayers who are 1 percent human or 100 percent human is perfect. God's plan is fair, righteous, and loving. God's plan is perfect! MARVI-RPIA's plan: not perfect, but marvi-lous.

HELL 3—POSTSCRIPT

Now, again, the reminder that *Connecting The Dots Of Identity* is NOT theology, but art. Still, the temptation to refute 2,000 years of orthodox teaching will arise. *Modern Abstract Religious Verbal Impressionism*, MARVI-RPIA, is meant to give the same kind of inspiration, stimulation, and elation you get from other art forms. Music, movies, architecture, dance, literature, etcetera, all do this.

However, when you're presented with orthodox theology that does NOT inspire, stimulate, or elate you, you might complain, critique, or dismiss it as illegitimate. In the case of Reformed theology, it's important to point out NOT to do this. Though you may want to walk out in the middle of a sermon, delete your religious videos, or debate Christian friends, try to remain neutral. Engage where appropriate to clarify positions but don't advocate CD1/CD2 as theology. Christian Reformed Impressionism may help to present theology, but only as art, never orthodoxy.

Some of the most noted, scholarly, representatives of Christian Reformed theology teach very stridently about Hell. All too often, it seems their doctrine of Election and Hell is inconsistent. There will be plenty of reasons why a follower of Christian Reformed Impressionism would want to walk out of an orthodox sermon.

Notable scholar Dr. X made the following statements:

> If you, as a Christian, don't warn people about Hell, you SHOULD and WILL burn in Hell. Why shouldn't you? If you KNOW what's in store for the sinner, you have an obligation to tell them the way to avoid Hell at all costs. He goes on passionately about people going to Hell every single day, and Christians doing so little to bring Hell to the forefront of people's thinking. Dr. X says no one mentions Hell these days.

Continuing, the other points of the sermon are as follows:

1) If you are a Christian, you're saved. But you might still go to Hell if you neglect to warn people of impending damnation.

2) People in Heaven will be aware of people in Hell as further blessing of avoiding Hell.

3) Satan, himself, will be tormenting people in Hell.

That first point implies you can lose your salvation by not warning. Were you ever saved if you could lose your salvation?

The second point is a summation of what Dr. X thought was a distinct possibility of what Heaven could be. You may be able to rejoice in Heaven KNOWING your family, friends, or associates are tormented in Hell, because this glorifies God's JUSTICE for the evildoers and glorifies God's GRACE for believers. You are a witness to this from the splendor of Heaven!

The third point characterized Satan as an impresario in Hell as he commands his demons and tortures his human subjects. You may have heard this from the pulpit for years. You certainly see it portrayed in nonreligious imagery.

The church has taught us to avoid Hell at all costs. It's doubtful if half the world's population believes in Hell, the Devil, or demons. The church has taught us to strive for Heaven at all costs. It's doubtful if half the world's population is truly motivated by any descriptions of Heaven. It's doubtful if half the world's population even believes in an actual afterlife.

This is why art is the means of communicating with you. Religion leaves a lot to be desired for many of us.

The Bible is replete with verses on election-predestination. There are 100 verses listed in Chapter 6. If you are elected, chosen, set apart, recognized, and identified by God as being saved before the foundation of the world, you should NOT ever lose that salvation.

The second point, as noted in the upcoming chapters on Heaven, is that the Bible indicates you will NOT ever be exposed to former negative things of the past. Does God expect people in the magnificence of Heaven to observe those in the horrors of Hell? Hell no! That is—no, it's unlikely God would expect that. Think of Lot's wife. She was safe in Zoar! She looked back. She looked back on damnation from a place of rescue and reward. She became corrupted.

And third, are we to believe that Satan is like a manager at the gym? He brings in weak, out-of-shape sinners and torments them on the excruciatingly diabolical fitness equipment. It's always Satan as the grand master, directing his demons on the finer points of punishing the damned sinners.

However, it's far more likely that Satan and the demons will be the ones receiving the torture. They won't be presiding over anything. They will be reduced to the lowest level of existence as they endure the specific result of opposing, accusing, and objecting to the will of God for their lives.

Yes, we have an obligation to introduce God to the ungodly. We do so by our actions and our lives. We do so by speaking of the attributes of God. We do so by speaking and explaining the scriptures. The strategy of warning people about Hell should always include a way of addressing the inability of avoiding Hell by "works." Grace has to be presented in a way that encompasses patience and confidence that God will save them, no matter how ridiculous election-predestination seems.

You can't do anything to avoid Hell. I can't do anything to prevent you from Hell. Only God does the work, and the work was done before the foundation of the world.

Don't take *Connecting The Dots Of Identity's* word for it. This is art. Read your Bible. Think for yourself. Wait patiently on the Lord. He's around. He's omnipresent.

> And it came to pass, when they had brought them forth abroad, that he said, Escape for thy life; look not behind thee, neither stay thou in all the plain; escape to the mountain, lest thou be consumed ... But his wife looked back from behind him, and she became a pillar of salt (Genesis 19:17, 26).

CHAPTER 40

HEAVEN—PART 1

Heaven—the crowning beauty of *Connecting The Dots Of Identity*! Everyone goes to Heaven because everyone is already there. No one goes to Hell who is fully human. Only nonliving, eternal spirit-beings, angelic or subhuman, will abide in Hell.

By the magnitude and significance of scripture attesting to the veracity of the Pre-Life Elect, we can have confidence that salvation was bestowed on individuals before the world was created. Those individuals have a distinct, definite, designation with the Lord. They have no access to the roleplay identities in the physical world and vice versa. The Pre-Life Elect are not "alive" but have spiritual ontological existence—whether in the "mind" of God, a specific spiritual essence, or a particular indescribable presence with the Lord remains obscure.

So, what is the reason for life on Earth, inside time and space?

This is where the mural of Free Will Roleplay and Identity Array comes in. As illustrated in the preceding chapters, God instituted a Demonstration. The Demonstration regards the Free Will of flawlessly created beings. *Will they exercise Free Will to act in the interests of the creature, or in the interests of God?* The Demonstration applied to God's human creatures, but God's angelic creatures previously posed a similar inquiry. Angels implored God to grant unlimited behavior to them based on God's omnipotence and omniscience, to correct any transgressions as they may occur in the life of the angel.

God admonished them. Free Will to behave without omnipotence and omniscience violates the spirit of life for oneself, for others, and for the environment. Life is love. God awarded one of the most precious gifts He possesses to His creatures—life. This is God's love. We are to honor and cherish our gift by glorifying the Giver and sharing the gift with others. We are not to first seek honor and glory for ourselves.

The Demonstration scenario takes place in a flawless environment. The environment contains a test in the figure of a tree, the Tree of the Knowledge of Good and Evil. The interests of God are for Adam and Eve. Do not partake of the tree. The interests of Adam and Eve should be the interests of God. It didn't turn out that way. Adam and Eve did partake of the tree. The penalty is death. They begin dying.

The angels are in observance. The angels are the ones who initiated the question of a creature's desire for freedom. In the case of angels, it was freedom to behave—omnipotence. In the case of humans, it was freedom of knowledge—omniscience.

Seeing the behavior of humans choosing their own interests rather than God's interests gave the angels reason to marvel at human conviction. Adam and Eve chose death rather than restricted Free Will. Being no longer flawless creatures, God also cursed the environment so that flawed creatures didn't confound the flawless environment.

Astonishment came to the angels when God made Adam and Eve a promise. Their colossal error would be corrected by procreation in the future. God will send a Redeemer to reclaim human flawless life.

A group of angels considered a strategy whereby they also may exercise Free Will in opposition to God's will for their lives. *The quest: proceed to obtain a redeemer for angels.* Imitate humans. Facilitate procreation via human females. From the Book of Genesis, we see the plan fail. God causes the Flood. Life begins anew with Noah and his family.

From Noah to Abraham, Abraham to Moses, Moses to David, David to Jeremiah, Jeremiah to Jonah, and Jonah to Malachi, the last book of the Old Testament, there has been plenty of drama. Along with the drama comes death. Too much death, we daresay. But no matter how bad it seems, it's all worth it when we reach the New Testament. We reach Jesus Christ.

Jesus proves He is the Messiah. He teaches we are not our bodies; we are spiritual creatures. The kingdom of Heaven is at hand. We now have our flawless life, guaranteed restoration by His magnificent testimony of words and deeds.

As Roleplayers living an existence dictated by circumstances of heredity, environment, and experiences, who we are on earth is not our true identity. We don't fully realize this until God intervenes in our life. God shows us the plight we're in is due to Adam and Eve. Sin corrupts our understanding. We are simply acting out the error of thinking and behaving in our own interests, rather than the interests of God. This is a Demonstration of Free Will. The flawless humans failed. A large group of flawless angels failed also.

Two other groups did not fail:

1) The Pre-Life Elect before the foundation of the world

2) First-Class Angels who refused to exercise Free Will in pursuit of their own interests.

Another group to consider is those who are reverently referred to as martyrs. They died in service and in honor of the Lord. Perhaps the Pre-Life Elect ones are with the martyrs, or with the general Elect who are deceased. That is doubtful. The Pre-Life Elect are not thought to be alive or have been alive at any time. Their status may be inactive—inanimate.

You may wonder about the status of life for the Elect who are deceased. The Christian Reformed Church, and many other churches, follow the general principle asserted by Apostle Paul:

> We are confident, I say, and willing rather to be absent from the body, and to be present with the Lord (2 Corinthians 5:8).

In other words, when an Elect person dies, they go immediately into the presence of the Lord. Another scripture is from Luke. The dying thief will be in Paradise that very day.

> And he said unto Jesus, Lord, remember me when thou comest into thy kingdom. And Jesus said unto him, Verily I say unto thee, Today shalt thou be with me in paradise (Luke 23:42-43).

It's a comfort to be told that all Elect persons are immediately in the presence of the Lord at death. But is that the case? Why would it not be the case? Being absent from the body implies death. Not a question there. A question arises concerning the phrase "presence with the Lord."

The Lord is omnipresent. The very definition of God includes this attribute. Most every religious person affirms that. The Lord is present with you right now. You are not dead. The Lord is present with me. I'm making words appear. The Lord may not actually be occupying all locations, as in being everywhere at the same time. He does not have to be. His omniscience has an awareness of all space(s). The point is that there may be more to the destination of the Elect than the phrase "presence with the Lord." *We have all been present with the Lord from the moment of our conception. Maybe even before conception.*

The other matter in the image of MARVI-RPIA is the day the thief on the cross joins Jesus in Paradise. On the day 100 percent human Jesus (not 100 percent God Jesus), and the thief on the cross are declared dead, they both have access, that day, to Paradise. Since there is no time in Paradise, a "day" is one continuous time. Human or Divine Jesus could spend three days in the grave and still join the thief "later" when it is "always today" in Paradise.

When we think of time, it's with the assumption of a "whenness" in a sequence of events. Then, now, and later for example. Where there are no timekeepers in place, such as the sun, moon, and stars, it's harder to conceptualize time. In your dreams and in your imagination, you may go forward and backward in time, but it's always in the context of conventional timekeepers.

Where God is the timekeeper, outside conventional time, the standard of light, dark, and the awareness of whenness has changed. An hour, a day, or a year doesn't have our definition.

> But, beloved, be not ignorant of this one thing, that one day is with the Lord as a thousand years, and a thousand years as one day (2 Peter 3:8).

Are people enjoying Heaven right now? What is right now when there isn't a now, then, or later?

- They are with the Lord.
- The Lord is omnipresent.
- They are enjoying the Lord's presence.
- At death, the conventional timekeepers cease.

- God is the new Timekeeper of Heaven, including the New Testament verses of the New Jerusalem.

Describing Paradise, Heaven, is impossible. Well, it's possible, but not likely to be accurately defined. Considering MARVI-RPIA is not theology, but art, it could still be uplifting. It should be uplifting. Thoughts of Heaven should come up off the page you're reading and fill your heart with the Lord's presence, His omnipresence.

This is quite a challenge. Does any spiritual imagery really lift your heart? Does the Bible do that for you? If it doesn't, shouldn't it? Is your church service boring? Is your worldview boring? Is your worldview joyous? Is your worldview reflective of who you really are? Who are you?

We've now had a little introduction to Heaven. So, let's continue with a Minister of Art portrait of Heaven.

HOW CAN THIS BE HEAVEN?

One day, The End comes! The trumpet(s) sound, the environment changes, the deceased Elect arise, and the living Elect arise. They meet Jesus in the air (1 Thessalonians). Presently, God creates a new heaven and new earth—a New Jerusalem-type environment. We are provided with a new body for the new environment. It's possible we will have the flexibility to be spiritual and physical, like the angels.

However, even though looking through the rose-colored glasses MARVI-RPIA creates, all is not what may be expected of Heaven. What's one thing we all hear people say they expect to do or see once in Heaven? *Greet loved ones*. They want to meet and see people (or animals) from the recent past, or even the ancient past. Adam and Eve, Noah, Moses, Enoch, Elijah.

They want to see their mother, father, siblings, relatives, friends, and lovers. They want to see their pets, musicians, celebrities, teachers, pastors, and the martyrs.

Now, a question for you. *Why do you want to see them?*

Probably because you want to *confirm they're in Heaven.* You're happy for them and confirming they're with you makes you happy. You also want to *share memories* of the Free Will Demonstration of the past life with the ones you loved.

Share memories of the previous life?

There are no negative memories of former things in Heaven. Former things regarding your inauthentic identity and the inauthentic identities of others would hardly seem appropriate in Heaven. People, places, and things of the former life are all tainted with sin. Born-again Christians have no pleasure in the people, places, and things regarding their former identity. The person of the past is an utterly regretful reminder of what made me the person I came to be. God interrupted and I became reborn.

The particular scriptures that confirm selective memory retention aren't always clear if God or the people of God are in view. For example:

> For, behold, I create new heavens and a new earth: and the former shall not be remembered, nor come into mind. But be ye glad and rejoice for ever in that which I create: for, behold, I create Jerusalem a rejoicing, and her people a joy. And I will rejoice in Jerusalem, and joy in my people: and the voice of weeping shall be no more heard in her, nor the voice of crying (Isaiah 65:17-19).

In either case, although you want to be a part of a super-reunion of people you love, admire, and respect, that may not happen as you have heard.

And what will everyone look like? Will they have a chronological age? We hope not. If no chronological age, how will we know them? Will all my relatives appear to be eighteen years old? Will my stillborn child appear one week old? My husband was six foot seven. Will everyone be the same height? My fiancée had red hair and lots of curves. Is she still the same?

> For the Lord himself shall descend from heaven with a shout, with the voice of the archangel, and with the trump of God: and the dead in Christ shall rise first: Then we which are alive and remain shall be caught up together with them in the clouds, to meet the Lord in the air: and so shall we ever be with the Lord (1 Thessalonians 4:16-17).

> And I saw a new heaven and a new earth: for the first heaven and the first earth were passed away; and there was no more sea. And I John saw the holy city, new Jerusalem, coming down from God out of heaven, prepared as a bride adorned for her husband (Revelation 21:1-2).

> For, behold, I create new heavens and a new earth: and the former shall not be remembered, nor come into mind (Isaiah 65:17).

Isn't there some sort of comfort to be found in the scripture about David and his deceased child?

> And he said, While the child was yet alive, I fasted and wept: for I said, Who can tell whether God will be gracious to me, that the child may live? But now he is dead, wherefore should I fast? Can I bring him back

> again? I shall go to him, but he shall not return to me (2 Samuel 12: 22-23).

What about King David? The usual consolation given is David indicates he will be going to Heaven and seeing his deceased child there. That could be true. However, David is likely speaking of going to the child at the time of his own death. How is seeing an infant in Heaven good for the infant? No infants are in Heaven. No fetus, no newborn, no toddler. For David to see an infant in Heaven or an adult in Heaven, knowing this is his child, how is that helpful? Knowing the child is Elect? That's God's business. Does a child grow up in Heaven? Is there a progression of time there?

> There shall be no more thence an infant of days, nor an old man that hath not filled his days: for the child shall die an hundred years old; but the sinner being an hundred years old shall be accursed (Isaiah 65:20).

Does Bathsheba want to see the deceased child she had with David? Does Bathsheba want to see her former husband Uriah? Does Uriah have to be separated from David in Heaven because of what happened on earth? What happened? King David had Uriah murdered as a military scheme so he could marry his wife Bathsheba. Does Abel have to be separated from Cain? Cain killed his brother Abel. God killed Er, Onan, Eli, Uzzah, Nadab and Abihu, Nabal, Ananias and Sapphira, and Herod Agrippa. Are they enjoying any rewards in Heaven? Are they second-class citizens there?

These persons were examples of Free Will. They were victims of roleplaying dictated by circumstances. They had brains, but those brains were created and provided involuntarily, without permission or knowledge of the recipient. Same situation for the body. No choice.

It would seem apparent that Elect Roleplayers, such as Noah, David, and Apostle Paul would not retain memories of their roleplay identity. Aren't memories the continuous essence of your identity? If you suddenly lose all your memory, who are you? How can you be you without reference points from the immediate past to the distant past?

In Heaven, the Bible indicates there will be no memory of former things. All former things? Select former things? If select former things are retained and transferred to Heaven, what would qualify? Your spouse? Children? Parents? Friends? Occupation (pastor, artist, nurse, doctor, judge, musician, celebrity, chef, pilot, CEO, etcetera)? Hobbies? Preferences?

Arguing that select former memories qualify for transfer to Heaven becomes weak. No former memory can compare to the immediacy of Heaven, which will obliterate the most treasured, esteemed memory. That includes your memory of spouse, children, family, occupation, reputation, or possession. Is this true?

> But we speak the wisdom of God in a mystery, even the hidden wisdom, which God ordained before the world unto our glory: Which none of the princes of this world knew: for had they known it, they would not have crucified the Lord of glory. But as it is written, Eye hath not seen, nor ear heard, neither have entered into the heart of man, the things which God hath prepared for them that love him. But God hath revealed them unto us by his Spirit: for the Spirit searcheth all things, yea, the deep things of God. For what man knoweth the things of a man, save the spirit of man which is in him? even so the things of God knoweth no man, but the Spirit of God (I Corinthians 2: 7-11).

What about Jesus saying we will be able to sit down with Abraham, Isaac, and Jacob in the kingdom of heaven?

> And I say unto you, That many shall come from the east and west, and shall sit down with Abraham, and Isaac, and Jacob, in the kingdom of heaven (Matthew 8:11).

Jesus taught in parables. Many will come from the East and West. Not all? East and west of where? In Heaven, there won't be any strangers. Why do only some sit with the men? Will there be men and women in Heaven? Gender differentiation? What purpose will that serve since procreation isn't necessary? Identity? Won't we be like the angels? They have an identity without being male/female. Will people sit down in Heaven? What is the purpose of sitting?

We can know ourselves without earthly memory. We know this by the nature of a Pre-Life Elect identity promised to exist before the identity created by Adam and Eve on Earth. At the end of the Free Will Demonstration, on the Last Day, when we are all changed in the twinkling of an eye, our Elect Roleplay Identity (HSID) will join our Pre-Life Elect identity. Our pristine heavenly identity will be who we truly are.

When Adam and Eve were created, did they have a blank memory? When the heavenly hosts were created—the angels—did they have blank minds? Obviously, God programs the mind. Who you are will NOT be an inauthentic identity based on heredity, environment, and experience. You will join your authentic identity based on the direct heredity of God, the environment of Heaven, and the experience of eternal life!

We will all know each other as intimately as if we were all married to each other. This marriage is based on love that is pure and holy. Unimaginable relationships on that side of Heaven will exist. We just have to trust it will eclipse what we have now.

This is not meant to imply you won't know people you knew before. You may interact with your spouse, children, parents, etcetera, but you may not know them in the same relationship you knew them before. That shouldn't make you sad or apprehensive. You will not miss your former relationships. Why? Because now you're related to everyone in Heaven. Their love for you, and your love for them, will be completely open, innocent, and trusting. It will be natural, authentic, and intuitive. It will be a transcendent, magnificent, super-social adventure.

Remember, you will be in the actual presence of the Trinity! The Father, the Son, the Holy Spirit! Your attention, your fullness, your delight, your joy, and your world will be on Them. Everyone there will feel the same way, including the angels. You will not have lost anything from your transition to Heaven. All is gain.

Okay, you still feel cheated by MARVI-RPIA because you have always had your heart set on meeting certain ones in Heaven. Every preacher has said as much. You're so looking forward to the Virgin Mary, Adam and Eve, King Solomon, John the Baptist, Esther, Daniel, and both Josephs. You want to hear the stories, ask questions, and relive the drama of Old and New Testaments.

That's gone? I won't be able to talk with them? Noah, Enoch, and Elijah—there are so many people I looked forward to meeting. Apostle Paul, Apostle John, Ruth, Bathsheba, Moses. Oh, and there are celebrities, my favorite musicians, childhood friends, and personal heroes. My children won't be there? I'm unable to greet my ancestors who contributed to who I am but died long before me? Fifi, Fido, Spot, and Puff won't be there?

My long list of questions I'm holding for Heaven won't be answered? This can't be! Please, don't take all this away from us. We really, really, really expect these things!

Don't worry. MARVI-RPIA is just an impression. Next, Heaven Part 2.

Wait. Please don't end the chapter here. Go over this again.

Is this saying my memories won't transfer to Heaven? But if in Heaven I can't remember what happened on Earth, that means I'll have AMNESIA. I won't have a consecutive link that defines how I've come to be who I am. No yesterday, last week, or last year. No heredity. No experiences. No identity.

You might ask yourself if Adam and Eve had amnesia as they gained consciousness on Day One. Did they know who they were? Did they have a personality? What memories did they have? Adam and Eve were programmed with functionality to think, reason, and self-actualize. They could walk, talk, sit, stand, run, and jump. They didn't require weeks, months, and years to mature. They were complete.

If you were to suddenly show up in Heaven and expect to retain your Earthly inauthentic identity, then yes, you would look for your mom and dad, spouse and children, family and friends. Your memory is of the PAST. The past is PHYSICAL. However, you are now SPIRITUAL—a new creature.

How do we know which people bring which memories? Do all people bring all memories? Do certain people bring certain memories? Do you possess limited recall? Do you possess total recall in Heaven, the ability to remember everything that ever happened to you? If so, that would be horrifying. What if you were aborted, stillborn, or miscarried? What if you were poverty-stricken, diseased, handicapped, mentally impaired, in prison, divorced, widowed, molested, raped, committed suicide, or murdered? Remembering the past is RELIVING the past.

Some very bad people become born again. They were gang members, pedophiles, alcoholics, drug addicts, prostitutes, and lawyers. Whoops, and politicians. Whoops. (Don't forget to delete these last two typos).

Can you control how far you regress? Is there a cutoff range similar to what we experience in attempting to recall memories of being less than one year old? What if you're able to relive being in your mother's body before birth? You relive being born. You relive not being able to feed yourself, walk, talk, read, or write. You're incontinent. You don't know right from wrong. You are not reborn by the Holy Spirit. Is this at all constructive?

The conventional teachings are that you WILL retain memories of your former identity. However, former memories will be overwhelmed by the beautiful magnificence of Heaven. If so, why bring the earthly baggage to Heaven? Exclude it. If you have access to the past, you will access it. If you can't, why bring it? What's the point? *You're a NEW person—brand-new!*

The argument against CD1/CD2 is it isn't orthodox. It's heretical. It deprives people of lifelong aspirations of being greeted with loving open arms by family, friends, great people of God, and the heavenly saints. We will all know each other as we are known. The CD1/CD2 impression opposes the orthodox view of Heaven. It's against OUR view of Heaven.

Yes. That's right. To most theists, Heaven is about ME. My spouse, my family, my friends, my pets. Without them in Heaven, I'm nobody. Well, I'm somebody, but only to God. I don't know God as well as I know my family, my friends, my pets. God understands.

This is related to the concepts of Ego-Skepticism and Ego-Centracism (Glossary).

Ego-Skepticism – Who am I without the guaranteed love of a spouse, children, family, friends, and pets? Nobody! God can't keep me company. He's a spirit. I'm flesh and blood. Besides, God Himself said of Adam, it's not good that man is alone.

Ego-Centracism – Life is all about ME! My family, love, romance, sex, fun, travel, games, entertainment, fame, food, music, looks, brains, skills/talent, possessions ...

Unfortunately, the imagery of spouses, children, and families as the method God instituted to correct The Error of Adam and Eve is obscured. Procreation was only in case Adam or Eve exercised Free Will to eat from the Tree of the Knowledge of Good and Evil. If they did, the whole human race doesn't die—only Adam and Eve. If Eve disobeyed and Adam refused to accompany her, God may have created another female.

The point, as mentioned previously, is that Adam was never LONELY. *Adam all by himself as a representative of humanity meant no arrangement in place to prevent Adam from ending the human race if he ate of the Tree of Knowledge of Good and Evil. That was the "not good" in the Garden.* The Bible says Adam was not deceived (1 Timothy), but that doesn't mean that Adam would *never* have been deceived.

As Adam and Eve procreate to reach the Promise of the Redeemer, roleplayers are produced. They exemplify The Error of exercising Free Will. God's will for flawless human beings is superior to their will for themselves. Discovering the knowledge of good and evil was all about THEM. They lost the enthusiasm for their two imperatives—the Garden and God.

The inauthentic you in this present life is all about you until God opens your spiritual eyes. The authentic you in the afterlife is all about a brand-new you. It's a brand-new you that awakens before God like Adam and Eve. How will you recognize people, places, animals, and things? Heaven knows. No need to worry. You woke up here on Earth without your knowledge, permission, or desire. Life is a mystery. So is the afterlife. All will be well. God's Plan A implied by the CD1/CD2 Plan B should comfort you. If not, trust in the God that you know.

CHAPTER 41

HEAVEN—PART 2

None of the descriptions of Heaven ever seem to be the dominating reason people follow Jesus Christ. Avoiding Hell usually takes first place. They're both fairly unimaginable as eternal destinations. Does *Connecting The Dots Of Identity* render a reliable image from the Bible we can anticipate? No.

However, it continues with Christian Reformed Impressionism. It will paint Heaven with words that may change the way you think of Heaven. Here is a typical "day" in Heaven, where there are no days or nights, per se:

Morning Praise – Hymns. Songs. Music. Sounds.

You join in with angels, as there is singing for the Lord and perhaps with the Lord. Everyone contributes to the music. Everyone has perfect pitch. Everyone has a musical instrument, if musical instruments are provided. The music goes on for "hours" with no bad songs and no unpleasant genres. It's as if the concert is specifically written for your heart and your ears, if you have a heart and ears. And it seems specifically written. They're your favorite songs! They're created as they're meant to be performed, now with the perfect context for enjoyment. These are like sounds you feel, touch, taste, smell, see, and hear. They're almost alive.

Morning Prayer – Worship. Silent gratefulness. Audible gratefulness. Holy Spirit leading.

You participate in spiritual and mental activities of devotion, reverence, and gratitude. This is a specific holy time of acknowledgment and recognition of the One who is above all and yet for all. The Lord has this quality time with YOU for communication, companionship, and education.

Morning Refreshment – Delights of the Senses: Taste, Touch, Smell, other.

You assume a body of your choice from a menu of bodies. From the body's point of view, you eat, drink, and make your heart merry without regard to gluttony, drunkenness, getting fat, or getting sick. Champagne, beer, and whiskey with your cereal. No obligations afterward. No dishes, flossing, or payment. Yes, you may smoke afterward. Cigars, cigarettes, and all manner of exotic plants. Why not? No illness here, no judgment here, no sin here.

You may enjoy refreshments in all kinds of locations. Skyscrapers, space stations, mountain tops, undersea aquariums, roller coasters, exotic temples, the moon, other planets, etcetera. Why not? You'll be able to eat while your heart is in your throat, or while in precarious positions.

Whatever you do, it's fun. It's joyous. It's a wonder of wonders.

May the morning refreshments include sex?

Sex? Sex in Heaven? Let's think about that for a few seconds.

Yes! Heaven is a very special place. On this side of life, we would not expect sexual intercourse in Heaven. But again, why not? Well, you know why not. Sex, shall we say, seems so out of place in Heaven.

Okay. What about this? New Jerusalem. The new Heaven and the new Earth. Is that better? Perhaps on a special "menu" in Heaven will be the New Jerusalem location. You go there to participate in scenarios where the laws of physics differ from Heaven. This subset of Heaven may compare to our earthly dream identity (DID) versus our earthly mental identity.

New Jerusalem is found in the New Testament book of Revelation. It's a reference to the City of God, in the afterlife, when God creates a new Heaven and a new Earth. Heaven and New Jerusalem are metaphysical and spiritual components of God's essence as much as His omnipresence. They have no location. He/They abides with His creation in unique concepts of interactions that fulfill a loving and meaningful relationship. This is love. This is the beauty of a relationship. This is life where every day is today, and it does not end.

Many of you will abhor sensual images presented in God's holy realm of worship and reverence. That's understandable. We are not given substantive details of Heaven or New Jerusalem. It may be best NOT to presume with so much detail. I apologize. No, not to you. To God.

> And I saw a new heaven and a new earth: for the first heaven and the first earth were passed away; and there was no more sea. And I John saw the holy city, new Jerusalem, coming down from God out of heaven, prepared as a bride adorned for her husband. And I heard a great voice out of heaven saying, Behold, the tabernacle of God is with men, and he will dwell with them, and they shall be his people, and God himself shall be with them, and be their God. And God shall wipe away all tears from their eyes; and there shall be no more death, neither sorrow, nor crying, neither shall there be any more pain: for the former things are passed away. And he that sat upon the throne said, Behold, I make all things new. And he said unto me, Write: for these words are true and faithful ... And he carried me away in the spirit to a great and high mountain, and shewed me that great city, the

> holy Jerusalem, descending out of heaven from God ... And the city had no need of the sun, neither of the moon, to shine in it: for the glory of God did lighten it, and the Lamb is the light thereof. And the nations of them which are saved shall walk in the light of it: and the kings of the earth do bring their glory and honour into it. And the gates of it shall not be shut at all by day: for there shall be no night there. And they shall bring the glory and honour of the nations into it. And there shall in no wise enter into it any thing that defileth, neither whatsoever worketh abomination, or maketh a lie: but they which are written in the Lamb's book of life (Revelation 21:1-5, 10, 23-27).

Reading the Bible is a literal, figurative, and spiritual adventure. Besides me, the other John writing the Book of Revelation makes use of vivid imagery. Among the illustrations, John pictures Heaven as the New Jerusalem. I do too.

However, John's inspired scriptural impression is 100 percent legitimate. It's God's holy word.

Modern Abstract Religious Verbal Impressionism is NOT legitimate, not even 1 percent legitimate. I'm not a theologian, a pastor, or a teacher. I'm an artist. MARVI-RPIA is not theology. It's an impression. It's art.

And keep in mind what scripture says about Jesus Christ:

> 34 All these things spake Jesus unto the multitude in parables; and without a parable spake he not unto them: (Matthew 13:34).

And keep in mind what the author says of this work:

Connecting The Dots Of Identity is not real. It's also a parable. A parable. A parable!

Parables are NOT REAL.

So, now, continuing with Heaven ...

MORE OF HEAVEN

Sex in Heaven? Absolutely! Are you concerned about clothing? Privacy? Reverence? Don't worry. You and your choice(s) may have your own sex island, sex skyscraper penthouse, sex luxury yacht, or even sex Learjet. Why stop there? Sex jump jet, roller coaster, or spaceship. Enjoy. It's HEAVEN—or a new Jerusalem! Sex isn't what it was on Earth. Somewhere, there are new heavens and a new Earth.

This seems a bit much. Sex on a recreated earth makes sense, but sex in space? In Heaven? Doesn't seem right. Will we be naked during sex? That doesn't seem right either. So far.

The difference is nakedness on Earth is an absence of clothing. Nakedness in Heaven is an absence of earthly clothing. The clothing in Heaven consists of spiritual garments, appropriate for each situation and individual.

Sex in Heaven is not the rudimentary custom of sex on Earth. In Heaven, sex is new, it's wholesome, it's holy, it's pure, it's refined, it's filled with wonder, joy, and love. It's the BEST of what was formerly GOOD. All its wrongs are now made right.

Of course, this topic probably would be considered rather crude, irreverent, and even disgusting if it were coming from the pulpit on Sunday. But I'm not a pastor. I'm not a theologian. This is not church. This is not a place of Sabbath Day worship. I'm just an artist. This is an abstract impression of religion. Don't believe it for a moment. Believe whatever you want to believe about Heaven. For now, this is a follow-through on an abstract impression of how Heaven may appear to an artist.

By the way, some of you may wonder how sex in Heaven compares to sex in the Garden of Eden? The MARVI-RPIA imagery paints a picture of the purity and innocence of Adam and Eve in the Garden. They had no knowledge of sexual intimacy. There was no need for procreation between flawless creatures. Procreation was only a "fail-safe" protocol to produce the Redeemer if Adam and Eve failed. So, no sex In the Garden (see also *Connecting The Dots Of Identity-2*, Chapter 29, "Question and Answers #6").

Does that contradict the imagery just painted of sex in Heaven? We'll also have purity and innocence there.

No. Sex for Adam and Eve was an inherent, unrealized roleplay feature of Free Will. Sex, or procreation, was a backup system so that death and life could coexist. In Heaven, no backup system is necessary. In Heaven, sex won't be for defense. It will be for scoring.

No ... that doesn't sound quite right. It'll be proactive rather than reactive. Yes, that's a little better. You get the idea. Also in Heaven, if genitalia is somehow transferred there, there won't be a waste removal function. No waste in Heaven.

Does this mean gender differentiation in Heaven? Genitalia? Hormones? Women's breasts? Or is this a part of the "menu system" of choosing a body to facilitate "missions"?

Yes. And as much fun as it is to describe Heaven, I don't want to spend too much time on this one topic.

The Bible seems to suggest we will have no memory of depressing, disgusting, unpleasant thoughts in Heaven. There will be no tears, no embarrassment, no ugliness there. No sexual awkwardness, no uneasiness, no apprehension, no dread, no coercion, no manipulation, no pain, no faking, no dissatisfaction.

Leaving the realm of sex, some things from our former life have a reasonable chance of being renewed in Heaven. Things like what?

Cooking. Eating. Drinking. Music. Singing. Dancing. Running. Racing. Swimming. Diving. Hiking. Fishing. Skiing. Flying. Travel. Games. Animals. Vehicles. Buildings. Much more.

Let's return now to the next morning event of the day.

Morning Task One – Artwork, construction, architecture, theme parks, temples, gardens, etcetera.

You will participate in personalizing the mansion Jesus made for you. You'll also help with other projects made for you and made for others. You manage and maintain a heavenly "infrastructure." It's work, but it's fun.

Noon Prayer – Similar to Morning Praise

Noon Refreshment – Similar to Morning Refreshment. (Yes, sex is again included on the menu, you hedonist.)

Task Two (Continue from Task One)

Recreation – Playtime. Hobby time. Travel time.

Once again, you assume a body from a menu of bodies. From the body point of view, you participate in activities from a menu. The menu includes hyper-realistic details and word-for-word scripts supplied for authenticity.

If you lack imagination regarding fun, thrills, mystery, entertainment, and surprise, Heaven produces something for you.

Travel to distant planets, galaxies, and dimensions. Engage in realistic fantasy worlds where you have superpowers. Go back in time, forward in time, in and out of time. Be a musician, athlete, dancer, pilot, race car driver, gymnast, mountain climber, circus performer, king, or queen. Remember, you have access to the special menu of bodies. You can assume an identity and, from that point of view, engage in a wide variety of activities. You can get married! You can have a baby! You can be the MVP of a sports game.

There is no sin there. No body is being harmed. You "assume" a "body," and other bodies are not real bodies, either. No harm, no foul, no exploitation of others. Your heart is in the right place in honesty and love to do as you desire. Whatever that desire, God understands. He has the epitome of a sense of humor, the spirit of fun, and the patience to permit experimentation and exaggeration.

Day Praise – Similar to Morning and Noon Praise

Day Prayer – Similar to Morning and Noon Prayer

Task Three – Continue from Tasks One and Two

Evening Praise – Similar to Morning, Noon, and Day Praise

Evening Prayer – Similar to Morning, Noon, and Day Prayer

Evening Refreshment – Similar to Morning and Noon Refreshment

Task Four – Continue from Tasks One, Two, and Three

Night Praise – Similar to Morning, Noon, Day, Evening Praise

Night Prayer – Similar to Morning, Noon, Day, and Evening Prayer

Night Recreation – Similar to Noon Recreation

Night Refreshment – Similar to Morning, Noon, Evening Refreshment

SPECIAL DAYS

From time to time—in a place of no time, remember—*God will have rewards for you.* It's your Special Day! Like a wedding day, your birthday, or a surprise party in your honor. God has something special just for you on your special day! Maybe just the two of you, or four of you—the Father, Son, and Holy Spirit. Maybe you and a favorite angel. Maybe you and a legion of angels.

You and the Trinity. The four of you. Think of that. Even in Heaven, you won't be able to comprehend God in all His essence. Even though your five senses of sight, sound, touch, taste, and hearing were feedback for the earthly environment, they aren't enough for Heaven.

You may have ten sensory features in Heaven. Perhaps an additional five senses that help ascertain the magnificence of God.

God is so omnipotent that it's frightening to consider the enormity of just a few of His accomplishments. The universe. Stars. Planets. Time. Velocity. Subatomic reality. Angels. Humans. Me.

To be in the presence of the Trinity may be like standing outside in the sunlight. The acknowledgment that it is daytime and not night is the ability to sense light, heat, and daytime activity. The Father, Son, and Holy Spirit are the dynamics that make this moment comprehensible. I'm alive because They are alive. They gave me life. They made me. I am extremely complicated. I'm so complicated that there is a significant percentage of me that I can never know. Only the Trinity knows all of me.

In Heaven, I may know more of the Trinity, and the Trinity may tell me more of myself. The me that God identified and saved before He created the world.

There you have a little slice of Heaven, rendered by Christian Reformed Impressionism. There is no day or night. Naming the segments by the time of day was just for contrast. An actual segment may have an appearance of time for the sake of the present experience in Heaven.

For those who have that nagging sensation that Heaven will be too much like a church on earth, unfortunately, that is the church's fault. Churches don't convey much to look forward to. *On top of that, many church services are boring.* People aren't rushing to return after the morning worship service. When all Sunday services end, they are almost happy. That is a disappointing fact. There are exceptions, but how many are there?

When you love someone, and someone loves you, spending time with that someone is incomparably fulfilling. The adventure of romance, discovery, and surprise is delightful. Bliss, happiness, and anticipation make each day a wonder. Your relationship with the Lord in Heaven will have similar characteristics.

But in Heaven, this will be to a much greater degree. It will be like an adrenaline rush. It will be like falling in love. Day after day (every day is today) of the most intimate, most loving relationship. We can barely imagine it. And the love is pure. True. Total.

God's love for you is complete because He knows everything about you. Anyone who loves you as a Free Will Roleplayer doesn't really love you. They don't know everything about you. They love aspects of you. There are aspects of you that are not loveable. You and your lover reach an agreement on what is acceptable to form a bond. Some bonds hold, some bonds don't.

It is very exciting to contemplate the things which God could have prepared for us. Whatever we imagine can't be better than what God has. It's almost an invitation, a challenge to look into our hearts and dare contemplate something better than God's plan. MARVI-RPIA is delighted to dare.

> But as it is written, Eye hath not seen, nor ear heard, neither have entered into the heart of man, the things which God hath prepared for them that love him (1 Corinthians 2:9).

HEAVEN 2—POSTSCRIPT

You may be familiar with the teaching that God has rewards for certain ones once they are in Heaven. This idea gets its proof from several Bible verses, added below. It may be helpful to focus on three points these verses may suggest.

Reward: merit, honor, praise.

Reward tier: based on the quality of "works" in the former life on earth.

Works transference: the buildup of works points on earth that transfer to Heaven.

Why would this be challenged? The reason no one would be rewarded in Heaven for their roleplay on Earth is that:

a) Personhood is an inauthentic identity dumped in your lap at conception. Roleplay based on heredity, environment, and experience isn't about optimizing identity so as to gain rewards in the afterlife. Roleplay is simply the demonstration of Free Will.

b) How can you lose or gain rewards when you have no way of knowing right from wrong until God opens your spiritual eyes to objective morality? That may not happen. Life is about proving the error of NOT knowing right from wrong until God intercedes.

As an example, the human embryo certainly has no grounds for rewards. What has it done? Nothing.

But as a person, it is no less deserving than Noah, the Virgin Mary, or John the Baptist. An embryo is just as deserving as the Apostle Paul, Saint Augustine, Thomas Aquinas, Martin Luther, John Calvin, Jonathan Edwards, Billy Graham, you, or me, because we all have a role to play—even if we die before birth. If we had no role, we would not have been conceived.

You might wonder: If a female becomes pregnant, doesn't know she's pregnant, and loses the baby without any indication of the loss, is this considered roleplay? The father is not informed, the mother isn't aware, and the baby never gains sentience. Similarly, for persons who die after fertilization as a zygote, blastula, embryo, or fetus, how do rewards apply to these persons?

In such a case, yes. It's still roleplay of Free Will, inherited from the parents. If no roleplay was necessary for the additional life of one more person in the world, whether in the womb of the mother or outside the womb, conception would not have occurred.

Should the Virgin Mary and the aborted baby have the same reward in Heaven? No? Maybe? Yes?

Would they know reward differences in Heaven? Are rewards strictly private between God and the recipient?

Rewards may be an analogy to how roleplay on Earth has its practical applications. It's problematic to believe how rewards translate to Heaven when no memory of the former things on earth remains. You don't remember what you did, or said, or thought that would win any reward. At that point, we simply enjoy rewards as Heaven makes them available.

The "talents" we receive after HSID matures in us is to apply objective morality to the world. This is how we embody the "enhanced" Demonstration of Free Will.

We redirect our will toward godliness. We make use of whatever we can in order to make life better for ourselves and for others.

Not doing what we should do brings hardship. This happens whether we are Elect or non-Elect. The non-Elect receive more beatings and more stripes as a consequence of proving the error of Free Will. This continues unless and until the Holy Spirit intercedes that makes the person a new creation. From this point of view, rewards and stripes are in the context of God's election program. We don't merit rewards or stripes. We demonstrate Free Will. We are in God's hand.

> For the Son of man shall come in the glory of his Father with his angels; and then he shall reward every man according to his works (Matthew 16:27).

The reward is Heaven.

> And, behold, I come quickly; and my reward is with me, to give every man according as his work shall be (Revelation 22:12).

The reward is Heaven.

> For we must all appear before the judgment seat of Christ; that every one may receive the things done in his body, according to that he hath done, whether it be good or bad (2 Corinthians 5:10).

The reward is Heaven.

> Now he that planteth and he that watereth are one: and every man shall receive his own reward according to his own labour (1 Corinthians 3:8).

Roleplay and the demonstration of Free Will are good and bad earthly rewards.

> Lay not up for yourselves treasures upon earth, where moth and rust doth corrupt, and where thieves break through and steal: But lay up for yourselves treasures in heaven, where neither moth nor rust doth corrupt, and where thieves do not break through nor steal: For where your treasure is, there will your heart be also (Matthew 6:19-21).

Roleplay. You can't do anything for the sake of Heaven until HSID.

> *I the LORD search the heart, I try the reins, even to give every man according to his ways, and according to the fruit of his doings (Jeremiah 17:10).*

Roleplay. God initiates grace that influences the works of Roleplayers.

> And that servant, which knew his lord's will, and prepared not himself, neither did according to his will, shall be beaten with many stripes. But he that knew not, and did

> commit things worthy of stripes, shall be beaten with few stripes. For unto whomsoever much is given, of him shall be much required: and to whom men have committed much, of him they will ask the more (Luke 12:47-48).

Roleplay on Earth. Not Heaven and Hell.

EPILOGUE

Your intuition tells you that God is love, God is righteous, and God is doing everything He should be doing. But you have doubts because everything in the world seems to be uncontrolled, disorganized, and perplexing. The church says this is because God is INCOMPREHENSIBLE. They say "Don't worry; God has a marvelous plan for you."

And even though Jesus was here teaching about God with 100 percent accuracy, the Person who is the most intelligent 100 percent human being is also 100 percent deity. Jesus is also INCOMPREHENSIBLE!

The takeaway is that Jesus is incomprehensible, but we are given what is needed to fulfill God's plan. This includes the document we have conveying God's words to us: the Holy Bible.

So now what? Do you say the Bible doesn't seem like such a great cause for celebration? You would have a good point. Genesis, the first book of the Bible, introduces us to the catastrophe of all catastrophes. Adam and Eve fall and take all of us with them. Then, in that same book, God kills everyone in the Flood except eight people. Following this, God confuses the universal language and scatters the population. As if this wasn't enough to end any celebration of the Good News of the Bible, racial differentiation was added to the human being project. All this without further complicating the story with the infiltration of evil angelic beings, the Nephilim.

So goes some of the headlines of the "Good News." Why aren't people a turning cartwheel in merriment every Sabbath Day? The whole point of procreation was to produce the Redeemer, Jesus Christ. He arrived. We are redeemed. Hooray! Now turn cartwheels? Not yet.

Jesus was executed by people He was born to redeem. How ironic. And we can't forget about Hell. Adam and Eve brought death to humanity. That wasn't bad enough. No. Hell is the final penalty for sin. Now can you cheer about the Good News of Jesus Christ? Not yet.

How good is the Good News? How high can Christians jump for joy?

Is this challenge the fault of the religious leaders who proclaim the Good News? Is this God's fault for not opening our spiritual eyes? Or is this our fault somehow, even though what we know or what we do doesn't contribute to our salvation?

Connecting The Dots Of Identity is meant to help you trust your intuition about who God should be. What you've heard about God from theists, atheists, and agnostics may be misleading. MARVI-RPIA paints God as an impression of spirituality. This doesn't mean the impression is better than your religious worldview, your atheist worldview, or any other worldview. The impression is simply building on your intuition.

Is your intuition positive? Is your intuition negative? Is your intuition neutral?

Modern Abstract Religious Verbal Impressionism-Role Play Identity Array.

Great News about the Good News. Is it great? It doesn't matter. Intuition matters.

You don't have to put 100 percent trust in your intuition. You don't have to trust the author of this book. Your 100 percent trust should be in Jesus

Christ. Do you know who He is? If you do, your trust is exactly where it should be.

If you don't know who Jesus Christ is, *be patient. He knows you.*

DOOMILOGUE

Connecting The Dots of Identity-1. Connecting The Dots of Identity-2.

Danger! There may be DOOM on the horizon.

Initially, CD1/CD2 seems innocuous. It seems actually pretty great. Everyone goes to Heaven, and no one goes to Hell, except the Devil and his angels. What's not to love about that? But after two years, five years, ten years, what may develop is a cult-like following that blossoms into a full-fledged religion. *A religion of doom!*

Oh, yes, the author says he doesn't believe it. It's only an artistic impression. You don't believe in art. You should believe in theology. Believe your Bible. He says he's only SHARING his views about Christian Reformed religion, not TEACHING. However, we have only to look at world history to see the result of objectionable religious ideals. Well-meaning people, hopeful people, and gullible people will follow all manner of myths, beliefs, and teachings. They bet their lives on yet another questionable belief system that may be worse than others.

The argument can be made that the religion of Universalism also teaches everyone goes to Heaven and no one goes to Hell. Loosely held beliefs similar to Universalism must have existed for hundreds of years. Their underlying belief is God loves everyone and no one will be tormented in Hell forever.

Atheism professes a related view in that God doesn't send people to Hell forever. God doesn't send anyone anywhere. There is no God. And for every Christian person, there are probably just as many non-Christian persons. They conclude it's not reasonable to assume life is based on stories from the Christian Bible. This is why atheism is popular, along with billions of people in non-Christian religions.

So how much devastation has Universalism and atheism caused? How much harm have the ten to twenty major world religions caused? How much harm will CD1 and CD2 cause? *The worst harm has to be HELL!* Advocating there is NO possibility of Hell when there IS a possibility of Hell is the ultimate irresponsible proposition. Think about it. The WORST harm!

And then, if authentic identity is in Paradise and inauthentic identity is in the present, why continue life? What's the point? To prove Free Will is an error? Adam and Eve proved it. They lived 900-plus years. Two weeks outside the Garden of Eden would have them saying 1,000,000 times, "We are so sorry! We were wrong! We admit God's Determined Will for our life is better than our choice for Free Will. We are dying. The earth is dying." And dying each day continues.

So many millennia after creation, and 2,000 years after Jesus Christ, humanity should know by now to accept God's Determined Will. But our Free Will is a corrupted Free Will inherited from Adam and Eve. We must be born again by the Holy Spirit. Otherwise, there is no interest in God's Determined Will. We can't speak for the angels. They don't have a Redeemer. Their identity is authentic. Their Free Will is final for all eternity.

Meanwhile, a human ontological identity, as defined by CD1/CD2, is the identity referred to as existing before the foundation of the world. This conclusion is altogether without precedent. Such an assumption is considered heresy—a direct opposition to orthodoxy. The author makes frequent disclaimers that CD1/CD2 isn't theology. It's art.

This "art" hopes to reduce suicide, reduce abortion, reduce despair, depression, and hopelessness. *What if it does the opposite?* What if the thought of assurance in Paradise produces a "disconnect" with present life? The present life has no eternal consequence.

Don't steal, rape, rob, or murder. That's bad. If you get caught, you must pay the earthly penalty. If you don't get caught, you're a bad person to do bad things, but you will be forgiven. It was done in ignorance. You will be forgiven in the afterlife.

And it's possible the people that do continue going to church could become disillusioned with orthodoxy after the influences of CD1/CD2. *People walk out in the middle of the sermon.* People don't attend other church services. Doubt about orthodoxy begins its progressive advance.

The orthodox erosion begins with large-scale churches. Then the medium to smaller-scale churches fall off in membership. *Finally, erosion begins in the Christian Reformed Church itself, the very church that professes election and predestination.*

The orthodox church expects everyone to follow tradition. You must do this, you must do that, you must do the other things to please God. The whole system is based on performance. When hearing of CD1 and CD2, God has already saved you, why go to church? The identity you embody in the present is only to demonstrate the error of Free Will. There's NOTHING you can do in the present that contributes to your salvation. That was done in the past, before the foundation of the world.

So, why go to church?

Why participate in the sacraments of baptism and communion?

Why join the choir, go to Bible study, or become an elder or deacon? Why encourage a pastor whose teachings are less convincing than CD1/CD2?

Why encourage a pastor whose teachings are against CD1/CD2?

Doom! People stop going to church, stop reading their Bible, and stop supporting religious organizations. They may stop working, stop having families, stop being good. Eat, drink, and be merry. Pie awaits in the sky. I'm not me; I'm a construct of heredity, environment, and experience. So what if World War III starts next week?

If I am one of the so-called SANE, I'm not able to open the spiritual eyes of the UNSANE. Only God can. In the interim, the unsane are taking over the world. The polls always show there is a large segment of the world population that affirms a Christian identity. However, when taking a deep dive into the particulars of what Christianity is, a great number don't understand Christianity. Why?

It's a multitude of factors, perhaps led by Christian immaturity. The church itself carries a large portion of the blame for that. With the lack of leadership in Christian education and in converting the unsane, what else should we expect? God uses Christians to assist in the unsane becoming sane. If CD1 and CD2 come to prominence, will that be beneficial or detrimental to the world?

Beneficial if the concept is godly, detrimental if it is not.

Will the orthodox church be undermined by yet another "improvement" on the word of God?

Will other churches suffer also? Time will tell.

Connecting The Dots Of Identity. Bloom, doom, or never blossom?

Doom!

CLOSING PRAYER

Prayer changes things. In the scriptures, there are some twenty verses encouraging prayer. For what should we pray?

It's not unreasonable to see that the unsane people in the world are gaining the advantage in key areas of influence: finance, politics, business, academia, media, entertainment, etcetera. What are sane people to do?

One, commandeer those segments of society for THEISM, or at least for NEUTRALITY.

Two, pray for God's intercession into the hearts of the unsane.

Commandeering those segments of society will take time. How much time do we have?

And for what SPECIFICALLY should we pray?

How do we prepare for the possibility of Hell or Heaven in the afterlife? How do we prepare for World War III, a fatal global pandemic, or an overthrow of humanity by artificial intelligence?

The general public would probably be the last to know of an impending global catastrophe. In the background, people who have no moral objectivity, the unsane, forge ahead without regard for ethical consequences.

There may be automated vehicles on the highway with human-appearing drivers. Human and nonhuman persons may have already replaced their well-known counterparts. The smart device we own may be hypnotizing us through gradations of euthanasia.

This doesn't necessarily mean the end has begun, *but the end has begun.* Previous CD1/CD2 chapters illustrate a breach in God's natural order of procreation that caused the Flood, the first end-of-the-world scenario. Do we have 120 years before the second end-of-the-world scenario? Do we have 120 months? 120 weeks? 120 hours?

> And the Lord said, My spirit shall not always strive with man, for that he also is flesh: yet his days shall be an hundred and twenty years (Genesis 6:3).

> But as the days of Noah were, so shall also the coming of the Son of man be.
> For as in the days that were before the flood they were eating and drinking, marrying and giving in marriage, until the day that Noe entered into the ark,
> And knew not until the flood came, and took them all away; so shall also the coming of the Son of man be (Matthew 24:37-39).

We know conclusively that people who were DIRECTLY related to Adam, Eve, Seth, Jared, Enoch, and Methuselah were alive at the time of the Flood. How much closer to godliness could anyone be? Yet all these people drowned in the Flood. Executed. Apparently, godly human males and females didn't recognize the seriousness of the present breach in the natural order of procreation. They didn't question, investigate, interrupt, or stop the Nephilim operation … until it was too late.

Are we in a simi'ar situation?

Is pregnancy and delivery by human males any more preposterous than angels and humans creating offspring?

Is procreation by angels and human females, the Nephilim, any more unbelievable than human and artificial intelligence producing less than 100 percent human offspring?

By the way, many people are so desperate to become pregnant, they may not care if the child is slightly less than 100 percent human. Worse than this, they may not be informed that the child will be less than 100 percent human. Meanwhile, scientific references to reproductive technology, which include issues of impotence, infertility, human cloning, and advancements in transhumanism, read like science fiction. In the years 1970 to 2000, reproductive science outgrew science fiction to become science nonfiction. From the year 2000 to the present day, science nonfiction is now science EXTREME reality.

Most of us have heard about the most famous End of the World scenario—the return of Jesus Christ. It is both beautiful and dreadful in its essence. Believers in Christ transition to Heaven, and nonbelievers will transition to Hell. Believers have been known to pray earnestly for this Last Day. They finally have their reward for trusting in His name. It is regretful that many of their family, friends, and associates didn't believe. The whole nonbelieving world will now suffer forever in a fiery lake of torment. They were warned.

Part of the impression MARVI-RPIA paints is that:

1) The End may be brought about by humanity itself, as in the Flood; and

2) The End could be when Jesus Christ has reached the perfect number of Roleplayers. The Error of Free Will needs no further proof.

In the sense that prayer changes things, CD1/CD2 could propose influencing The End by diminishing further roleplay participation. We finally agree that God's will is best, not our own will. *We surrender the directive to continue creating more Roleplayers via procreation.* No further proof of The Error Adam and Eve committed is necessary. Of course, if it's NOT about proving The Error of Free Will, and it's NOT God's will to decrease procreation, it certainly won't happen, whether we surrender our right to procreate or not.

Then again, people who love CD1/CD2 might advise a reluctance to discontinue procreation. It may not be the prudent direction to pursue. Significant decreases in the population of any first-rate country come with consequences. This means discussion among those in first-rate countries to articulate details of the consequences. Oh, and there's the point of an extremely powerful human impulse for love, family, and … sex.

However, if enough of us come to accept some version of what is illustrated by CD1/CD2, we could possibly influence God to bring The End BEFORE we cause our own gruesome downfall. *We can now pray for The End with a clearer conscience than before.* We don't have to worry about human beings going to Hell forever. Hell is only for Satan and his devils.

Keep in mind that *Connecting The Dots Of Identity* is just an impression. It is not theology. *However, if prayer changes things as scripture indicates, and if we don't feel comfortable praying for The End, shouldn't we at least pray that God's Plan A will be as good or better than CD1/*

CD2 Plan B? God's Plan A as taught by orthodox theology for 2,000 years may be appropriate, but is it comprehensive? Think of Salvation, Election-Predestination, and Hell.

Final words of a rather long closing prayer: God's Plan A will be as good or better than CD1/CD2 Plan B.

Isn't that a worthwhile prayer? Let's pray together …

AFTERWORD

War is raging in the world. War is ALWAYS raging in the world. It may not affect us today, or it may cause our death tomorrow. It's such a tragic situation. People don't seem to be willing to take the legitimate steps to de-escalate the tension between warring factions. If there is a willingness to negotiate a resolution, the "war machine" intervenes. Money and power are major Influences in continuing the hostilities. Another major factor is the cultural identity of the groups in conflict.

Cultural identity meaning the interests of the *people-in-general* or the interests of the *people-in-power.* The people-in-general have personal interests represented as a cultural history. Their ethnicity, family traditions, family legacy, and local property, make up present-day life. They feel obligated to preserve this.

The people-in-power are represented by special interest groups who pursue an agenda that seeks to maintain power and wealth. They have no true allegiance to their constituents. It's all rhetorical posturing. Their personal integrity was long ago compromised.

Wars continue as long as the people-in-general tolerate the people-in-power. By the time objection to the powerful reaches a point of conflict, removing them is usually too late to save the situation. When leadership is replaced, the new leadership may not be much of an improvement. The people-in-general must have the integrity to evaluate integrity in leadership. After that, there have to be enough people with integrity to develop a platform of integrity.

A method to minimize conflict between warring factions or nations could be characterized by a political figure who employs the imagery of

MARVI-RPIA. Historically, such an idea could be summarized by the concept of the *Philosopher King.* This is attributed to ancient Greek philosopher Plato three hundred years before Jesus Christ.

The impetus to pursue the concept of a philosopher king is to support a person who embodies the principles of pursuing truth, knowledge, and logic while utilizing political strategy to achieve progress and well-being for the populace. There are two major obstacles to such a political structure:

1) The initial establishment of this person in power.

2) Groups that attack the establishment of this person.

Hope for national integrity must begin with you and me. The quest for a unifying factor that promotes integrity might begin with a version of a philosopher king—such as an Artist King. *A Minister of Art. No, not me. You!* Yes, you. You don't have to do all the work. We will assist you. We will support you.

But when people-in-general look in the mirror, what do they see? They see their family, their race, their ethnicity, gender, culture, height, weight, and age. Underneath, or on top of this, they see their religious identity, their national identity, and their occupation. These things and many other things are reflected as they look at who they think they are—who they're told they are.

CD1/CD2 paints a picture from scripture that means all these images are NOT you. They all DIE. *They die because they are not REAL.* The real you were identified before the world was created. You are safe in Paradise. *The real you NEVER dies because the real you are SPIRITUAL!*

The people who say they KNOW what reality is do not all agree. There are many worldviews. There are theists, nontheists, and agnostics. None of their worldviews are invulnerable. They all have significant misgivings. Of course, they do; they're not omniscient. They're guessing. Jesus, as a Person of the Trinity, wasn't guessing. He was omniscient. He arrived in time and space to teach us that we are spiritual beings, and that Heaven is at hand.

CD1/CD2 also has significant misgivings. However, if more of us contribute to promoting and improving the image, perhaps we can improve the integrity of people. A believable image of God as the epitome of moral objectivity helps refute human beings in that role. A believable image of Christian Reformed Impressionism, based on 100 Bible verses, helps put God back on the throne. Everyone 100 percent human is already in Heaven. Only the Devil and his angels go to Hell. Less than 100 percent humans cease to exist.

In the meantime, life goes on. Then, one day, out of nowhere, while out shopping in various cities across the nation, groups of terrorists roll into selected shopping centers. Guns drawn and firing, they murder people and capture hostages. Retreating to designated locations, they make their demands known. War has come to each of those cities ... and the nation.

What am I supposed to do? Fight back? Yes, some would. Some would be killed. Some hostages would be killed. This could happen this year, next year, or in two to three years.

However, by challenging the insistence of an inauthentic identity based on past life as authentic, it may be possible to redirect our focus on forgiving the past and upgrading the future. It will be imperative to purge corrupt people and organizations currently in power. As we become more adept at being responsible for our own identity, it will be easier to evaluate, defund, and prosecute corrupt persons. By our irresponsibility, we put them in power. Now we must remove them.

But who's willing to give up their ideology? Their religion? Their worldview? Very few. To a great degree, the family you are born into defines your worldview. The country where you grew up defines your worldview. The formal and informal education you receive defines your worldview. CD1/CD2 paints a worldview that disassembles the imposed inauthentic identity. In its place in an identity that absolves the past. That person was not you. That person was a compilation of heredity, environment, and experience. With a renewed outlook on identity based on the future, the present is rediscovered.

You're not locked in to continue on a course based on the past. You can make a clean break and start anew. Forgive the past. Build a present and future based on moral objectivity—integrity. It may be possible if enough people accept the Great News about the Good News.

Just imagine if the youth of certain countries began to disassociate themselves from the religious identity that heredity, environment, and experience have imposed on them. They agree to open up their religious location, culture, and relics to the world. Religious descriptions of God should NOT be based on heredity, environment, and experience. God doesn't require strict adherence to customs, rituals, or appearance. There is no need to ostracize, shame, condemn, berate, or kill in the name of religion. We presume God does not require us to behave as though we are special and everyone else is not.

But hostility will continue because it's the ideology of past generations and the present generation. Our physical land on the world map is our physical and metaphysical identity. Who we are is where we are. *Only the next generation of people can break the cycle of an imposed identity based on custom, ritual, and genealogy.* You would have to say: I am me, an individual. I am not all of you. I am not my ethnic progression of ancestors.

A Muslim cannot convert a Jew, Christian, Hindu, Buddhist, or atheist to Islam. And they cannot convert a Muslim to their religion. There are exceptions, but this is the natural order of humanity. This is what God achieves with a Demonstration of Free Will.

If God of the Bible created humans flawlessly but they became flawed, isn't it possible for God to have a plan for flawed humans? Wouldn't such a Plan be similar to CD1/CD2? It's okay if there are many religions. It's okay if there are atheists and agnostics. *We're all demonstrating Free Will. We CAN'T all have the same worldview.* It's not possible in a world of billions of people—people who identify by heredity, environment, and experience.

But fighting to death over property and doctrines is the situation in Israel, Palestine, Armenia, Azerbaijan, Ukraine, Yemen, and other nations and countries. The world sees that this behavior reflects religious diversity, religious disagreement, and religious acts of violence. It's a long history. People have deep-rooted memories.

They did this and that to us. We were innocent. The law says we have a right to exact vengeance. If we forgive or do nothing, they will assume that as weakness. They will exploit us. The law requires penalties for wrongdoing. Jesus taught compromise and forgiveness but accountability in matters of justice. We demand justice after years of restraint and patience. *If justice is delayed, inadequate, or unfair, then matters will be settled outside the law. But matters are never settled.* So, hostility never ends. Never say never?

Well, if a significant number of people are ALLOWED to open their spiritual eyes, here is what they could perceive:

If God is a God of love, honor, fairness, control, and forgiveness, He would NOT make distinctions in religion. The Muslim, Hindu, Buddhist, Jewish, Christian, and Atheist would ALL go to Heaven, none to Hell. How so? God knows they are all demonstrating the effects of heredity, environment, and experience. A person's religion, or absence of religion, is all a factor of when they're born,'where they're born, and to whom they're born. *There is no religion better than another. Yes, there's only ONE way to salvation, Jesus Christ, but He accomplished salvation before the world was created.* There were no religions then. Everyone is already saved.

Life has to be something similar to this to make sense. CD1/CD2 is a Plan B impression of God's Plan A. If there is a true God, He would make it obvious which religion was His choice for humanity. There wouldn't be ten major and fifty minor religions. We would ALL know which one God wanted us to follow. *But He doesn't make it obvious.* Why? *Possibly, so that flawed human beings demonstrate the result of flawless human beings exercising Free Will to disobey God.* There must be proof that *God's Determined Will (see Glossary)is superior to a flawless human beings' Free Will.*

It's 100 percent natural for people to base their worldview on heredity, environment, and experience. This is the expectation. Otherwise, why wouldn't God make Himself sufficiently known to everyone so none would be mistaken? Do you think He wants people to be mistaken? Well, He does allow it:

1) Certain people are spiritually immature.

2) Certain people are not 100 percent human.

3) Certain people are Roleplayers who have yet to meet the Holy Spirit.

Today, we simply glorify Him as having made provision for our salvation before the foundation of the world. Today, we simply make the best of what we know to improve the environment of people. Adam and Eve were given the task to maintain, be fruitful, and multiply the Garden of Eden. The Tree of the Knowledge of Good and Evil was there as a test of Free Will. While going about their tasks, Ego-Skepticism set in. Who am I? Why am I here? What is reality? They had doubts. They began to trust themselves rather than God. This is what we may do when we don't trust Jesus Christ, sent by God, to confirm we are spiritual beings, temporarily in physical time and space.

The Promise to Adam and Eve after the Fall has been fulfilled. Jesus arrived. Love God. Love your neighbor. Love your enemy. Love yourself. If we don't change our perspective on how we understand God, religion may be the cause of the ultimate act—the end of the human race.

Please don't allow heredity, environment, and experience to continue dictating your religious worldview. That is your inauthentic identity. Your authentic identity is known by God before He created the world. The present is only a Demonstration of the Error of Free Will versus God's Determined Will.

Religion isn't about war. Religion isn't about God loving us and wanting what we want. Religion isn't about us being the best people. Religion is love. Compromise. Cultivating the Garden of People. When the response is to Old Testament examples of God commanding wars, strict rules of behavior, and one chosen people, it was to direct a path leading to specific individuals.

The dots must connect from Adam to Noah to Abraham to Judah to King David to the Virgin Mary to Jesus Christ.

In the Old Testament Book of Deuteronomy, the other nations had developed associations with evil spirits. How did they get involved with spirits? No, not Third-Class Angels. They're in chains of darkness—the Abyss. Second-Class Angels are suspects. Also, the ancestors of the Giants, the Nephilim, are suspects. They're not 100 percent human. So both would be candidates to influence 100 percent humans to practice the occult.

God forbade Israel from doing so. Nothing must interfere with the path to Jesus Christ. Angels collaborated with human beings in the days of Noah. The Nephilim was the result of angel and human female offspring. This defined the violation of God's procreation law. Such violence could be the reason God brought the End of the World—the Flood. This kind of violence must not end the world before the promised Messiah is born.

> There shall not be found among you any one that maketh his son or his daughter to pass through the fire, or that useth divination, or an observer of times, or an enchanter, or a witch. Or a charmer, or a consulter with familiar spirits, or a wizard, or a necromancer. For all that do these things are an abomination unto the Lord: and because of these abominations the Lord thy God doth drive them out from before thee ... For these nations, which thou shalt possess, hearkened unto observers of times, and unto diviners: but as for thee, the Lord thy God hath not suffered thee so to do. The Lord thy God will raise up unto thee a Prophet from the midst of thee, of thy brethren, like unto me; unto him ye shall hearken (Deuteronomy 18:10-12, 14-15).

The nations who were harmed by God to prevent them from interference were simply demonstrating Free Will. God was working through that to accomplish His Promise. *No one who was 100 percent human was damned to Hell. They were just Roleplayers.* They will transition to Paradise. The damnation was a result of Free Will, and the damnation was death.

Once Jesus is on the scene, He says "I am the Promise. I'm God. I'm human. I'm roleplaying. You're roleplaying. This is all a Demonstration of Free Will from Adam and Eve. I am the new Adam. You're a result of heredity, environment, and experience. This creates an inauthentic identity. You're a spiritual being in physical time and space. Your authentic identity is spiritual. *I arrived to fulfill God's promise of a Redeemer to Adam and Eve. I arrived to affirm salvation was accomplished before the foundation of the world."*

Jew and Gentile don't matter. Male and female don't matter. This generation or that generation does not matter. Love God. Love your neighbor. Love your enemy. Love yourself. *That's your religion!*

Man-made? The Bible doesn't say this. Jesus doesn't say this. Bible scholars don't say this.

CD1/CD2 says this. God structured religion to guarantee the appointment of Jesus Christ. Then Jesus spoke in parables. PARABLES! And religion was re-created. CD1/CD2 is a parable.

We don't expect a one-world religion. We don't expect people to understand all religions, or no religions are the same. The differences are the Demonstration of Free Will based on heredity, environment, and experience. Religion gives us guidelines, structure, and history. *But religion is not our identity, and it doesn't save us. It's man-made.*

> There is neither Jew nor Greek, there is neither bond nor free, there is neither male nor female: for ye are all one in Christ Jesus (Galatians 3:28).

We have a hard time trusting God. The idea that He saved us before the foundation of the world only comes if He opens our spiritual eyes. One hundred Bible verses from *Connecting The Dots Of Identity-1,* Chapter 6, are not persuasive. Those who do see cannot open the eyes of others. We need the Holy Spirit to initiate the process. CD1/CD2 is trying to open your spiritual eyes. *What do you see?*

Please help make this worthy of consideration for young children, teens, and young adults. They don't have all the investment in ideology that adults are protecting. We have a chance of averting the ongoing steps to WWIII. *WWIII is going to happen!* It's just a matter of when. On purpose. By accident. By a thousand cuts …

BOOK REVIEW

A popular AM radio station in the USA has a morning show hosted by a fascinating fellow and his producer. Here is an impression of him giving *Connecting The Dots Of Identity* a book review. It might come across in one of his morning segments as follows:

"Okay, coming up in the nine o'clock hour, we're going to spend some time talking about a book that recently came out with an odd twist on a religious theme. The title is *Connecting The Dots Of Identity*. The working name is MARVI-RPIA which is the subtitle. This acronym stands for Modern Abstract Religious Verbal Impressionism-Role Play Identity Array. What's it about? Well, it's supposed to be a way of making written religious material represent imagery of the Bible—like a mural on a building. MARVI-RPIA is the paint, the Bible is the building. But MARVI-RPIA is not claiming to teach the Bible. It's just an impression of the Bible.

We'll take a quick break and be right back with the story. This is the *Famous Fascinating Fellow Show.*

(Commercial)

"We're back. I guess the first thing I'll say about *Connecting The Dots Of Identity* is that I don't know if it really works or not.

Producer: Did you actually read the book?

Host: No, it's really not my cup of tea, you know, religious books. So, I dug around on the internet. As everybody knows, we do infotainment here, and a religious book would be bor-ring to our listeners. Two of the sources I used were the reviews on N5Sense Books and on 10 AM Books.

Producer: Yeah, I don't know, the whole idea seems hard to get your head around. I did buy the book but haven't yet read it. I'm intrigued by how I have those eight roleplay identities and won't get that one-way ticket to the hot place forever.

Host: Yeah, and no Hell might be the reason people would read this. Well, that and also everybody goes to Heaven. Wow! What a concept. Everybody goes to Heaven. Nobody goes to Hell.

Let's start with this. The author, John Louis Thomas, has developed religious imagery he calls art. He bills himself as the Minister of Art. It all begins with a rather obscure religious doctrine called Christian Reformed theology. Thomas takes artistic liberty to offer a modern abstract impression of the doctrine. Reformed theology isn't a new spiritual concept. It goes all the way back at least to Saint Augustine (400 AD), up through Saint Thomas Aquinas (1200 AD), then sees a great re-emphasis by Martin Luther (1500 AD). The re-emphasis brought about the Protestant Reformation. This marked the opposition to the Catholic Church, which held great power from the Middle Ages.

Following Martin Luther's belief system in re-establishing the definition of salvation and the means of salvation, John Calvin (1500 AD) expanded and further defined the tenets of "grace" rather than "works" for salvation. Grace means God's gift of salvation and works means you acquire salvation on your own. You may have heard of Calvinism. It has an infamous reputation in religious circles owing to its hardline regarding so-called predestined persons. Predestination is a term for God selecting certain people for salvation before He created the world. These people are guaranteed to go to Heaven. The corollary is that those not chosen cannot go to Heaven. That only leaves Hell.

Seems unfair. Right? Right! And this is one of the many reasons why people don't become religious; they become agnostics or atheists. God is not fair. Life is not fair.

Now, back to MARVI-RPIA. Thomas says yes, God does say quite plainly in scripture that He has predestined certain individuals to salvation before they were born. Thomas calls them Super-Spiritual Identities—SSIDs. But the Bible does NOT say God predestined others to Hell. But by not choosing others, what happens to them? The answer? Thomas says they may not be 100 percent human! I'll explain that when we come back from this short break. This is the *Famous Fascinating Fellow Show.*

(Commercial)

Host: Okay. We're back. I can't believe I'm talking about a religious book on the air. Well, I guess it's supposed to be an art book, but whatever.

Producer: Yeah, and the author says he doesn't believe it himself, even though he wrote it.

Host: Right. He doesn't believe it, the readers don't believe it, I don't believe it, but Okay, let's continue.

Now, how is it that people may not be 100 percent human? Here's how that goes. Before the world was created, God created angels. Lucifer, before he is Satan, humbly asks God if created beings are truly free if restricted in behavior? Lucifer advances the notion that God could allow unrestricted behavior and simply correct errors on the fly as beings are behaving. God reminds Lucifer that He is God and not a 24/7 repairman, but He will provide a Demonstration of Free Will using flawless living creatures—human beings.

God creates the world, our planet, the Serpent, Adam, and Eve. Flawless creatures reject God's will for their lives, choosing freedom or death. They die, but in God's mercy, it is a slow death. The greater mercy is a promise to provide an Antidote for their error through procreation. That would be Jesus Christ. The angels observe, and a group of them leave Heaven to seek a similar solution for angels should they ever disobey God. In the Book of Genesis, angels and human females procreate, creating children called Nephilim. The plan fails. The earth becomes corrupted. God drowns everyone in the Flood except Noah and his family. There are now three classes of angels.

First-Class Angels remain loyal to God's will for their lives. Second-Class Angels, led by Satan, do not abandon Heaven to mate with human females. They remain to accuse God of angel and human design flaws and favoritism toward humans above angels. Third-Class Angels, led by Abaddon, are the ones who leave Heaven in the interest of providing a fail-safe for angels like the humans are promised and "marry" human females.

Quite the drama, isn't it? Okay, let's keep going. It's pretty wild so far.

Producer: I'm a little confused, but not bored.

Host: Adam and Eve's offspring become Free Will Roleplayers. They inherit a flawed physical and mental identity in a flawed physical environment of air, water, land, plants, animals, weather, etcetera. Their consolation is one day a Savior will redeem humanity, and all will be flawless again. In the interim, the proof of the error of Free Will is depicted with real lives in an innumerable manner of combinations and permutations. Unless God intervenes to change any person's life, all lives continue in sin and damnation.

Because God has chosen people before He created the world, the Pre-Life Elect, they are safe in Heaven. The Free Will Roleplayers that are born again join with a corresponding Pre-Life identity at Judgment Day. Those who are not born again may also join their Pre-Life identity. They simply provided the contrast to show no one comes to God of their own will. Their roleplay ends. If a person has no corresponding Pre-Life identity to join, the implication is this person is not 100 percent human. This person is subject to the One-Drop Nephilim Blood Rule. This is a euphemism for a human with evil spirit ancestry. At death, they simply cease to exist. No soul. No spirit. No afterlife.

Producer: I think I know some of those people.

Host: Yeah, me too. Okay. You might be asking why does Jesus Christ arrive if salvation is already guaranteed to individuals? Well, because Jesus, Himself, is a Roleplayer. Jesus as 100 percent human arrives to save 100 percent humans—not angels, not angel-human hybrids, not aliens, not animals. He redeems Roleplayers as part of the Free Will Demonstration, which occurs inside time and space. The Pre-Life Elect individuals exist as a separate reality outside time and space. The focus is on the error of Free Will (from Adam and Eve that Jesus corrects) versus Determinism (God's Elect persons outside time).

So, what do you think? Any chance? In Thomas's defense, he doesn't claim to be a theologian, philosopher, teacher, pastor, or even a writer. He is an artist, a minister of art. MARVI-RPIA does seem to have a Dan Brown *Davinci Code* religious fiction about it. It is quite a stretch. But if it's just art, a mural on a building, you don't have to like it. In fact, Thomas is on record saying he himself doesn't believe in MARVI-RPIA. It's not a belief system. It's art. It's an impression. Speaking as a Catholic person, and my producer is a Jewish person, we don't see it.

When I was on the internet, one of the well-known church leaders made kind of an interesting observation. He said the Demonstration of Free Will is the whole reason for living. The ability to disobey God is proof of a creature's autonomy and reason to continue life. If you ever suspect you are an automaton or a puppet of God, you will lose the will to live. This goes for angels, humans, and even animals, as proven by the Serpent in Eden. Proof of Free Will must be demonstrated with multiple life forms in multiple scenarios, in multiple permutations. And then, to show contrast, God intercedes in select people's lives, showing that unless God changes that person, interrupting their Free Will, that person will always choose their own will rather than God's will for their life.

Of course, *Connecting The Dots* says as much by implying the First-Class Angels and the Super-Spiritual Identities, the SSIDs, must also have God's determination for them, or they too wouldn't be safe. The SSIDs are the name for identities God saved before He created the world. They correspond to every 100 percent human conceived on earth. JLT's impression doesn't give them life, it gives them ontological status. Orthodox religion teaches the ones saved before the world was created are humans who are conceived here in the present. They're NOT humans who were never conceived, either in the past or in the future.

Okay, we're late for the break, and I think we're just about out of time anyway.

Producer: Okay, then I'll say this real fast. As far-fetched as MARVI-RPIA seems, the actual Bible stories are even further out there. This version seems more likable than what I hear from the churches.

Host: Well, it's not doing too bad. N5Sense Books has it at number nine in sales and 10 AM Books has it at number twelve. *Connecting The Dots Of Identity-2* just came out, and it follows up on *Connecting Dots-1* with commentary on sex-ed, abortion, and politics. I think a lot of readers may be put off by any religious slant on those topics, including me. Well, there you go. We're way late for the break. This is the *Famous Fascinating Fellow Show*. Be right back.

QUOTES OFF THE RECORD

(1) "How ya gonna keep 'em down on the farm after they've seen Paree?"
78@RPMM

(2) "Modern Abstract Religious Verbal Impressionism. I may become a Minister of Art."
High School Senior

(3) "JLT overcomes so-so writing to reveal religion as it's never been revealed.
Connecting The Dots Of Identity is a life-giving event."
Glam Grammar Group

(4) "MARVI-RPIA isn't the right image, but the right image may not look better."
Bebopbrowser.link

(5) "You almost had us."
All Atheists All the Time

(6) "We don't believe it, but we teach it. Yes, we teach disbelief."
New Preachers of the New Years

(7) "Liberates people who were in religious doctrinal lockdown."
Fan of JLT

(8) "*Connecting The Dots Of Identity* is not defense of the faith. It's offense!"
Head Coach, Metro Ministers of Mystery

(9) "Thanks to the Creative Commons License, volunteers read selected CD1 and CD2 chapters online—including my young daughter. If enough people volunteer, it becomes a free audiobook."
Happy Parent

(10) "Religious gimmick! The author admits he doesn't believe a word he wrote. Why write if not for money? He'll soon be on the talk show circuit."
Anonymous

(11) "If religion is the automobile, CD1/CD2 is the flying car. If religion is Norman Rockwell, CD1/CD2 is Salvador Dali. If religion is a cruise ship, CD1/CD2 is a submarine. If religion is the jumbo jet, CD1 CD2 is the spaceship."
#R*E*D

(12) "CD1 CD2 is like the Leaning Tower of Pisa. As a work of art, flawed but attractive."
Editor – Art as It Ain't

(13) "This reminds me of Acts 17: 'These that have turned the world upside down.'"
Bible Neophyte

OVERVIEW

Thirteen Points of History

1) Life—angels and humans
2) Fall—angels and humans
3) The promise of redemption—humans
4) Nephilim—human and angel offspring
5) Flood—violation of God's procreation plan
6) Babel—language and communities created
7) Days of Peleg—earth divided, countries and races begin
8) Creation of God's chosen people Israel
9) Prophecy of Messiah
10) Jesus Christ arrives
11) Ongoing Demonstration of Free Will since the beginning of life
12) Judgment Day—End of Demonstration of Free Will versus God's Determined Will
13) Afterlife in Heaven, Hell, or Oblivion

Twelve Points of Christian Reformed Impressionism

1) Spiritual life is created as the heavenly hosts (angels)
2) Lucifer's Postulate—life may not be worth living while God restricts freedom
3) God proposes a Demonstration of Free Will—Elect are recognized (SSID). First-Class Angels trust God's will
4) The Serpent, Adam, and Eve initiate the Free Will Demonstration, exercising the choice to disobey God
5) The Fall of Adam and Eve brings about roleplay/identity array from heredity, environment, and experience

6) Third-Class angels seek an angel redeemer via offspring with human females, causing the Flood
7) Proof of the error of Free Will and inability to choose God is shown by the Holy Spirit's arrival or not
8) Proof of the error of Free Will is illustrated by the contrast of objective morality to subjective morality
9) Afterlife refers to 100 percent humans, less than 100 percent humans from Nephilim, and Satan with his angels
10) Heaven, Hell, or Oblivion as destinations in the afterlife
11) *Connecting The Dots Of Identity* is an impression of God's relationship with angels and humans.
12) Modern Abstract Religious Verbal Impressionism is the art of Christian Reformed theology.

Seven Shortcuts of Christian Reformed Impressionism

1) Life Created
2) Lucifer's Postulate of Freedom
3) Demo of Free Will excluding SSIDs and First-Class Angels
4) Roleplay ID Array based on Heredity, Environment, and Experience
5) Less than 100 Percent human beings derived from Nephilim
6) Objective versus Subjective Morality as Sane versus Unsane worldviews
7) Afterlife as Heaven, Hell, or Oblivion

Seven Shorter Shortcuts of Christian Reformed Impressionism

1) Life
2) Lucifer
3) Demo
4) Roleplay
5) Nephilim

6) Unsanity

7) Afterlife

IMAGE GALLERY PORTRAITS

|*Lucifer's Postulate*|

|*Pre-Life Elect*|

|*Ego-Skepticism – Ego-Centracism*|

|*Designationism – Creationism – Traducianism*|

|*Heredity – Environment – Experience*|

|*First-Class Angels – Second-Class Angels – Third-Class Angels*|

|*Nephilim*|

|*SSID – HSID – SID – ESID – MID – PID – CID – DID*|

|*Objective Morality – Subjective Morality*|

|*Authentic Identity (Future) – Inauthentic Identity (Present)*|

|*General Revelation (Nature) – Special Revelation (Scripture)*|

NOTES

Chapter 1—Pre-Life Authentic Identity

15 CD1 CD2 Plan B Highlights.

Views of reality and identity (human and angel).

Chapter 2—Designated Roleplay

Impressions of spiritual reality.

Group A persons outside time—Group B inside time.

Chapter 3 —Second Best News

R.C. Sproul. *Defending Your Faith. Four Steps Backward.* Message 4. YouTube. 2020.

Chapter 4—Bible As Merit

Council Of Chalcedon. https://www.britannica.com/event/Council-of-Chalcedon.

Accessed April 10, 2021.

R.C. Sproul. *Hath God Said.* Ligonier Ministries. 2021.

Additional support for the Bible as God's word to man.

General Revelation. Special Revelation. Romans 1:20, Psalm 19:1,2.

Illiteracy. Bloody Bible. Written by men. Government fears.

Harmonic Atheist. YouTube. Tim Mills. 2023.

Family Radio. Familyradio.org

Refnet. https://listen.refnet.fm

J. Warner Wallace. *Person Of Interest.* Zondervan. 2021. Cold Case Christianity. David C. Cook. 2023

R.C. Sproul. *Defending Your Faith Series.* Ligonier Ministries. 2001. Or YouTube.

Chapter 5—Christian Reformed Theology Part 1

Stephen C. Meyer. *The Return of the God Hypothesis.* HarperCollins. 2021.

Christian Reformed Theology. Saint Augustine. Martin Luther. John Calvin. Jacobus Arminius.

Reformation. Election. Less than 100% human.

Nave's Topical Bible. MacDonald Publishing Co.

Chapter 6—Christian Reformed Theology Part 2

Predestination-Chosen-Election. *Holy Bible*. Authorized King James Version. World Bible Publishers. 1989.

Chapter 7—Christian Reformed Theology Part 3

Supralapsarian. Infralapsarian.

J. Ellis McTaggart. *The Unreality Of Time.* Mind A Quarterly Review of Psychology and Philosophy. October 1908. The Nature Of Existence. Volume 2. Cambridge University Press. 1927.

Jacobus Arminius. Dutch theologian. 1560-1609. The proponent of remonstration to Christian Reformed Theology (Calvinism). https://biography.yourdictionary.com/423habad423-arminius. October 2021.

Reformation versus Remonstration.

Chapter 8—Election/Predestination

John 3:16. Whosoever believes. Bible is difficult on purpose.

Instagram. A young girl confronts Christianity. April 2021.

Harold Camping. Family Radio. *Open Forum* Program. 1992. (familyradio.org)

Pinterest. Space Dyke (Twitter) one-panel cartoon. April 2021.

God starts over multiple times. Preachers teach grace but add works.

Chapter 9—General Revelation – Special Revelation

Monism. Physicalism. Overcoming faulty worldviews. Why God doesn't appear.

David Hume. 1711-1776. Scotland. Philosopher. Author. Christopher Hitchens.1949-2011. Great Britain. Philosopher. Author. Sam Harris. 1967-present. USA. Neuroscientist. Lawrence Krauss. 1954-present. Canada/USA. Physicist.

Hell created for the Devil and his angels.

Chapter 10— Trillionaire

What is a trillion?

Don't want to be a Christian.

Chapter 11—Who Am I?

Early personal influencers – Baba Ram Dass (Richard Alpert), Sigmund Freud, Emile Durkheim, Max Weber, Lao Tzu, Roy Masters, Garner Ted Armstrong, J. Vernon McGee, Dr. Walter Martin, Jim Bakker, Dr. Gene Scott, George Vandeman, Hal Lindsey, Dr. Wayne Dyer, Harold Camping. Especially Harold Camping.

What makes JLT write CD1/CD2?

Chapter 12—Minister Of Art

Jesus is not recognized by religious scholars.

General Revelation. Special Revelation. Romans 1:20, Psalm 19:1,2.

Minister of Art. John Louis Thomas (author). Rewrite of Bible by hand. Fear of heresy.

Margaret Hungerford. Beauty in the Eye of the Beholder.

https://www.irishcentral.com/roots/history/duchess-who-wasnt-day-margaret-wolfe-hungerford

Mentalfloss.com. Sources: en.wikiquote.org/wiki/Ai Weiwei; Art and Its Significance; Concise Oxford Dictionary of Art Terms (2 ed.); Crofton, Dictionary of Art Quotations; La Cour, Artists in Quotation; Oxford Essential Quotations; Gabrielle Selz, Unstill Life.

Famous painters: Pierre Auguste Renoir. Claude Monet. Alfred Sisley. Frédéric Bazille.

Christian Reformed Impressionism. Glossary. 2021.

Chapter 13—Marvi Stages

Hell created for the Devil and his angels.

Stages 1-8 of MARVI-RPIA background.

Chapter 14—MARVI Identity Array

8-part/10-part. Roleplay Identity – SSID, HSID, SID (Neg/Pos), PID, MID, CID, DID, ESID.

Less important identity images are named.

Chapter 15—Super-Spiritual Identity (SSID)

SSID details of impression.

Ontological Status and proponents. Aristotle. Saint Anselm of Canterbury. Rene Descartes. Alfred North Whitehead. Willard Van Orman Quine. Edmund Husserl. Wikipedia – the free encyclopedia. Ontology. Reality and Actuality. Alfred N. Whitehead. Footnote [196]. "Citations Needed" notation. (March 30, 2021).

Book of Life. Lamb's Book of Life. Psalm 69:27,28. Daniel 12:1. Luke 10:20. Philippians 4:3 Revelation 3:5, 13:8,20:15, 21:27.

Max Tegmark. M.I.T. professor. January 10, 2014. Scientific American. EXCERPT. *Our Mathematical Universe: My Quest For The Ultimate Nature Of Reality*. Random House/Knopf. Copyright 2014. Accessed April 2021.

Jan 4 '16 at 14:35 by Jumblegreen 11 1. *"What Is A Number?"* Math.Stackexchange.com. April 2021.

J.P. Moreland. *Scientism and Secularism: Learning to Respond to a Dangerous Ideology.* September 30, 2018. Crossway Publishing.

"virtual." Merriam-Webster.com. Merriam-Webster, 2021. 3/31/21.

"virtual." Languages.oup.com/google-dictionary-eu. Oxford languages and Google. 3/31/21.

"virtual." Vocabulary.com. 3/31/21.

Chapter 16—Jesus's Number One Message

5 Most Hated Christian doctrines.

The controversy of Mark 16:17,18 (these signs shall follow them that believe).

Harold Camping. Family Radio. Franklin, TN. Familyradio.org.

Jesus (100% man) as a Roleplayer.

Artist uses A.I. to recreate the faces of Jesus Christ and other famous figures. Medium.com. Alexander Keane. July 2020.

Resting in bed: Me, Jesus, Apostle Thomas.

Chapter 17—Role Play Identity Array

Identity scenarios.

Trillion $ Treasure – Good News (Jesus Christ) and Great News – Everyone goes to Heaven. No one goes to Hell except the Devil, his angels, and those less than 100% humans.

Universalism is a heretical religious idea.

Patrick Henry. Founding Father United States. Politician. 1736-1799.

God's moral character, especially regarding Old Testament.

Insanity Chart.

Blind Eyes Chart

Chapter 18—MARVI Details

Why not sin if there's no Hell?

Hitler, Stalin, and Mao are in Paradise but babies in Hell?

Non-Elect babies to Hell?

Status of less than 100% humans. N1, N2, N3 Nephilim families.

Chapter 19—In Beginning(s)

Lucifer's Postulate (to God) before God created the world (Glossary of Colors).

Class 1, 2, 3 angels.

God proposes Free Will Demonstration with human beings. God retains other non-angelic beings outside time. Lucifer's assessment of God's Eden demonstration.

Chapter 20—Marvi As Art

Why is there no previous mention of the ontological status of the identities God saved before the foundation of the world? CD1 as heretical art?

John Calvin's interpretation of the Apostles Creed. *"Ask R.C."*. R.C. Sproul. Ligonier Ministries. *Did Christ descend into Hell?* 2020.

Chapter 21—Adam And Eve, No Satan

Why Adam being alone is not good (not what you think).

Controversial image of Serpent in Eden – including eating from Tree of KG&E.

Eve is the only female in the world (country of Eden/Garden of Eden). All created beings are (probably) male.

Tree of Life was good for food and enhanced dynamic attributes.

Is King of Tyre, Adam, or Satan? Ezekiel 28.

Satan as accuser.

Ego-Skepticism. Ego-Centracism (Glossary of Colors).

Chapter 22—Serpent & Class 1, 2, 3 Angels

Eve eats from Tree of KG&E. She realizes she was deceived – and worse.

Adam eats of Tree of KG&E.

Serpent as innocent bystander ambushed by Satan? God curses the serpent – no mention of Satan.

Three classes of angels emerge – First-Class, Second-Class, Third-Class – Glossary of Colors.

The Serpent as a first-class monster.

Chapter 23—Nephilim Part 1

Angels see 1) Adam and Eve chose knowledge over life 2) God promised a Solution to death 3) Angels speculate on the seed of woman and the seed of the serpent.

Ego-Skepticism. Ego-Centracism (Glossary of Colors).

Chapter 24—Nephilim Part 2

Abaddon/Apollyon. Does a redeemer redeem everyone – humans, and angel-human hybrids?

Features of First, Second, and Third-Class Angels.

The Serpent is Satan?

Chapter 25—Nephilim Interim

22 Traditional Christian Principles.

Chapter 26—Nephilim Part 3

Enoch and Elijah are deceased. *Where Are Enoch and Elijah?* By Herbert W. Armstrong (1892-1986) 1973.

Str.org. #strask. *If Wages Of Sin Is Death…*Amy Hall. Gregory Koukl. December 16, 2021.

https://www.cgg.org/index.cfm/library/booklet/id/469/where-are-enoch-elijah.htm.

Chapter 27—Nephilim Part 4

Nephilim Opinions 1-4.

Angel's points of view.

Eve was a sucker and a fool?

Adam and Eve dialogue.

Who are the sons of God?

Chapter 28—Nephilim Part 5

10 Reasons to believe angel/human offspring produce Nephilim.

One-Drop Rule (a reference to the discriminatory practice of mixed-race persons based on a "drop" of Negro blood) – Glossary of Colors.

Noah cursed Canaan – not Ham. Genesis 9:24-26.

Which relative of Noah's family continued Nephilim (giants)?

Are angels sexless? Matthew 22:30.

Harold Camping. *1994?* Vantage Press. 1992. Calendar of the Bible (Years from the creation of the world to the birth of Jesus Christ – Page 295-298).

Satan as the Accuser.

Chapter 29—The Flood 1

Abaddon and Third-Class Angels. Lucifer and Second-Class Angels.

Noah, Missus Noah, Noah's sons, Noah's son's wives. One-Drop Rule regarding Nephilim.

Giants pre-Flood and post-Flood.

Free Will Demonstrations 1) Garden of Eden, 2) outside Garden in Eden area 3) post-Flood Noah and family.

Chapter 30—Flood 2

Noah and wine.

https://www.visualcapitalist.com/visualizing-worlds-deepest-oil-well/

https://oilprice.com/Energy/Energy-General/*The-Truth-About-The-Worlds-Deepest-Oil-Well.html.*

People of Pre-Flood days. The urgency for children to produce redeemer.

The Flood of Noah's day caused sudden death to plants, animals, and HUMAN BEINGS by water. Oil, gas, coal, and other organic material are found all over the world.

The appearance of age – oil, gas, and coal require millions of years to produce.

Connecting The Dots Of Identity paints 10-Plus "beginnings".

Why only eight saved in the Flood?

Chapter 31—Flood 3

Nephilim genetic dominant/recessive traits.

10 trillion pre-Flood population from Nephilim families.

The Flood as a blessing. No Flood – no oil, coal, or gas.

10-point profile of less than 100% human.

Naming a less than 100% person.

Nephilim chromosome markers.

Class 1, 2, 3, angels as proof of spiritual reality.

Chapter 32—Flood 4

10,000,000,000,000 (ten trillion) pre-Flood population figure.

10 TRILLION POPULATION AT TIME OF FLOOD (Bible-Science Guy)

https://biblescienceguy.wordpress.com/2014/06/18/4-*population-growth-how-many-died-in-noahs-flood/* Dr. William Pelletier. BibleScienceGuy.wordpress.com.

Why pre-Flood people were corrupted.

Flood in the last days – last seconds.

Demon possession today.

Chapter 33—Babel

The figure of Nimrod (Noah's descendant) was instrumental in leadership.

One-world language is confused to ensure human diversity. Human diversity to ensure Free Will Demonstration.

Reiteration of MARVI-RPIA identity models – less than 100% human, identity pre- and post-Holy Spirit intercession.

Chapter 34—Peleg

Earth divided by language and/or land mass?

Morris, John D. 1993. *What Happened in the "Days of Peleg"?* Acts & Facts. 22 (10).

Racial Differentiation? Birth-defect incidence?

Chapter 35—Chosen People

Three groups of chosen people 1) Pre-Life Elect 2) Elect Roleplayers (HSID) 3) Israel.

"Jew" https://www.chabad.org/library/article_cdo/aid/640221/jewish/What-is-the-Meaning-of-the-Name-Jew.htm.

Genealogy of Jesus—Matthew/Luke.

Depiction of Old Testament life.

Chapter 36—Identity Array Continued

More details regarding 8 of 8 Identity Array models.

Demon possession, demon oppression.

Jesus couldn't die naturally.

The longest sentence in the book.

God starts over for Adam and Eve.

General Revelation and Special Revelation access to the world.

End of Free Will Demonstration/Judgment Day indication?

Chapter 37—Hell Part 1

4-Point MARVI-RPIA worldview.

Is Hell a deterrent to evil?

Identities that are less than 100% human.

If Jesus taught more about Hell than other things, how can *Connecting The Dots Of Identity* claim everyone goes to Heaven?

Levels of crime against authority.

Hell is incompatible with the God of love. Punishing or Punishment?

Parable of the rich man and Lazarus regarding Hell.

Chapter 38—Hell Part 2

Is Hell Necessary?

When was Hell created? Where is it?

What is death for a flawlessly created being?

Angels act of suicide. Adam and Eve's act of suicide.

Do thoughts linger after death?

Chapter 39—Hell Part 3

Who goes to Hell? Why?

Progression of offspring derived from Nephilim (Nephilam, Nephilom, Nephilegion).

"One-Drop Rule" (evil-spirit immaterial-genetic-substance) – Glossary of Colors.

Less than 100% human identity chance of salvation?

Dr. X teaches Christians MUST warn of Hell or go there. Heavenly view of people in Hell.

Chapter 40—Heaven Part 1

Overview of Free Will Demonstration. Angels request omnipotence. Humans desire omniscience.

Contrast fallen humans and fallen angels to the Pre-Life Elect (SSID) and First-Class angels who didn't fall.

Heaven's expectations.

Absent from the body present with the Lord?

Chapter 41—Heaven Part 2

A Day in Heaven.

Rewards in Heaven

Quotes Off The Record:

"How ya gonna keep em down on the farm after they've seen Paree (Paris)"

Popular song. Composer: Walter Donaldson Lyrics: Sam Lewis, Joe Young. 1919.

ABOUT THE AUTHOR

Born in Los Angeles, California (1947), John Louis Thomas grew up in Anchorage, Alaska. He returned to Los Angeles before retiring in 2009, then relocated to New Mexico in 2017. For twenty-five years, he's been a member in good standing of Christian Reformed churches. During the pandemic of 2020, church attendance was suspended and hasn't yet resumed. Single. No children. Ketogenic diet since 2012.

He is an advocate of the "Rewrite the Bible by Hand" project, having completed all twenty-seven books of the New Testament in 2020. Incomplete writings from Genesis to 2 Samuel exist. He has completed writings from Genesis to Deuteronomy and 1 Kings to Malachi. Currently, he is rewriting the Book of Joshua (2024).

Back of the book cover photo – 2023.

Contact:
John Louis Thomas
900 Pinetree Rd SE #15730
Rio Rancho, New Mexico 87124-9998
johndeuce442@gmail.com
Business inquiries:
Chad Mulligan
rednlove2@gmail.com

Other books by John Louis Thomas:

Connecting The Dots Of Identity-2. 2024

Websites:
unorthodoxtemple.com

rednlove.com
johnlouisthomas.com

www.ingramcontent.com/pod-product-compliance
Lightning Source LLC
LaVergne TN
LVHW020647110826
845149LV00012B/1939

* 9 7 9 8 9 9 0 7 4 8 7 0 5 *